The March of Time, 1935-1951

The March of Time, 1935-1951

Raymond Fielding

New York
Oxford University Press
1978

Photographs appearing on pages 44, 47, 48, 51, 54, 55,
60, 61, 140, 152, 157, 164, 179, 182, 189, 190, 191,
192, 193, 294, and 295 are from the March of Time,
courtesy of Time Incorporated, the copyright proprietor.

Photographs appearing on pages 12, 13, 14, 16, 27, 42, 65,
88, 93, 94, 96, 103, 116, 117, 121, 122, 141, 215, 247, and 298
were furnished by Time Incorporated to the author for
research purposes. However, Time Incorporated assumes no
responsibility for their publication in this book.

Library of Congress Cataloging in Publication Data

Fielding, Raymond.
The March of Time , 1935-1951.

Bibliography: p.
Includes index.
1.   Moving-picture journalism—United States—History.
2.   The March of Time (Motion picture)   1.   Title.
PN4888.M6F53   791.43′53   76-51711
ISBN 0-19-502212-2

Printed in the United States of America

To the Memory of my Father

Acknowledgments

The author gratefully acknowledges the assistance given him in the conduct of this study by numerous individuals over a period of several years.

Surviving *March of Time* members made themselves available for extensive interviews, most of which were tape-recorded. Listed alphabetically, these were Edgar Anstey, Jack Bradford, Julien Bryan, Louis de Rochemont, Richard de Rochemont, Mary Losey Field, Jack Glenn, Peter Hopkinson, Roy Larsen, Tom Orchard, Morrie Roizman, Jack Shaindlin, James Shute, Albert Sindlinger, Arthur Tourtellot, Harry Von Zell, and Lothar Wolff.

Other individuals who provided information and assistance included James G. Stewart, Richard Harkness, William Goetz, Roy Brown, and William Melnitz.

At Time, Incorporated, executives Roy Larsen and Arthur Murphy, and archivist Lillian Owens made corporate records, still photographs, films, scripts, memoranda, and other materials available for this publication. Ms. Owens' thoughtfulness and patience were especially appreciated. However, none of these individuals nor any other officials or employees of Time, Incorporated, have expressly or impliedly approved or endorsed this book or the accuracy of its contents.

Acknowledgments

Individuals at both private and public archives and libraries were unfailingly helpful in identifying and retrieving materials for the study. These included William Murphy and Rose Ann Ernst at the U.S. National Archives; John Kuiper, David Parker, and Paul Spehr at the Library of Congress; James Spears at the Smithsonian Institution; Brenda Davies at the British Film Institute; Bernard Karpel, Eileen Bowser, and Margareta Akermark at the Museum of Modern Art; Betty Franklin, Lillian Schwartz, and Mildred Simpson at the Library of the Academy of Motion Picture Arts and Sciences; and the library and archival staffs at Temple University, the University of Southern California, the University of California at Los Angeles, the National Film Board of Canada, La Cinématèque québéçoise, and the Columbia Broadcasting System.

Photographs and other illustrations were provided for the book by Time, Incorporated, and by several former *March of Time* staff members, all of whom are credited in the captions of the illustrations.

Raymond Fielding

Philadelphia
March 1977

Contents

The March of Time, 1935-1951

1

The Beginnings of Time

"We know the end before we consider the beginning and we can never wholly recapture what it was to know the beginning only."

C. V. Wedgwood

Journalism, like ice sculpture, yields products of transient value. The news fades, the ice melts, and so does our memory of each of them. Less than a decade has passed since the last American newsreels flashed upon motion picture screens, and yet one generation of citizens has nearly forgotten what they looked like, while the next doesn't even know they existed.

For the benefit of both—the newsreel was a nine- or ten-minute collection of more-or-less newsworthy footage, comprising eight or nine items, each subject separated abruptly from the others by a title, all of them backed up by a noisy musical score and a high-speed, invisible narrator. The issues in which they appeared were released serially, twice a week, to more than 15,000 theaters throughout the United States.

There were five great American newsreels, the first of which, Pathé's Weekly, was introduced by the U.S. branch of a French firm in August 1911 (a European version having appeared earlier). There were more than thirty competitors in America during the next half-century, but only five of these survived for any length of time, each owned by one of the major motion picture production-distribution-exhibition organizations: Fox Movietone News, Pathé News (later, Warner-Pathé News), Universal News, Hearst International Newsreel (later, Hearst Metrotone News, then News of the Day), and Paramount News.

At its height, in the United States alone, the American newsreel was seen weekly by at least 40 million people, and throughout the world by more than 200 million. For many people, especially the illiterate, it was a principal source of news until the coming of television, providing the imagery with which to perceive and conceive the nature of political and military events, distant geographical locales, technological innovation, and foreign people and cultures.

By the middle of the 1920's, American producers dominated the international newsreel business, employing a world-wide network of news-gathering facilities, hundreds of cameramen, contact men, and reporters who often gained headlines themselves in their competitive struggle to make motion picture records of newsworthy events in time for exhibition deadlines.

With the commercial introduction of talking pictures in 1926-27 the newsreel acquired a voice. It was a scratchy and sometimes incomprehensible voice at first, but a thrilling one nevertheless. The sound camera could now bring the comments of kings and commoners, the sounds of battle, the roar of a motor car race, perfectly synchronized with the moving image, onto the screens of thousands of theaters.

For more than half a century, theater patrons got the newsreel with every feature film they paid for, together with a Mickey Mouse cartoon, a Pete Smith Specialty, a Grantland Rice sports reel, or a Fitzpatrick Traveltalk.

And then, dinosaur that it proved to be, the newsreel began to disappear, its numbers shrinking from year to year. Warner-Pathé went out of business in 1956, Paramount News in 1957, Fox Movietone News in 1963, and Hearst's News of the Day and

Universal News in 1967. There are no more theatrical newsreels in the United States, and we shall probably never see their like again. Accurate figures are hard to come by, but so far as one can tell American newsreel cameramen alone shot more than a *half a billion* feet of negative during its fifty-six-year history. Astonishingly, at least half of that total still survives.

A number of factors led to the newsreel's demise. These included the Justice Department's breaking up, in the 1940's, of the American film monopolies, within which system the newsreel had played an important role in the design of the "block-booked" program which was offered to theaters; the economic hardships which the film industry suffered in the late 40's and early 50's, at which time the studios jettisoned their least valuable properties and programs; and last but not least competition from television news programs, which were both faster and more thorough in their coverage. The newsreels had never made any money for anyone, and so they were the first to go.

Actually, one is astonished not that the newsreel disappeared but that it survived as long as it did. The form and style of the newsreel had become petrified shortly after the introduction of sound in the late 1920's, and had it not been for the explosive, tension-filled news events of the 1930's on which the newsreel fed, it would probably have soon become apparent that there was nothing new in the newsreel.

Both in the United States and in Europe, newsreels were compromised from the beginning by fakery, re-creation, manipulation, and staging. None of these practices is necessarily inappropriate in certain types of documentary films, but all are certainly suspect in a medium that tries to pass as reportorial journalism. The early years of the news-film and newsreel were the worst in this respect, with regular, outright faking of scenes such as the San Francisco earthquake and fire, the eruption of Mt. Vesuvius, the battle of Santiago Bay, the Boer War, the Spanish-American War, and the First World War.

The newsreel acquired a voice in the late 1920's, but rarely had anything of consequence to say. Although exciting and amusing at times, its content for the most part was trivial and devoid of

5

intellectual substance. Oscar Levant, the American humorist, once described it as "a series of catastrophes followed by a fashion show."

Many critics considered the newsreel fundamentally flawed as a journalistic medium because of its producers' reluctance to deal with controversial subjects. The contemptuous attitude of the American film industry toward its own newsreels was never more succinctly expressed than by Martin Quigley, influential editor of the trade paper, *Motion Picture Herald,* in a June 1937 editorial:

> . . . newsreels have no social obligations beyond those of the amusement industry and theatres they are supposed to serve. Newsreels have an obligation, if they are to be purveyed as entertainment in theatres, to be entertaining. They have no obligation to be important, informative. They can successfully present neither one side, both sides, nor the middle of any social condition or issue.

Critics also felt that the newsreel failed to present a thorough treatment of current news events. Because of its brief 9-10-minute length and its coverage of so many different subjects, the treatment of any one event was sketchy and inadequate. Andrew Buchanan called the newsreels "jumpy little post-card collections," and suggested that "For some reason or other, probably through lack of time, newsreels are never produced—they merely happen."

The newsreel was part of America's collective communications experience. Many people loved it, much as one might love a backward, hyperkinetic child—happy to share its curious, convoluted joys, while apprehensive for its future. In the end, it proved a witless form and an embarrassment to the journalistic family in which it claimed membership. "From the beginning," wrote British film critic John Grierson, "we have had newsreels, but dim records they seem now of only the evanescent and the essentially unreal, reflecting hardly anything worth preserving of the times they recorded. . . . The newsreel has gone dithering on, mistaking the phenomenon for the thing in itself, and ignoring everything that gave it the trouble of conscience and penetration and thought."

Clearly, by the mid-1930's the time had arrived for an "interpretive newsreel"—one that would explore selected news events, sketch in backgrounds, and give meaning within the social and political context of contemporary life.

In the publishing field by the 1920's, at least one magazine was attempting such an appraisal of current events—a summary of the week's news which interpreted it in the light of past events, social and political trends, and prognostications of future change. The publication was *Time the Weekly News-Magazine,* introduced in 1923 with a modest investment of $86,000 by Henry Luce and Briton Hadden. A financial success from 1928 onward, the magazine won enthusiastic approval from the reading public, provided the cornerstone for an immense publishing empire, and provoked a rash of imitations.

The magazine's journalistic style was an odd blend of newspaper brevity and magazine exposition—economical and pithy in its choice of words, yet reasonably descriptive and analytical in its treatment of news items. The editors pioneered a new type of dynamic, high-tension magazine writing, full of word-pictures and thought-provoking phrases. As with most newspapers, the magazine was presented to readers as an organic whole, for individual articles were rarely signed. "Like all machines," wrote critic Dwight MacDonald, in the May 1, 1937, issue of the *Nation,* "it is vastly impersonal. Its products bear the name of no individual author, appearing as pronouncements *ex cathedra,* with the whole weight of the organization behind them."

In the beginning, *Time* generated precious little of its own news coverage. Most of its information was lifted without acknowledgment or payment from the pages of the *New York Times* and other leading newspapers of the day.

The magazine managed to irritate nearly everyone who counted in the intellectual/communications establishment: elitists because of its enormous popularity with middle-class Americans; the well-bred because of its vulgarity and scandal-mongering; journalists because of its editors' appetite for other people's coverage; liberals and leftists because of its noticeable but erratic conservatism; and literary purists because of its "barbaric" style—a preposterous kind of sentence structure in which subjects, predicates, adjectives, and other components of the English language all ended up in unpredictable and grammatically unauthorized positions. "Backward ran sentences until reeled the mind," wrote *New Yorker* parodist Wolcott Gibbs in his celebrated November 1936 analysis of "Timespeak." "Where it all will end, knows God!" concluded Gibbs.

Encouraged by the spectacular success of their news magazine, and seeking greater diversity in their journalistic ventures, the corporation began publication in 1929 of *Fortune,* a high-priced, quality-printed monthly magazine devoted to the celebration of American business, industry, and commerce. Despite the incongruity of *Fortune*'s appearance during the lean years of the depression, it proved to be a moderate financial success and was widely acclaimed for the uncommonly good quality of its photographic illustrations and layout.

By 1929, the year of young Briton Hadden's untimely death, the corporation's future was assured. Although it would never rival the *New York Times* in the gathering of news, it would, with the passing of years, become one of the world's largest and most profitable dispensers of the product.

It is not our purpose here to chronicle the history of either Henry Luce or the corporation he headed; the creation of the *March of Time,* on both radio and film, had nothing to do with Henry Luce. It was entirely the work of Roy Edward Larsen, originally circulation manager and then general manager of *Time,* later publisher of *Life,* for many years president of Time, Incorporated, and in the long history of the corporation the most influential and important figure after Luce.

Well educated and multi-talented, Larsen is described by his associates as a Renaissance man and one who probably would have succeeded in anything he tried. An excellent writer with an early interest in the dramatic arts, he decided to bring his various talents to bear upon a career as a creative businessman.

The son of a newspaperman (and sometimes motion picture theater manager), he was born in Boston in 1899, educated first at Boston Latin School, and then at Harvard University, from which he graduated in 1921. While at Harvard, he managed the college's literary magazine, the *Harvard Advocate,* increasing its circulation dramatically and returning the publication to solvency.

The Beginnings of Time

After leaving Harvard he worked briefly at the New York Trust Company, a position which he later said he detested. In 1921, two Yale men, Henry Luce and Briton Hadden, mindful of Larsen's success in developing the *Advocate*'s readership, invited him to join them as advertising manager of their new experimental magazine, *Time*. "I worked in a bank and I was ready to do anything to escape banking," said Larsen, who considered Luce's offer, rejected it, reconsidered it, and then, in 1922, joined the two young publishers as circulation manager and *Time*'s first noneditorial employee. The new magazine was introduced shortly thereafter. Under Larsen's supervision its circulation rose from 25,000 in 1923 to 200,000 in 1928, by which date the corporation had begun to make a substantial profit. Originally hired at $40 a week, Larsen had become, by 1936, the corporation's second largest stockholder. His association with the enterprise turned out to be a long-term one. Half a century after he had been hired, long after Luce and Hadden had departed the scene, Larsen was still around as vice-chairman of the corporation to celebrate his golden anniversary with *Time*.

Dwight MacDonald described Larsen in the *Nation* on May 22, 1937, as "quiet, impersonal, realistic and inhumanly efficient," a description with which Larsen's colleagues seem to agree. They remember him as a handsome, dynamic executive, a happily married family man, a soft-spoken gentleman in his dealings with others, a firm but fair boss to his subordinates. Larsen, according to MacDonald, "doesn't take the racket too seriously. To Luce journalism is a crusade, to Larsen a game."

Larsen enjoyed the excitement involved in *Time*'s journalistic adventures and was responsible for initiating many of the corporation's communications innovations. Although educated for and occupationally based in conventional print journalism, Larsen was also what theorist Marshall McLuhan has termed an "electric man," sensitive to the newer media of communication, the novel modes of transmission and perception involved in their operations, and their impact upon contemporary society. As early as 1924, Larsen had brought *Time* into the infant radio business with the broadcast of a fifteen-minute sustaining quiz show entitled "Pop

Question," which survived until 1925. In 1928, in association with radio executive Fred Smith, Larsen undertook the weekly broadcast of a 10-minute program series of brief news summaries, drawn from current issues of *Time* magazine, and featuring what Larsen later described as one "hair-raising" news event in each broadcast. For this news program, which was originally broadcast over 33 stations throughout the United States, Larsen coined the term "newscasting."

"Newscasting" was soon converted into a new series named "Newsacting," which featured dramatic sketches performed by professional actors with accompanying sound effects, illustrating current news items. In this series each broadcast lasted 10 minutes (later 15 minutes) and was offered free of charge to radio stations in return for publicity for *Time* magazine. The series was intended by Larsen to stimulate magazine circulation. Although more than a hundred stations subscribed to the program, Larsen and Smith grew dissatisfied with its modest format and proposed to Luce that *Time* produce a well-financed, half-hour show on network radio. Conscious of the competing *Literary Digest*'s established news broadcast series featuring Lowell Thomas on NBC, Luce nervously assented to the expenditure of substantial amounts of money for experimentation.

According to *Time* historian Robert Elson, Fred Smith had asked for "the ten best radio actors," an "announcer extraordinary," a "splendid orchestra," and a "clever director." In time, he and Larsen got them all.

The title of a Harold Arlen song, "The March of Time," which had been written originally for a Broadway production of Earl Carroll's *Vanities,* was selected for the series, as was the lively song itself for the *March of Time*'s opening "logo" music.

Larsen told me that, during the period of experimentation on the show, he had gone to a stage performance of *Grand Hotel,* and was struck by the role of the telephone operator, or "narrator," around which the play revolved. The narrator, as he saw it, was the key to *Time*'s new radio show, providing exposition, setting the scene for the actor's performances, and punctuating the whole sequence with periodic repetitions of what was to become a most memorable expression: "Time—Marches On!" Without the "Time Marches On" gimmick, said Larsen, they wouldn't have gone on the air. As it was, no one else in the corporation's editorial group liked the idea.

On February 6, 1931, after several months of expensive experimentation, a pilot program was piped by CBS from their studios to Larsen's home, where Luce, Larsen, the managing editors of *Time* and *Fortune* magazines, William Paley of CBS, and other important corporation figures listened critically. Hardly anyone was happy with what he heard. The show was not editorially smooth like the company's magazines. Larsen said his editorial associates were "mad as hell" at him. They felt he had misused and degraded the *Time* trade mark. They thought the whole venture presumptuous of him.

Fortunately, neither Luce nor his advisers really knew what to make of such a radical departure in *Time*'s affairs. Reluctantly, they approved the project, with broadcast of the first show scheduled for March 6, 1931, over the CBS radio network. Bruce Bromley, *Time*'s legal counsel and one of the few people present at Larsen's home that evening who was enthusiastic about the project, was asked by Larsen whether the company faced legal problems in dramatizing news events and impersonating famous people over the air. Bromley said to forget the legalities and to go ahead with the project. In the end, said Larsen, "It was the lack of restrictions that let us proceed."

A perfectionist in all matters, Larsen had looked around for an "announcer extraordinary"—a distinctive and powerful voice for the crucial pivotal role of the "Voice of Time." Over the years, he found three different men to play the part: Ted Husing, Harry Von Zell, and Westbrook Van Voorhis. Von Zell recalled his work on the series:

. . . as "The Voice of Time" my challenge there was great because I was, in effect, a disembodied voice: THE VOICE OF TIME! And, as such, there could be no frog in the throat, there could be no slip of the tongue, and my delivery had to be similar to that of a teletype machine—crisp, flat: "Today, in the news, so-and-so-and-so-and-so. TIME MARCHES ON!

11

The *March of Time* on radio re-created current news events with professional actors and impersonators, sound effects technicians, and a full studio orchestra. On the air from 1931 to 1945, it was one of radio's most popular shows, heard regularly by millions of Americans. (Courtesy Time, Inc.)

For Larsen's "clever director," Arthur Pryor, Jr. (and at other times, Don Stouffer) was acquired while the "splendid orchestra" was conducted at different times by Donald Voorhees and Howard Barlow. Elaborate sound effects were designed and executed for the show by CBS expert Ora Nichols. These included, on one occasion, the sound of a decapitation.

Finally, New York's "ten best actors" (and then some) were hired to play the well-known celebrities whose voices were impersonated in *Time*'s re-creations of the week's news. These included Agnes Moorehead, Nancy Kelly, and Jeannette Nolan (all of whom were to play Eleanor Roosevelt from time to time); Art Carney, Bill Adams, and Stats Cotsworth (all of whom played Franklin Roosevelt); Dwight Weist (Adolf Hitler), Edwin Jerome (Josef Stalin and Haile Selassie), Ted de Corsia (Mussolini), Peter Donald (Neville Chamberlain), Jack Smart (Huey Long), Maurice

Technicians re-created a wide variety of both well-known and exotic sounds for the show, including, on one occasion, the sound of a decapitation. (Courtesy Time, Inc.)

Tarplin (Winston Churchill), Gary Merrill, Kenny Delmar, Arlene Francis, Ray Collins, Pedro de Cordoba, Porter Hall, Arnold Moss, Paul Stewart, Juano Hernandez, John McIntire, Everett Sloane, and the very young Orson Welles. Welles played many roles on network radio in those days. In 1938, he startled the country with his radio version of H. G. Wells's science fiction story, "The War of the Worlds," using techniques similar to those of the *March of Time.*

The *March of Time* radio program was presented in various formats, sometimes three times a week, running 15 minutes per show; sometimes once a week, in a 30-minute format; and at various times on either the CBS or NBC networks. It is reported that its production required the work of 75 staff members and 1000 man-hours of labor to get each issue on the air.

New York's finest actors performed regularly for the *March of Time* on radio, imitating well-known political officials, military leaders, entertainers, sports figures, and other celebrities in the news. Here, Everett Sloan plays a part. (Courtesy Time, Inc.)

Great care was taken to secure transcripts of authentic statements and comments of the celebrities who were impersonated on the program. In those cases in which these could not be obtained, writers were given the dramatic license to contrive and "re-create" such dialogue as seemed appropriate to the characters and situation.

Care was taken to coach the actors, whether professional or amateur, to mimic exactly the voice patterns, inflections, and characteristics of the figures impersonated. Sometimes these attempts backfired. Harry Von Zell, who was present at the re-creation, recalled an instance:

> . . . one time we ran afoul of this problem of reproducing a voice . . . with Chiang Kai-shek when he entered into the news of the world. We had no member of that amazing, versatile cast that could produce [an impersonation] to the satisfaction of Arthur Pryor, who was the producer and director . . . and it looked like

14

they were up against their first insurmountable problem when somebody finally suggested: "Well, we have a Jewish theater, we have a Hungarian theater, every kind of theater in New York, there must be a Chinese theater." So they looked in the telephone book and, sure enough, there was a Chinese theater, so they called and told them what they wanted was a native-born Chinese, an actor, who could speak just enough English to be convincing. And we had acetate discs of Chiang Kai-shek's voice, and the voice itself was easy to reproduce, but the dialect was the important thing. And we found an actor and his English with the Chinese inflections were just perfect, and we used him. And the first program upon which an episode appeared featuring Chiang Kai-shek speaking at length, the switchboards lit up, the telephones were tied up—people complaining. And the gist of the complaint was to the effect that the *March of Time*, of all people—to put a voice like that on the air that's supposed to be Chinese—that is not even *close* to a Chinese! *And it was the actual living thing!* What they wanted was the pidgin English that they were used to in movie Chinese characters. We had given them the real thing and they didn't like it one bit.

Larsen recalled only one celebrity who complained about the impersonations, and that was President Roosevelt. F.D.R. became annoyed, said Larsen, because he was getting calls and notes from political advisers regarding statements and remarks spoken on the *March of Time*'s radio show by the Roosevelt impersonator. These statements reflected Roosevelt's policies, but, in fact, had never been uttered by the President. Larsen said that this was an unnerving development because F.D.R. was their "star" impersonation, featured regularly on the show. *Time*'s staff was also worried that if F.D.R.'s objections became widely known they might provoke other celebrities to complain. By 1937, states *Time* chronicler Elson, White House complaints grew so firm that the *March of Time*'s radio producers ceased imitating Roosevelt altogether.

A few of the subjects which were presented during the first year of the series follow:

The political victory of Chicago mayor "Big Bill" Thompson.
The legalization of 4 percent beer and repeal of prohibition.

An expensive production, the *March of Time* required as many as 75 people to put each show on the air. Harry Von Zell (center) was featured as the Voice of Time while Westbrook Van Voorhis (left) played the Voice of Fate. (Courtesy Time, Inc.)

Devil's Island penal colony.

Investigation of the murder of Vivian Gordon and of vice ring operations in New York City.

"Flat-world" advocates and their activities.

The Communist rebellion in Cuba.

Political trials in Moscow.

Mahatma Gandhi and civil disobedience in India.

Military rebellions in Spain and Nicaragua.

Speedy divorces in Nevada.

The shooting of "Legs" Diamond in the Catskills.

Professor Piccard in a balloon.

Fascist students attacking Christian institutions.

The sinking of the submarine *Poseidon*.

The taking of Mukden by Japanese soldiers.

Charles Lindbergh in China.
The death of Thomas Edison.

Although a bit "campy" by today's standards, these dramatized "re-creations" were vastly entertaining in their own time. Here is an excerpt from a 1931 program which described the real-life visit of an American tourist, Mrs. Hattie Belle Johnston of New York, to India, and her brief meeting with Mahatma Gandhi:

VOICE OF TIME

New Delhi, India!
Today, round-the-world, tourists look forward to their stop at India—to the possibility of seeing India's first citizen—world-famed Mahatma Gandhi. In New Delhi, several hundred American tourists from the world-cruising S.S. *Belgenland* have joined the vast crowds of Hindus to hear Saint Gandhi speak. One of the tourists, Mrs. Hattie Belle Johnston of New York, has sought out and found mouselike Mrs. Gandhi, who takes the American tourist and several of her friends to the speaker's platform.

(Great crowd noises which fade)
MRS. JOHNSTON *(gushing)* Oh, Mrs. Gandhi, we want so much to speak to the Mahatma.
MRS. GANDHI *(slowly, sweetly, with Oriental accent)* Very well—I think that now is a good time to do so—But first excuse me, I am curious about something.
MRS. JOHNSTON Oh . . . what, my dear?
MRS. GANDHI What kind of clothes do you American women wear? Is it silk or satin, is it handmade or factory made?
MRS. JOHNSTON *(nonplussed)* It is factory made.
MRS. GANDHI *(very earnestly)* Ah, you American women must wear homespun garments and emancipate yourselves from slavery to style just as the women of India are doing. Here—now's your chance to speak to Mr. Gandhi!
MRS. JOHNSTON Come on, girls! . . . Oh, Mahatma, when are you coming to America? They'll go wild about you there . . . simply wild.

GANDHI   I shall come after India has her independence.

MRS. JOHNSTON *(quite excited)*   How long will that take?

GANDHI   Oh, perhaps not so long as it took America to get her freedom.

ANOTHER AMERICAN WOMAN   Oh, Mr. Gandhi—won't you please write your name in my autograph book?

MRS. JOHNSTON   Oh, yes—here's mine, too.

GANDHI   You may as well ask me for a lock of my hair.

MRS. JOHNSTON   Oh—how amusing, the Mahatma is so bald! Isn't he a dear! Oh, Mrs. Gandhi—maybe you wouldn't mind signing my autograph book!

(Crowd noises and music up and down)

Concluded the Voice of Time, thirty minutes or so later:

What news will the next seven days bring? *No man can say!*

In India, will threats to end the life of nut-brown little Mahatma Gandhi be carried out?

In New York City, what will be the result of the attempted investigation into the administration of Mayor James John ("Jimmie") Walker?

In Spain, will it be necessary for King Alfonso once again to appoint a Dictator who will coerce the Spanish people into submission?

Whatever happens, you can depend on one magazine to summarize for you at the end of the week *all* the news of *all* the world —to tell it vividly, accurately without bias—That publication is TIME—the weekly newsmagazine. A new issue goes on all newsstands every Friday.

TIME MARCHES ON!

The *March of Time* was enormously successful. Described by *Variety* as "the apex of radio showmanship," it reached millions of Americans during its 14-year history, provided publicity for *Time*'s publications that was of incalculable value, and was consistently rated in industry-conducted polls as one of network radio's most popular dramatic programs.

Intended as advertising for *Time* magazine, the show did not *make* money, it *cost* money. By the end of the second series, in late 1931, it was reported to have cost *Time* $211,000. Luce, never overly enthusiastic about nonprint communication, announced that the series would be discontinued early in 1932. To Larsen's delight, over 22,000 listeners wrote to the network and to *Time* to protest Luce's decision. The corporation found itself in an awkward position. In a two-page spread in *Time* on February 29, 1932, Luce thanked its public for their support of the series, then asked: "Whose the responsibility to continue it? *Time's*? *Time's* subscribers? the radio chains? a philanthropist's? the government's? . . . Obviously *Time* cannot be expected to buy advertising when it does not want it, in order to perform public service."

Following this remarkable display of listener loyalty, embarrassed CBS executive William Paley arranged for the network to support the show for a while, with editorial control remaining in the hands of *Time*. Said Larsen, "We got the credit, however, because of the big play accorded the announcement, 'Presented by the Editors of *Time*.'" In the years that followed, some commercial sponsors were found for the series, including Servell Electrolux, Remington Rand, and Wrigley (chewing gum). Wrigley's sponsorship came to an end in the late 1930's, according to Larsen, because of protests from German groups who complained about *Time's* growing anti-Nazi positions. The series was suspended in 1939, revived in 1941, and, with a new format, lasted until 1945, when it disappeared from the air.

In view of Larsen's flair for journalistic innovation, it was inevitable that he would consider translating the *March of Time* into a film series. Furthermore, "pictorial journalism" was a notion that interested Luce. One of the publisher's great enthusiasms during this period was for a "picture magazine" similar, perhaps, to the *Illustrated London News,* which would exploit the journalistic potential of the still photograph. In the early 1930's, research and development on a magazine called *Parade* was undertaken by the corporation. The new magazine was intended to extend the integration of photographs and text which had already been initiated in *Fortune*. In 1934, however, Luce decided that the project had not developed satisfactorily and suspended it.

Larsen is reported to have begun planning a motion picture version of the *March of Time* as early as 1931. In the next three years, a number of "wildcatters" sent him proposals and outlines for such a film series, but he was not impressed with any of them. None of the proposals explained how such a series could be put together and made to work. "A thousand people had an idea for me," said Larsen, "and most were wrong." More important, Larsen had not yet found the right man to produce such a series.

In the end, the right man turned out to be a veteran newsreel cameraman/producer named Louis de Rochemont, who had begun his film career while a teenager and by the 1930's had risen to become head of short subjects and producer of the *Magic Carpet* and *Adventures of a Newsreel Cameraman* series at Fox Movietone Corporation. De Rochemont had also introduced and produced, for Columbia Pictures, a novel film series entitled *The March of the Years,* which, with professional actors, re-created news events of the past, such as the Lizzie Borden murder case and the notorious career of Boss Tweed.

"I was fascinated with the *March of Time* radio," said de Rochemont, "and a friend said, 'Why don't you come in and see *Time*— this is too good to be!' So we made a date to go in and talk about it."

In later years, neither de Rochemont nor Larsen could remember who the individual was who had introduced them and then, just as suddenly, disappeared for good from their affairs. The man's name was Chester Withington, and his brief but important role was remembered by the late Celia Sugarman, executive secretary to Roy Larsen.

Sugarman was one of *Time*'s senior salaried employees when she retired in 1969. In 1955, she prepared, at the corporation's request, a history of the company and its leadership, as she remembered it. That history is now secure in the corporation's archive. I was allowed to examine the section of her memoirs that dealt with the entrance of Louis de Rochemont into the affairs of Time, Incorporated. It was a rare privilege. In a scene reminiscent of the Thatcher Memorial Library sequence in Orson Welles's *Citizen Kane,* one reads of her first contact with film maker Louis de Rochemont.

The Beginnings of Time

In the spring of 1934, Mr. Chester Withington approached Mr. Allen Grover [head of research for *Fortune*] on behalf of a friend or client . . . who had an idea for producing a movie based on items in *Time*. . . . Mr. Grover referred the whole thing to Mr. Larsen, who thus met Mr. Louis de Rochemont. Mr. de Rochemont was at that time with Fox Movietone News, where he was producing short subjects, among them *The Magic Carpet,* an excellent newsreel series. The early Larsen-de Rochement-Withington meetings were held outside of the office—one of them, I think, for the purpose of screening various issues of *The Magic Carpet* for Mr. Larsen, who was particularly impressed by Mr. de Rochemont's technique of keeping the commentary to a minimum and so editing the pictures that they spoke for themselves. Before long, Mr. de Rochemont and Mr. Withington were coming openly to Mr. Larsen's office for their sessions. The first time they came, Mr. Larsen was unexpectedly tied up and obviously going to have to keep them waiting. Since we were then on the same floor as the reception room, I usually went out to explain such delays in person; and, as we had no pages, I almost always went out to act as guide. So this small ceremony of explaining that the guests would have to wait a few minutes provided my first meeting with Mr. de Rochemont, whom I found to be a big, burly, deep-voiced, pleasant individual.

Larsen was impressed with de Rochemont's energy, insight, and expertise. Above all, Louis had a clear idea of how the *March of Time* could be put on film. It became obvious that if such a film series were to succeed, it would have to integrate substantial amounts of newsreel footage with specially photographed material. And Louis knew the Fox Movietone News film library inside and out. "It was love at first sight," said Larsen forty years later. "I felt he had everything the movie business had to offer. . . . I said, 'Louis, you're for me!' . . . Within one week, he was on the team."

Perhaps Larsen's greatest administrative asset was his ability to combine an entrepreneur's optimism with a businessman's caution. He insisted that de Rochemont and he put together a sample *March of Time* issue so that he could see, at first hand, exactly how much time and money it would cost.

Larsen and de Rochemont set to work at once, with Louis instructing Larsen at every step in the art and technique of film making. Then, as later, Larsen worked side by side with de Rochemont at the editing tables and in the screening rooms. When Lothar Wolff, later chief film editor of the *March of Time*, first joined the organization, he was flabbergasted to discover that the man at the editing table, laboriously rewinding 35mm film, was a principal officer and one of the largest stockholders in *Time*'s publishing empire.

"We could hardly contain ourselves," recalled Larsen. "We could hardly wait to get out the sample reel. After a couple weeks, we were bold enough to show our work to Harry Luce, who was wondering where I was." Luce looked at the film, bewildered. "It's terrific, but what is it?" he said to Larsen in a memo. "Please spell it out for me; what is this all about?"

Larsen prepared a prospectus for Luce which Luce reedited and perfected, and it was Luce who brought the prospectus to the board of directors—he felt that Larsen was too emotionally involved to do the job properly. The board approved further experimentation so Luce authorized expenditures reported to total nearly $200,000 for research and preparation.

Within a month of Luce's authorization, de Rochemont and Larsen rented the second floor of Fox Movietone News's New York headquarters at 460 West 54th Street, took over a projection room, carved out some studio space, installed production equipment, and began auditing tens of thousands of feet of 35mm newsreel footage from which they hoped to take the raw material of their series. De Rochemont succeeded, at this point, in going over the head of his former boss, Truman Talley, and securing the right to buy footage from Fox Movietone's archives. Access to this material was absolutely crucial to the *March of Time*'s early operations. In the years that followed, the *March of Time* built up its own library till it contained more than 10 million feet, but without Fox Movietone's footage, Louis could never have made the series work. It was a sensational coup, and one for which Truman Talley never forgave de Rochemont. "I kept telling [Talley] that the newsreels weren't any good," said Louis. "And he said, 'Oh, the *March of Time* is a waste of time.' "

Larsen and de Rochemont screened thousands of feet of newsreel film, staged scenes with impersonators for their first experimental reels, then waited anxiously for Henry Luce's judgment. "It's terrific," said Luce, "but what is it?" (Photo by Alfred Eisenstaedt, Life Magazine; courtesy Time, Inc.)

Early news of the experimental work reached the public in November 1934, through Daniel Longwell, then assistant to Henry Luce. It was announced in the *New York Times* on November 24 that, if produced, the series "would bear the same relation to the present type newsreel as a discursive magazine bears to the newspaper." At that time the corporation had not yet decided to commit itself to production, and arrangements had not yet been made for distribution.

After several months' work, three experimental *March of Time* reels had been completed, each running approximately 20 minutes and covering the following subjects:

No. 1: 1. Indianapolis auto race; 2. Lloyd's of London; 3. The Dionne quintuplets; 4. Albert Einstein; 5. Tojo and the Pacific navies.

No. 2: 1. Vatican City; 2. Bubonic plague; 3. Chinese eastern railroad; 4. Dolfuss-Hitler; 5. The drought of 1934.

No. 3: 1. Bergoff, the professional strike breaker; 2. Moe Buchsbaum; 3. Sinking of the *Morro Castle;* 4. The stroboscopic camera; 5. Smiukse (who vandalized a WPA mural in New England); 6. The Saar.

Each of these experimental reels incorporated both newsreel and "re-created" scenes, the latter of which were based upon real-life events which were performed by impersonators who looked like the political figures, scientists, artists, military leaders, and other celebrities selected for these issues. Some of the very earliest *March of Time* issues were shot silent, and later, back at the studio, the dialogue was dubbed by actors and actresses who sounded like the celebrities on the screen. The object was superior sound recording quality and a saving in time and money. This approach proved unworkable, however, and much more expensive than synchronous "on-the-spot" sound recording, and after a short period of time it was abandoned.

Though crude and unpolished, these experimental reels showed promise as a new type of motion picture reportage. Impressed, the directors of Time, Incorporated, approved a schedule of commercial release, and preparations were made for the launching of *Time*'s fourth major publishing venture. The experimental shorts themselves were never released in their original form; however, several of the sixteen sequences were later included in the commercial releases.

The *March of Time* was founded in 1934, separate from but under the control and ownership of Time, Inc., with business offices and general headquarters at 135 East 42nd Street in New York. Heading the new corporation were Roy Larsen, president and treasurer; John S. Martin, vice-president; Louis de Rochemont, vice-president; and John R. Wood, Jr., secretary and assistant treasurer. Contracts were signed with First Division Pictures, a small distributing organization in which the March of Time, Inc., had bought a controlling interest. As it turned out, this was a mistake. First Division was nearly bankrupt. "We didn't know *what* we were doing," recalled Larsen. "Breaking into the film business was even worse than into the radio networks."

The production staff was gradually enlarged to include a permanent complement of cameramen, research workers, editors,

Richard de Rochemont, Louis's brother, was chosen to head up European operations. Like Louis, a veteran newsreeler, Richard had been editor and Paris manager for Fox Movietone News. (Courtesy Tom Orchard)

writers, and technicians. Production of film issues were increased to provide for a projected distribution schedule of one issue per month. Richard de Rochemont, Louis's brother, was selected to head European operations. Although only 32, Dick de Rochemont had already had a long career in the news gathering business as a reporter, newsreel editor, and manager for France of Fox Movietone News.

An intensive publicity campaign, through the pages of *Time* and *Fortune* magazines, the radio version of the *March of Time,* and local-level advertising, prepared the public for the coming series. In a widely circulated publicity brochure *Introducing the March of Time,* the corporation outlined the contents of the first issue, revealed plans for future releases, and carefully differentiated between the *March of Time* on radio and on film:

> Is the *March of Time* a promotion scheme for Time Magazine? No. The motion picture is a distinct, independent project. A separate company, THE MARCH OF TIME, Inc. has been formed to produce the picture. This is sold to motion picture exhibitors on its own entertainment value. It must pay for itself or it will be discontinued.

By January 26, 1935, some 509 theaters had booked the series in advance.

With the first issue of the new series completed, future issues already finished or in preparation, and the prerelease publicity campaign drawing to a close, the stage was set for the introduction of the *March of Time* to an eager and expectant public.

2

One Man in His Own Time: Louis de Rochemont

In March 1975, I had a three-hour lunch with former *March of Time* director Jack Glenn at a pleasant French restaurant on the east side of New York City. With my tape recorder running, we sat at the back of the restaurant where we would not disturb the other patrons with our prolonged conversation and our more or less continuous laughter, as Glenn reminisced about the experiences he had had at the *March of Time* and the strong and oftentimes contrary personalities who were his colleagues and bosses at the organization.

As we sat talking, an attractive woman in her mid-thirties came into the restaurant alone and took a table close to ours. We lowered our voices, but it was obvious that she listened with interest to Glenn's remarks. After an hour or so, she completed her meal, rose, and departed, never to be seen by us again. Moments later, the proprietor returned to our table with a note from her. It read:

Being able to listen to your conversation has been the high point of my first day in New York.

But—who is Louis?

Who indeed?

One Man in His Own Time: Louis de Rochemont

Louis de Rochemont was born in Chelsea, Massachusetts, on January 13, 1899, the eldest son of Louis L. G. de Rochemont, a Boston attorney, and Sarah Wilson Miller. He was subsequently raised and schooled nearby in Winchester. A distinctly New England product, his family derived its name from French Huguenot ancestors who had settled in New Hampshire in the 1820's.

From childhood onward, the values, imagery, and expectations that he brought to his life and work derived substantially from his New England experience. In the years that followed, he became one of the world's most traveled men, moving familiarly through what were then the farthest and most exotic reaches of the earth. But whenever he put a film together, everything always came out looking like New England.

As a youngster in Winchester, Louis's hero had been a literary character named Gallegher, from the Richard Harding Davis novel of the same name. Gallegher was a teen-age news reporter—a resourceful, hyper-thyroid, never-say-die kind of kid whose principal aim was to obtain "scoops" for his newspaper. For Louis, such a life seemed grand. He canvassed the town of Winchester, unearthing "scoops" about its citizens and their affairs. If he couldn't find any real news, he would manufacture it. "I used to bring in scoops that had never happened," he said, "and tell them, for instance, that the Germans were putting poison in the cattle. I'd do anything."

By the age of thirteen, he was working as a freelance motion picture newsreel cameraman, supplying regional movie houses with scenes of local citizens and events, using a 35mm camera which he'd purchased from a film maker in Worcester. Prophetically, one of the films that young de Rochemont sold was to Roy Larsen's father, then manager of Keith's Theater in Boston, in 1916—it was a 1000-foot short of the Harvard-Dartmouth football game of that year.

While still in high school, he attracted widespread attention with his coverage of the arrest of Werner Horn, a German saboteur charged with the demolition of a bridge at Vanceboro, Maine. Following the announcement of the apprehension of Horn, de Rochemont and other news cameramen rushed to Portland, the scene of the arrest, where they discovered that they were too late to film the actual incarceration that had taken place earlier in the day. De Rochemont remained at the courthouse until his disappointed competitors left, and then persuaded both the sheriff and the saboteur to "re-create" jointly the imprisonment exactly as it had occurred earlier. The sixteen-year-old cameraman cranked away on his camera as the official obligingly led a cooperative Horn outside the jailhouse and pantomimed the seizing, handcuffing, and jailing of the saboteur.

This was de Rochemont's first attempt to "re-create" reality by reenacting actual events. In doing so, he secured exclusive motion pictures of an important news event, hundreds of feet of which were bought and exhibited by both the Mutual and Universal newsreel companies. His outraged competitors charged the youthful film maker with fraud and charlatanry. De Rochemont defended himself by arguing that newsreel cameramen had the same right to reenact events with film as the newspaper reporter and rewrite man had with words. In the years that followed, he argued that reenactments were "frequently sharper and more detailed than the 'real' thing." It was something to think about.

The European war was well under way when Louis graduated from high school in 1916. He enlisted in the Naval Reserve, quickly became a yeoman second class, and was sent to officer's candidate school. His commission as temporary ensign came through shortly after the end of the war and he served as a deck officer in the U.S. Navy until 1923. During this period his commission was confirmed as a regular officer and he was promoted at least once. The history, traditions, customs, and values of this service had as profound an influence upon de Rochemont as did his New England upbringing. His love for the navy was passionate, and it lasted for a lifetime.

De Rochemont had served as a watch officer, not as a photographic specialist, but he always took his camera with him and shot thousands of feet of film of navy life and operations throughout the world, a great deal of which he sent on to the navy's recruiting office. The navy liked and remembered this gesture. While still on duty, he also shot newsreel material which found its way into commercial release, including the capture and burning of Smyrna by Kemal Ataturk.

In 1923, by which time he had been promoted to lieutenant, de Rochemont resigned his commission to return to civilian life and a position as newsreel cameraman for Hearst International Newsreel. De Rochemont then quickly discovered, if he had not already done so earlier, that in the newsreel business, no matter how devious the method of covering a major news event, the end was felt to justify the means. When the Byrd expedition to the North Pole tied up exclusive motion picture rights and granted them to a rival newsreel company, de Rochemont arranged to have the expedition's departure from Spitsbergen photographed from the Amundsen expedition's dirigible, *Norge,* and rushed his "stolen" footage to movie houses several days in advance of his licensed competitors. On another occasion, faced with a "lockout" which prevented him from filming a notable horse race at Belmont Park in New York, he smuggled a battery of cameras into the park inside a root beer truck and, from a vantage point next to the track, secured photographs of the entire race.

De Rochemont remained with Hearst until 1927, when he resigned in order to join Pathé News as assistant editor. Almost immediately, he secured leave from Pathé to produce a number of experimental recruiting films for the U.S. Navy as an independent contractor. At first he took with him as cameraman former navy seaman Bonney Powell. Later he took a former newspaperman named Jack Glenn with him as his writer, director, and actor. Together, Louis and Jack traveled throughout the world, producing short silent travelogues designed to stimulate navy enlistments. The films were comic, corny, and fun to make, with Glenn appearing in most of them, properly costumed, as an American seaman. Titles in the series included "Greece Through a Doughnut," "Paths in Palestine," "Hello Hawaii," "Egyptian Adventure," "Red-Hot Mummies," "In the Steps of Genghis Khan," "Down to Dalmatia," and "Shanghai Jesters."

In 1928, de Rochemont was ordered back to work on newsreels by Pathé and told to abandon his experimental short subject work. "The newsreels are stuck in the mud," he complained to Glenn. "They never get behind the news. What has led up to a given event? What does it portend? . . . Someday," he concluded, "I'm going to revolutionize the newsreel."

He resigned from Pathé in 1929 and joined the staff of Fox Movietone News. Still traveling widely, de Rochemont was in India during the terrifying Bombay riots of 1930. Although appalled by what he saw, he was professional enough to get it all on film. As he had assumed would happen, a British CID officer was knocking on his Bombay hotel door within an hour after the event to take possession of the footage he had managed to photograph. But Louis had already switched labels on the film cans; the riot footage was now in a can purporting to contain scenes of the annual Punah festival celebration. "I shed crocodile tears," recalled de Rochemont, and reluctantly handed over the travel scenes to the officer, who departed with thanks and professional sympathy. At once, like his youthful hero, Gallegher, Louis set to work to smuggle the negatives of his "scoop" back to the United States. He found an American nurse in Bombay, ill with a lung infection, who needed money for passage back to the U.S. Her friends were in the process of taking up a collection when de Rochemont appeared and pressed the necessary travel funds upon the bewildered woman, together with his precious can of film. Properly briefed, the girl departed with thanks and Louis's smuggled film en route to the U.S.A., via Genoa, Italy. Then Louis cabled Truman Talley, his boss at Fox, to prepare him for the handling and release of the riot newsreels. The film finally reached Fox Movietone headquarters, but the cable got misplaced along the way. Native festival scenes were a drug on the market, and since that was what the label said it was, the footage sat in Talley's office, undeveloped for weeks until Louis got back to New York. "I said, 'What in hell happened to my riot films?'" recalled de Rochemont. "They hadn't paid any attention to my cable." With Louis on hand they paid attention, and the film was quickly released, a little late but with spectacular results, to motion picture theaters throughout the world. The coverage was sensational, and Louis's reputation for aggressive newsreel reporting was further enhanced.

At Fox, Louis was made director of short subjects and editor of Fox Movietone's *Magic Carpet* and *Adventures of the Newsreel Cameraman* series. Fox Movietone News was the world's largest and best financed newsreel organization at that time. It had introduced the sound-on-film motion picture to audiences in 1927 and had an enormous staff scattered throughout the world. Its English-language version featured the very popular narrator, Lowell Thomas, and, at its peak, its foreign issues were released to 47 foreign countries in more than a dozen languages. De Rochemont worked closely at Fox with Movietone News's talented editor, Mike Clofine, who, de Rochemont recalled, was the man who taught him more than anyone else about the art of film making.

In 1933 de Rochemont ventured into independent film production with a 70-minute documentary feature entitled *The Cry of the World,* which he constructed from war and newsreel footage in the Fox Movietone library. The film was a powerful indictment of war and oppression, and provided an impression of the military conflicts that were still to come. Rita C. McGoldrick, in a May 14, 1932 article in *Motion Picture Herald,* said "There has been no picture ever that has brought to me so much of fearful reality as this 'Cry of the World' . . . Its message is unanswerable." It was one of the first sound-on-film compilage feature films to be produced, employing editing techniques that became increasingly popular during the 1960's and 70's with the release of historical documentary series on television. In 1933, however, it was both thematically and stylistically ahead of its time. Its production gave de Rochemont valuable experience in the integration of newsreel stock shots into documentary productions, but the film was a catastrophic financial failure and cost him a considerable amount of his own money.

Louis never looked back. He started work on an entirely new series, called *March of the Years,* which re-created historical events involving celebrated or infamous people, and which had been inspired, according to de Rochemont, by the radio version of the *March of Time.* Louis's aim was to "restage" the past in a manner that was both convincing and entertaining, using professional actors and actresses in the roles of well-known historical characters. Financial backing for the series was arranged, and a corporation was founded with Peter Naphen as president. Production was carried on in New York City, beginning in 1933, with the schedule calling for twenty issues a year. The series was billed as "The first different short feature since Mickey Mouse," and was successfully released through Columbia Pictures.

The first issue contained re-creations of Boss Tweed, "Czar of New York" in 1870; the birth of prohibition in 1880; the Lizzie Borden sensation of 1892; the invention of the airplane by the Wright Brothers in 1893; and the invention of an automatic hat-tipping device in 1896. Succeeding issues contained sequences on the kidnapping of a child named Charlie Ross, the British Crippen murder case, the opening of Japan by Commodore Perry, a gang-land killing involving the O'Bannion group, and the opening of America's first musical comedy. Clearly Louis's historical interests were catholic.

Most of the performers in Louis's new series were New York stage people, many of them appearing in films for the first time. These included Charles Coburn (who played Boss Tweed), Maggie Mullen (who played Lizzie Borden), Pedro de Cordoba, Marjorie Lytell, and many others. Some of Louis's production and technical staff on the series were people who would later figure in his production of the *March of Time*. These included editors Beverly Jones, John Dullaghan, and Morrie Roizman; director Jack Glenn; and musical director John Rochetti.

Such was the background of the man who, at the age of thirty-five, was hired to launch Roy Larsen's ambitious new venture into theatrical film production, the *March of Time*. For many of the old-time, print-oriented people at *Time* magazine and the parent corporation, the whole business of making films was a vast annoyance—something lower-class and vulgar, like the astrology and lonely hearts columns at the back of the big-city newspapers. What was a rowdy newsreeler like de Rochemont doing in a nice place like this? What kind of man were they getting for their money? What was his philosophy of journalism and how did it fit into the magazine's scheme of things? How would his films reflect upon the firm's name and reputation? Where it would end, knew only God!

They had a lot to worry about. In the first place, no one who ever worked with Louis ever knew for certain what he believed in. Politically and socially, his privately held beliefs were a mystery. Louis considered himself a journalist who happened to make films,

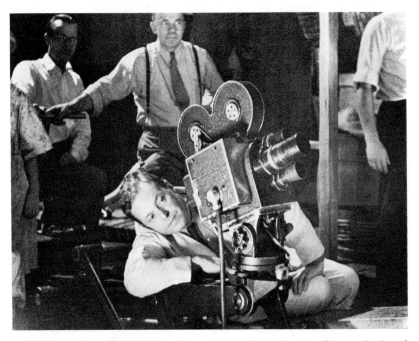

De Rochemont (crouched behind camera) may have been a disorganized and inarticulate administrator, but none of his subordinates ever doubted that he knew what he wanted in the way of a finished film. Single-minded to the point of compulsion, he drove his people very hard indeed, just as he drove himself. (Courtesy Jack Glenn)

and he liked to pretend that he merely reported the news as it happened. Like his youthful hero, Gallegher, he was high on Moxie and deficient in theory.

Within the huge, conservative bureaucracy of Time, Incorporated, the *March of Time* and its films were considered moderately left-wing. Indeed, there were a substantial number of liberal and leftist film makers on the payroll. Louis himself could not by the wildest stretch of the imagination have been considered part of any left-wing persuasion. And yet, the films that he created were consistently liberal, progressive, and militantly antifascist at a time when it took courage to attack "prematurely" the totalitarian adventures then under way in Germany, Italy, Spain, and Japan. His films were critical, though somewhat less vigorous in their treatment of Soviet communism. What did that make Louis? "Well," said writer Jimmy Shute, "he wasn't anything, either left-wing or right-wing. He was right-wing one day and left-wing the next. He was a highly emotional man."

His films consistently championed the racially oppressed and doggedly exposed theater audiences to the emerging horrors of anti-Jewish persecution and genocide. In the late 1940's, as a feature film producer, he made one of the first modern American fiction films that dealt with the second-class citizenship of black men and women in American society. The film was based upon a true-life story involving a young white-skinned man who discovered that he was racially black. Dated now, courageous then, it was called *Lost Boundaries*, and was well and widely received when it was released in 1949. And yet, if Louis, in his conversations, ever enunciated any kind of humanistic creed or sympathetic sentiments for racial minorities, no one can remember it.

Today, rarely granting interviews, virtually alone in his Newington, New Hampshire, estate, aloof, seldom visited, rarely photographed, he remains, as throughout his career, an enigma. In the end, we will judge him by his films, their impact upon society, and his role in the development of film journalism.

De Rochemont was such a colorful, chaotic, and contradictory personality that it is easy for the careless student of film history to miss the fact that he was also an enormously talented man.

He was an excellent film writer. Jimmy Shute, who became head of the *March of Time*'s editorial board, claimed that Louis was a far better writer than he "in that he always knew what to leave out. I wanted to get everything in, and so it would get talkier and talkier, and he'd cut out words, slashing to right and to left, and I'd be horrified at how much he'd leave out—but somehow, it didn't matter."

He was a born film maker with a fine visual sense. Tom Orchard, senior *March of Time* associate producer, called him "The Master Editor," whose specialty was making something out of nothing. Arthur Tourtellot, another associate producer, agreed: "He had this passion about editing film; it was a passion and it was a gift. . . . I think that Louis de Rochemont's great historical achievement is as a film editor."

36

He was an effective, if unorthodox, teacher. "Louis was my teacher," said Roy Larsen, and with a few exceptions, nearly everyone else admitted the same thing. Sometimes, even if Louis didn't like his colleague's work, he would praise it anyway. Jimmy Shute recalled him saying, "Gee, this is great. That's a wonderful line." And then, said Shute, "he'd put the whole thing aside and start writing a whole new one himself. And nothing that he ever mentioned with praise ever got into the final script."

He was a first-class journalist with a remarkable news sense. "He would decide, say in February, to go into something on Czechoslovakia," said Shute, "and everything would be quiet in Czechoslovakia. And then, suddenly, just the week our picture came out—Bang!—everything would explode! And I don't know whether he did that deliberately or whether it was just sort of instinct with him."

Above all, Louis had *velocity*—a gigantic, unmodulated kind of energy which, when focused through the lens of his obsessions, inevitably swept fellow workers and innocent bystanders along. It was not in Louis's case the kind of motion that one associates with a sleek train, a fast car, or a speeding bullet. It was more like the momentum of a maddened elephant, crashing through the underbrush at Time, Incorporated, raising lots of dust, making lots of noise, and leaving its mark on the intervening landscape.

So much for his talent and energy. His personality was something else. However liberal and progressive Louis's films may have seemed to audiences, in his own shop he was an absolute tyrant.

For those who worked with Louis to achieve his ends, it was bloody hell all the way. A few of his former colleagues remember him with something like affection. As for the others, the kindest thing that most of them can say of him is that he was a difficult man to work for.

Mary Losey, an early *March of Time* researcher, said, "I disliked him intensely. . . . I found him bullying, devious, and a very chaotic personality. And he certainly disliked me. It was very mutual." Losey was especially resentful of the inferior position of women in all *Time* divisions, for in those days only men occupied positions of responsibility and authority in the corporation. She said:

Louis was the first and, I think, most magnificent example of male chauvinist that I ever came across. . . . I think he disliked women more than he disliked men, but he preferred men who kowtowed to him, and he was very destructive.

Albert Sindlinger, the *March of Time*'s distribution and promotion head, was even more blunt:

Louis is a hell of a guy, but he couldn't control his ego. . . . He could have been a great man if he hadn't been such a God-damned egotist. . . . Louis couldn't give anybody else any credit for anything. Everything was *his*.

Because of his stocky build and 218 pounds, de Rochemont looked shorter than he was. In fact, he was well over six feet tall—a big man with a big voice, which he used at good volume much of the time.

When he wasn't shouting, he was growling, and when he wasn't growling, he was mumbling, a tactic he used with great artistry, together with unfinished sentences. According to his subordinates, Louis's mumbling could reduce the simplest set of operational instructions to mush. A group of five experienced film makers could walk out of de Rochemont's office with that many different ideas of what he wanted in a film and what they were supposed to do to provide it. He was a disorganized and inarticulate administrator, but none of his subordinates ever doubted that he knew what he wanted in the way of a finished film. And, just in case they got to thinking otherwise, he'd interrupt from time to time with incisive, authoritative questions, most of which required incisive, authoritative answers. All of this would have been faintly amusing had it not been for the fact that Louis had the power to hire and fire. And it was a power in those preunion depression days which he was capable of using with sufficient frequency and arbitrariness to keep the rank and file on edge at all times.

Louis drove his people very hard indeed, just as he drove himself. He was single-minded to the point of compulsion.

Here's a man, [said editor Morrie Roizman] who never played cards, never went out to do any athletics, never went to the theater, never went to the movies, never did anything—all he did was smoke, and work. . . . with Louis, it's nothing but work, work, work. And when you get through working, you work some more. And that's all there ever was. You know, it was really funny. He never could give up. There must be *something*, you know. He never saw his wife. He never saw his children. That's a rather strange way. There must be something *else*.

Jack Shaindlin, the *March of Time*'s musical director, found de Rochemont enjoyable to work with, and was one of the few people who consistently got along with him. This probably followed from the fact that he and his musicians were outsiders who worked by themselves, and that Louis, with his tin ear and ignorance of musical matters, was in no position to tell them how to do their jobs. Shaindlin describes de Rochemont as a complicated and difficult man, but unquestionably the driving force who had created and shaped the *March of Time* film series. "Louis either liked you or he didn't," said Shaindlin. "If he didn't, you couldn't come near him. If he liked you, after a while, he'd leave you alone." Shaindlin added as an afterthought that if anyone ever made a film about de Rochemont, the role would have to be played by Orson Welles—a bigger-than-life figure whose egocentricity and volatile temperament were matched in equal proportions by his energy, will, and talent.

Interestingly, Louis was a perfect host. He never allowed another person to pick up a restaurant check, and in his own home, with his wife Jinny, he was as considerate and thoughtful a person as one might wish to find in an otherwise imperfect world.

If anyone at *Time* magazine imagined they were going to keep Louis on a short leash—or on a long leash for that matter—he soon disabused them of the notion. Apart from the restraining influence of Roy Larsen, who loved the *March of Time* and respected Louis's vision, no one—not even Henry Luce—could tell him what to do. "In the end," said associate producer Lothar Wolff, "Louis is incapable, really, of working with anyone whom *he* doesn't control. He would resent anyone . . . and in each instance [in his career] there was a battle, really, with the people who were above him.

And that was the way it went, from the day de Rochemont arrived until the day he left. Like many other successful film producers, he functioned like a general, sending his men out into one hazardous battle after another, sustaining heavy casualties along the way, but somehow or other accomplishing the variety of missions assigned to him by the corporation.

In sum, the portraits which Louis's fellow workers draw of him are sharp, consistent, and vividly colored: a driven man, inspired but insecure; a dreamer who was painfully uncommunicative and contradictory in his relations with other human beings; a bully who was impossibly demanding of both himself and his associates; an oftentimes hard and humorless man who could be unpredictably generous in helping loyal workers.

Readers of a later generation, innocent of economic realities, may wonder why anyone would work for such a difficult man. They worked for him, and willingly so, because there were no jobs elsewhere. Thirty-five dollars a week may not seem like much today, but, as editor Morrie Roizman observed, there were always a lot of hungry guys outside on the street waiting to take your place.

Apart from economics, however, the *March of Time* was a wonderfully exciting place to work. It was unique in both journalistic and film-making circles. No one had ever attempted anything like it before, and no one would successfully do so again until the coming of high-quality television news and public affairs programming decades later. Tom Orchard, Louis's right-hand man, recalled the sense of the place:

> We loved it. . . . It was young. I hate that word, because I'm now older, and I loathe this "young" business. But at that time, we were all young, it was all new.

Even Mary Losey, no friend of Louis, agreed:

> I was right in it. As a matter of fact, that whole period of time for anybody who was in any of the media was very exciting. Whether it was the *March of Time,* or [later] the Canadian Film Board, or the OWI . . . you were right in the middle of the storm, and it was great fun.

Fun or not, it was 1935, and if you wanted to be part of the new motion picture journalism, you ended up at the *March of Time.* There was only one game in town, and Louis was running it.

3

The Time of Their Lives: First Year

On February 1, 1935, the first issue of the *March of Time* was premiered at the Capitol Theater in New York City and opened, almost simultaneously, at seventy first-run movie houses throughout the country. Running 1964 feet (22 minutes), it covered a wide variety of subjects in a style which the film's producers called "pictorial journalism."

The first sequence of the film described the role of Prince Saionji in Japan's internal struggle between democratic leadership and growing militarism. The second sequence revealed the devices and ruses used by the proprietors of Manhattan's famous "21 Club" to frustrate the efforts of federal agents during the prohibition era. The third showed the attempts of Britain's transport minister, Leslie Hore-Belisha, to erect traffic lights ("Belisha Beacons") throughout the country, despite the hostility and vandalism of British motorists. The fourth sequence recounted a foreign incident involving an American tourist, Moe Buchsbaum, who refused to pay a traffic fine in France unless the payment were applied to France's unpaid war debt to the United States. The fifth investigated the National Recovery Administration and the conviction of Fred Perkins, a small battery manufacturer, who had refused, as

First issue of *Time*'s news film series reached theaters in February of 1935. The promotion campaign included this walking "sandwich board" announcement on the streets of New York. (Courtesy Time, Inc.)

a matter of principle, to abide by NRA wage-scale directives. The last sequence, which incorporated the first sound pictures ever taken of the Metropolitan Opera, described the last-night performance, resignation, and retirement of Giulio Gatti-Casazza, general manager of the Metropolitan Opera for twenty-five years.

The film's continuity depended largely upon the frequent use of "re-creation." Excepting the first sequence, which dealt with Japan, the contents of the entire film were staged by *March of Time* directors and cameramen, who either persuaded the principals to reenact the incidents shown as they had originally occurred or used impersonators in their place. The sequence on Japan relied heavily on newsreel stock shots. However, even in this episode, at least one of the scenes of Prince Saionji was made in New York with a Japanese nonprofessional look-alike, who was paid $30 for his brief on-camera performance. Even when authentic newsreel material was available, impersonation was sometimes preferred by the film's editors in the interest of dramatic effectiveness. Though the *March of Time*'s producers had stated that "the principal characters in a news story . . . are perfect cinemactors," they found British transport minister Hore-Belisha's voice "indistinct and too English," and dubbed in a New York actor's voice. Clearly, the more or less literal format of the conventional newsreel had been abandoned for a more dynamic and dramatic motion picture treatment of current events.

Critics generally seemed pleased with it. Alistair Cooke wrote in the *Listener* on November 20, 1935:

> There are papers, and in a fainter way documentary films, that are intelligent. There are some that are energetic. There are some that are aloof. It has been left to *Time,* and now "The March of Time" to combine, for the first time in journalism, intelligence, energy, and aloofness.

Worries at the home office about the film's commercial potential gradually faded as the public endorsed the new series at the box office. *Variety,* the industry trade paper proclaimed on February 5, 1935:

> From the exhibitor angle, the cinematic "March of Time" . . . is boxoffice. . . . The same skillful news merchandising which has

43

Climax of the first issue was a sequence describing the last-night performance of Giulio Gatti-Casazza, retiring general manager of the Metropolitan Opera. The episode showed the first motion picture footage ever photographed of a performance at the Met. (Courtesy Time, Inc.)

distinguished the weekly news magazine finds a counterpart in the "March of Time" reel which may well become a No. 2 feature for the average exhib. It's more than a newsreel, and even the deluxers, playing single features, first run, may well be deemed offering a dual bill every month when the new "March of Time" rolls around.

With its first offering well-received, March of Time, Inc., released the second issue in its first-year schedule. By now, distribution of the series was well enough planned to ensure a fairly wide audience for the film.

Following each issue's appearance in key, first-run theaters, the prints were passed on to smaller houses throughout the country until, at the end of its run, the issue had appeared in 417 movie houses in 168 cities. The cost to exhibitors varied with the size and prestige of the house, the size of the city, and, of course, the nature of the release (i.e., first run, second run, etc.). First-run rates varied from $500 per booking for independent houses in Albany to $1500 per run in Philadelphia and $2000-$2600 (the top) at the Radio City Music Hall in New York City. Lower rates were quoted to houses belonging to large theater chains; lower still to theaters that ran it, weeks later, as second and third runs. The lowest price charged for a weeks'-late release to small theaters in out-of-the-way places was around $7.50. March of Time, Inc., optimistically predicted its average gross revenue from all 417 theaters during this first year at $200,000 per issue. This, as it turned out, was very optimistic indeed.

The second issue, unlike the first, was mildly controversial. One of its episodes was devoted to a sequence on Adolf Hitler, briefly describing his rise to power, political maneuvers, and preparations for war. Up to this time, photographs of Hitler had rarely appeared on American movie screens because of the film industry's reluctance to arouse its audiences and create controversy. The publishers of *Time* boasted on January 31, 1938, in *Life* magazine: "THE MARCH OF TIME flouted this taboo. . . ." And so they did, but in doing so, began a sixteen-year battle with what *Variety* euphemistically termed, "The Scissors Brigade"—the forces of foreign and domestic censorship.

The film contained one of the most celebrated shots ever shown of Hitler, made late at night as the dictator sat before a fireplace staring moodily into the fire. As it happened, the shot had been staged by the *March of Time* in its New York studios, with an impersonator. Over it, somber narrator Westbrook Van Voorhis intoned:

To a mountain retreat in the Bavarian alps, an ultimatum from the great powers of Europe sends a lone, strange man to brood over a bitter fact. He has just been forced to realize that he is the most suspected, most distrusted ruler in the world today. In two short years, Adolf Hitler has lost for his country what Germany had nearly regained—the world's sympathy.

From Canada, two sequences of this second issue were removed and shipped back to New York by Famous-Players-Canadian. The Ontario Board of Censors had found the Hitler sequence "warlike in attitude," despite arguments by de Rochemont that the film merely paralleled newspaper and magazine treatments of the European crisis.

Also deleted by the Ontario board was the second sequence of the issue—a description of the methods used by the *New York Daily News* in "scooping" its competitors with news of the Bruno Hauptmann death sentence. Deletion of the sequence by the Censor Board was in line with its general ban on all newsreel clips of the Hauptmann trial as being "in bad taste."

The remainder of the second issue was devoted to sequences on the Mohawk sea disaster; ex-convict, folk-song writer Huddie Ledbetter ("Good Night, Irene"); and Professor Edgerton's new slow-motion camera, this last sequence having first appeared in the third experimental *March of Time* reel.

If de Rochemont and Larsen were disturbed by the mild controversy that their second issue had provoked, it was not apparent. The third issue, released in April 1935, was still more controversial. It featured, first, a satirical study of Huey P. Long—political demagogue, former governor, and then senator from Louisiana. Wrote the reviewer in the April 24, 1935, edition of the *New York World-Telegram:* "It neither condemns nor ridicules deliberately, but by bringing together certain of the Kingfish's sayings and doings allows him to do this himself in a thoroughly devastating manner." On the same day *Variety* added: "The impersonal off-screen description is . . . not without its editorial influence in

RIGHT ABOVE:
Title logo for the first few issues of the *March of Time*. Distribution during this period was through a small exchange system in which Time, Inc., had bought an interest. (Courtesy Time, Inc.)

RIGHT:
By August 1935 distribution of the series had been given to RKO Radio Pictures and a new and more dramatic logo was designed.

just the right degree when it suits the 'Time' editorial-production staff's purposes. . . ."

In fact, the *March of Time* made a fool out of Long. The man's outrageous behavior and dictatorial control of his state's political apparatus were described in the most uncompromising fashion, from the moment of Van Voorhis's opening narration:

VOICE OF TIME

Almost like a foreign city in the midst of America is New Orleans. . . . This old-world city, in fact the entire state of Louisiana, is in the grip of a decidedly un-American dictatorship of the loudest character the national political scene has heard in a generation.

Long is the name, and long is the way this unusual man has come in the last seven years. . . . Frankly a demagogue, he has been elected through his appeal to the people up the Bayou.

The narration was written in a manner which would never get past today's cautious television-news editors:

VOICE OF TIME

To run his state, dictator Long puts in O. K. Allen, his good-natured henchman—new puppet governor of Louisiana. To his new friends in Washington, Huey boasts that back in Louisiana he has the best legislature money can buy.

The *March of Time* had managed to talk the "Kingfish" into appearing personally in sound-film sequences which were photo-

---

LEFT ABOVE:
One of the world's most famous trade marks, it showed a vast, unending line of marching men and women, many of them carrying banners, over which the *Time* (later *Time-Life*) name was superimposed, followed by the series title. (Courtesy Time, Inc.)

LEFT:
Also part of the famous head-title logo was this figure of a drum major leading the passing parade. (Courtesy Time, Inc.)

49

graphed in his Senate office. In addition, an impersonator was used to reenact some of Long's more obnoxious behavior, including an unbelievably crude affront to the commander of the visiting German cruiser *Emden*, whom Long received in his hotel room, dressed in pajamas. (After the officer had demanded an official apology, Long visited the ship to return the call and pay his respects.) Huey Long's bedroom "reception" was staged in a New York hotel room for the *March of Time*'s cameras, using a "look-alike" New York actor named Walter Baldwin, dressed in the rumpled pajamas the role called for. In the finished film, this scene was followed directly by bona fide newsreel shots of Long visiting the ship dressed in a tuxedo. The two scenes cut together beautifully.

VOICE OF TIME

Next day, in dress clothes borrowed piece by piece from friends, he returns the call and receives a governor's salute.

March of Time cameramen and editors had a hilarious time working with their sound-film footage of Long's personal secretary, whom he had officially appointed acting governor during his absence from the state, and who unwisely agreed to speak for the *March of Time* cameras. The inarticulate woman stumbled through several takes for the camera crew, the worst of which was purposely incorporated into the finished film. Its point could not have been lost on audiences.

VOICE OF TIME

His pretty typist he makes secretary of state and lets her run Louisiana when he is away.

SECRETARY: As the first lady governor of Louisiana, I want to take this opportunity to thank my friends for . . . er . . . [pause]— [Cut]

The *March of Time* staff also re-created an alleged true-life event in which the Kingfish, momentarily unprotected by his body guards, involved himself in a brawl in the men's room at a private

MOT's April release featured a devastating attack upon controversial Louisiana politician Huey Long. Long had collaborated in the film's production, re-creating a scene, here, in his Senate office. This was combined with other scenes of Long which the *March of Time* made with an impersonator. The Senator was not amused. (Courtesy Time, Inc.)

Long Island club, and ended up with a black eye. For this staged sequence, the *March of Time* again used actor Walter Baldwin. Adding insult to injury, the film featured a close-up of a medal, the striking of which had been paid for by public subscription shortly after the men's room incident: INSCRIPTION: By public acclaim for a deed done in private—Sands Point, August 26, 1933.

All of this was amusing, but one must remember that at this point in American politics Huey Long politically was not an entertaining figure. He was the most powerful demagogue in America, and was believed by many people to pose a serious threat to the reelection of Franklin Roosevelt. Had he not been assassinated in 1935, he might conceivably have become the thirty-third President of the United States.

Louis de Rochemont never doubted the real dangers that this

kind of motion picture ridicule involved. A few months later, while supervising a *March of Time* film on board a coast guard cutter off the west coast of Florida, he was struck down by appendicitis. The crew proposed to take him into New Orleans for surgery. Louis refused to go. The coast guard finally assigned a pharmacist's mate to de Rochemont, and he was rushed by train to New York City where surgeons removed Louis's diseased appendix. Louis had figured that whatever might happen, the odds would be better anywhere than in Louisiana.

The surviving *March of Time* staff members do not recall who directed this issue, although all express great pride in it. The production file's "dope sheets" (camera reports) do not indicate the director's name—but then, they rarely did. The cameraman on the film, Jack Haeseler, sent a brief, hastily scribbled memorandum back to the home office that gave a shrewd and prophetic appraisal of Long's totalitarian abuses in Louisiana, finding "so many parallels with revolutionary times that it is not at all funny. And it may result in civil war. Perhaps the only solution outside of his assassination."

The film concluded with a scene in which several newsreel shots of Huey Long giving a speech appear optically superimposed over each other, the very image of a modern demagogue, uttering what emerged on the sound track as gibberish. This, in turn, was followed by a brief but dignified statement by President Roosevelt. Speaking of this film forty years later, Roy Larsen referred to it as a classic "example of a public figure putting himself in the hands of the media."

When the film opened at the Loew's State Theater in New Orleans on April 16, patrons found the sequence on Huey Long conspicuous by its absence. Whether the Kingfish, who had rushed to New Orleans shortly before the print of the film arrived in the city, had directly ordered the deletion has never been made clear. The management of Loew's claimed to have run the print as they received it and denied any pressure from Long or his associates. According to the April 24 issue of *Variety*, F. F. Goodrow of the First Division Distribution Exchange "couldn't remember" whether his organization had delivered the print to the theater or whether the theater had received the print directly from Railway

Express. As for Long, *Variety* reported that he "flew into one of his rages . . . when questioned about it" and refused to answer the newsmen's questions. Shortly thereafter, Long introduced into the Louisiana legislature a bill, subsequently passed, which provided for censorship of motion pictures (including newsreels) in that state.

The second sequence in this controversial issue was an exposé of the meeting on the French Riviera of International Railmakers, revealed by the film's editors to be a conference of munitions manufacturers. The film incorporated exclusive "stolen" footage of Sir Basil Zaharoff, billed by the *March of Time* as the "wisest and richest of the dealers of death." The shots of Zaharoff had been made by a freelance cameraman and commissioned by Richard de Rochemont. By hiding an automatic camera in a railway fruit stand and wheeling it past Zaharoff, who was being escorted in his wheelchair to a train for Paris, the cameraman got the first newsreel shots ever made of the wealthy manufacturer. The finished sequence was politically simplistic but journalistically effective. The reviewer of the *New York World-Telegram* said on April 24 that it had "all the clarity and vigor and power of a war cartoon by Daumier."

The third sequence, a somewhat inflammatory description of alleged suppression of freedom of religion in Mexico by ex-President Calles, was attacked on July 9 by the left-wing publication, *New Masses,* as showing "A completely reactionary, chauvanistic and fascist tendency . . ." as well as offering a "direct approval of lynching."

The fourth and last sequence described the bridging of the Pacific Ocean by Pan American Airways' giant flying boats, then a marvel of aviation technology. Although ostensibly noncontroversial, the subject had profound geopolitical implications, for it reflected the United States government's resolve to maintain hegemony in the Pacific—a theme dear to Louis's heart. It also illuminated the economic cooperation that existed between Pan American Airways and the Chinese government—a theme dear to Henry Luce's heart.

Operationally speaking, the issue was unique in its approach, for whereas most *March of Time* issues *re*enacted events in the im-

Sir Basil Zaharoff (left), wealthy, rarely photographed munitions manufacturer, termed by the *March of Time* "the wisest and richest of the dealers of death," was photographed by a hidden camera while being wheeled through a train station on his way to Paris. (Courtesy Time, Inc.)

mediate past, this one *pre*enacted an event that had not yet taken place—the inauguration of scheduled flying boat service across the Pacific. It was released later, after the event, as an authentic record.

Shown in the film were the variety of stops that a typical Pan Am Clipper would make over a five-day period—at Honolulu, Guam, Manila, and the like. However, almost every shot in the issue was staged at locations along the Florida coastline. Associate producer Tom Orchard recalled its production.

> The trans-Pacific service had not yet gone into effect. So Louis and I went down to Miami and went out to the air base of Pan Am's. . . . There were, at that time, big flying boats called Brazilian clippers—they flew down to Rio de Janeiro. So we went to the Episcopal Church in Coral Gables. Father Silbert was the minister there. We said that we wanted to *pre*enact the flight across the Pacific. We needed some actors. So we got the Women's Auxiliary, and gave a donation to the church. That's what we used to do to

The April release also included an astonishing example of *pre*-creation, in which the inauguration of Pan American Airways new flying boat service across the Pacific was staged in Florida *before* the event occurred. Here, a steward calls passengers to the plane for the next leg of the journey. (Courtesy Time, Inc.)

get our people. So we had about 25 people from the church there. And Pan American gave us one of their two or three clippers for the interior shots. . . . We got some big welcome gates, which we had a sign maker make, saying, "Welcome to Guam," "Welcome to Manila," "Wake Island," that sort of thing. So we had our actors getting off the plane [in Florida]: "Wake Island." Then we'd change the camera around and we'd have the big welcome in Manila. And we got all the Filipino pullman porters from the Atlantic Coast Line Railroad down there in Miami to be Filipinos . . . dressed in their little shirtwaists, waving Filipino flags as our people came in. So we got across the Pacific that way.

Time's fourth issue, covering only three subjects, was surprisingly mild in tone considering the controversial nature of its featured subject—the Soviet Union. Simple-minded in its analysis, the film was both laudatory and sympathetic to the Soviet experiment, most of the footage having been photographed by freelance cameraman Julien Bryan. Missing were references to political purges then in progress, the well-known suppression of religious freedom throughout the country, the execution of political dissidents under Stalin, and the liquidation of recalcitrant peasant populations. What with smiling faces, well-dressed citizens, and joyous children throughout the film, only the most skeptical viewer could fail to see that the promised revolution had finally succeeded.

VOICE OF TIME

Through state recreation parks stroll the proletariat—aristocrats of the new order.

And the state provides fun! (*shots of children playing*)

The *March of Time* did concede, in one line of narration, that 150,000 anticommunist prisoners were being used as forced labor in the building of a canal linking the White Sea and the Baltic, but fitted this revelation into a series of statements regarding the astonishing progress being made in industrializing and modernizing the country. Concluded the Voice of Time: "That the young Soviet is doing a better job of nation-welding than the last of the imperial rulers none can deny."

Scattered charges of "communist propaganda" were heard from the Hearst press following the film's release, while liberal reviewers seemed to find it a fair and impartial presentation. *Variety,* less impressed, concluded on June 5 that "Even the American Communists who are attacking 'March of Time' as bourgeois, in choice of subject and treatment thereof, could scarcely charge that Russia failed to receive ample recognition of its accomplishments and a generous neglect of its failures at the hands of *Time's* editors."

The remainder of this issue was devoted to a review and explanation of U.S. Navy war games in the Pacific and a rather dull study of the Washington news corps, starring Secretary of State Cordell Hull and Pulitzer Prize-winning journalist Arthur Krock in speaking parts.

By now, some observers had begun to suspect that the *March of*

Time, rather than avoiding controversy, was deliberately provoking it. The appearance of a controversial newsreel was a new experience for film critics. Some were pleasantly surprised. Wrote the *New York World-Telegram* on April 24:

> Any doubts about the necessity of a supplementary newsreel like "The March of Time" . . . should disappear after a glance at the third issue. . . . By far the finest of the three already released, not only from the point of view of subject matter but treatment as well, the current issue shows anew how forceful and influential a well thought-out motion picture commentary on the current scene can be.

Others were less hopeful for its continued success. On February 20 the *Nation* warned:

> Sooner or later the producers will be forced to recognize the distinction between a news magazine, like *Time* or the *Literary Digest,* and a journal of opinion, like the *Nation* or the *New Republic.* And the moment that they realize the hazards which the latter choice would involve they will undoubtedly be forced to turn out a product which is not essentially very different from the old-fashioned newsreel. The choice is clearly between bare presentation and critical interpretation of the news; and only the most sanguine optimist can persuade anyone that the great motion-picture audience is ready for the latter.

In June 1935 contractual agreements between March of Time, Inc., and its distributor, First Division Pictures, were canceled by mutual consent. The disassociation, described as a "friendly break," resulted from the inability of First Division Pictures, a relatively small distributor, to offer a complete national and European release for the high-budget series. It was also felt that the *March of Time* alone could not support the company's exchanges. Shortly thereafter, the *March of Time* signed a new distribution contract with the R.K.O. distributing organization, thus ensuring intensive promotion and widespread release of the series. This relationship proved an agreeable one and lasted until July 1942. According to *MOT* staffers, Ned Depinet, R.K.O.'s distribution head, loved the *March of Time* and always gave its release special care.

57

As a result of the change in distributors, release of the fifth issue was delayed until August 1935. As if in apology for their procrastination, and the moderation of their last issue, the company released a politically explosive film that disrupted the film industry, provoked dissension between political factions, and plainly established that the *March of Time* had committed itself to a fearless, if sometimes sensational, examination of currently controversial subjects.

The 20-minute film, which covered three subjects, dealt first with Father Coughlin, the politically inclined Catholic priest; second, with the fascist French organization, Croix de Feu ("Cross of Fire"); and third, with mobilization maneuvers of the United States Army under the command of General Douglas MacArthur. A *March of Time* résumé summarized the first two subjects in the following manner:

> CROIX DE FEU—The second worst railroad wreck in history, scandalous collapse of a loan company, "suicide" of an international crook, Alexandre Stavisky, set the stage for widespread and turbulent protest in France against the wholesale political corruption thus exposed. Under Col. François de la Rocque emerges the anti-Communist Croix de Feu, numbering 400,000, and pledged to strong authority. "Be ready!" exhorts their leader. "Our hour is at hand! Tomorrow, or the next day, mobilization!"
>
> FATHER COUGHLIN—New in U.S. politics is the phenomenon of a Roman Catholic priest, Father Charles Edward Coughlin, actively involved in broadcasting his views by radio. His following, over 8,000,000, organized as the National Union for Social Justice, have paid for the million dollar Shrine of the Little Flower at Royal Oak, Michigan. The March of Time shows both his critics and his loyal supporters, speculates on his ultimate role.

For the third subject in this controversial issue, the *March of Time* asked General Douglas MacArthur to simulate an actual mobilization of the U.S. Army. "General MacArthur obliges," said a *March of Time* summary, "and before the MOT cameras go the men and mechanism of this modern Army, to stop an imaginary invasion through the St. Lawrence Valley." One curious sequence in the film revealed the odds that were then being offered by

Lloyd's of London on war breaking out anywhere in the world: 20 to 1 against a Russo-Japanese war; 100 to 1 against the U.S. being drawn into a major conflict; 500 to 1 against an invasion of the U.S. by any power on earth.

The Father Coughlin issue had been directed largely by Tom Orchard. It is hard to believe today that viewers would have considered it a piece of pro-Coughlin propaganda. De Rochemont had sent cameraman Charlie Gilson out to travel around the country with Coughlin in the latter's private plane, producing an intimate kind of coverage which is common today but was rarely exploited by newsreelmen in the 1930's. Orchard also staged several re-creations of incidents from the life of the priest, including Coughlin's alleged confrontation with a group of Ku Klux Klanners at a cross-burning ceremony. Coughlin cooperated in the making of the film.

In fact, the film had very little to say about Coughlin one way or another. In this respect, it encouraged audiences to read whatever meaning they wished into the scenes. It never referred to the priest as being fascist or anti-Semitic, but relied upon the familiarity of the general public with Coughlin and his "National Union of Social Justice." It probed, in some detail, Coughlin's position within the Catholic Church, concluding with the Voice of Time: ". . . the Roman Catholic Church is a very careful church, and able priests who become too conspicuous are sometimes made Bishops in far-away places."

As for the Croix de Feu, the political situation in France was quite unstable at this time. The organization was threatening to mobilize and to take over the French government. They told Richard de Rochemont, who had filmed the organization's activities, to delay the release of the finished *March of Time* issue until October. Richard passed the request on to his brother Louis in a memorandum dated July 8, 1935: "If this is impossible, I wish you would send me a letter which could cover me with them, as I should hate to get the castor oil treatment when, as, and if they become the masters of the situation." Louis went ahead and released the film in August as planned.

Richard could be as persuasive as anyone else on the staff in conning important political celebrities into appearing before

ABOVE:
Most controversial of the 1935 issues was released in August showing, first, a militant French fascist organization called the Croix de Feu ("Cross of Fire"), members of whom are seen here marching through Paris before their leader, Col. François de la Rocque. (Courtesy Time, Inc.)

RIGHT ABOVE:
Coughlin, who cooperated in the film's production, is seen here in a re-creation of an alleged confrontation with Ku Klux Klanners. (Courtesy Time, Inc.)

RIGHT BELOW:
Third episode in the controversial issue showed a simulated mobilization of U.S. troops by Gen. Douglas MacArthur (left) to stop an imaginary invasion through the St. Lawrence Valley. The entire issue caused so much controversy that Hollywood's Hays Office considered censoring the *March of Time*.

March of Time cameras. He said, "it would be rather naïve of me to go to Col. de la Rocque and tell him that we thought he was an apprentice dictator who was liable to make trouble. We wouldn't approach him like that. We crept up on him through some of the people who knew him, and we'd say, 'Well, now, what *is* this? Tell us more. This is very interesting, we'd like to know more about it.' Obviously, you don't produce a confrontation and expect them to

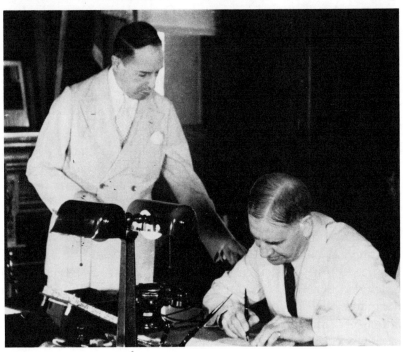

do anything." Richard was able to deal effectively with the left as well. For this particular issue, most of the French Communist Party's leadership, including Maurice Thorez, performed re-creations for him, but only, according to one of Dick's memoranda, "on condition that we make the picture in sound, as they did not want to run the risk of being misquoted. This was a some-what footless objection, but I nevertheless agreed, as this group has never been filmed before and since they were willing to put on an act for us."

Critical reaction to the film was explosive. "A formidable thunder rolled, from right to left, from the *Herald Tribune* to the *New Masses*," proclaimed George Dangerfield in the *New Republic* on August 19, 1936. Left-wing publications were particularly vocal in their denunciation of the issue. On September 3, 1935, Peter Ellis wrote in the *New Masses:* "This was the signal for The March of Time to unfurl their true flag; the swastika. . . . The political status of the March of Time is no longer a matter of speculation. . . . It is open and brazen fascism." Dangerfield felt that the film "was very kind to the Croix de Feu. . . . To have sent such an episode into so many theatres was an infuriating ges-ture, even if an unintentional one, and the evidence against its being unintentional was overwhelming."

In March 1936 an article by Hy Kravif appearing in the *American Spectator,* a journal of the radical left, charged, among other things, that the directorate of Time, Inc., included numerous Morgan connections and was part of the same business arrange-ment that included the Morgan-Harjes firm of Paris, allegedly linked to the Croix de Feu. Although the author's charges received little serious attention, they contributed to the confusion that fol-lowed the film's release. Liberal critic George Dangerfield, by no means a friend of the *March of Time,* called the charges "discon-nected truths and insinuations. . . . It is a kind of witch-hunting, it deduces the devil out of cloudy evidence and ugly and unrelated facts. . . . The films themselves don't bear it out." Dangerfield concluded that the *March of Time* issues "have no conviction in them, they are thrillers. That, I submit, is the real evil in the March of Time. It is neither candid nor passionate nor partisan, merely excitable . . . ; it is almost completely irresponsible."

The controversy was further aggravated overseas by British censorship of scenes in the Croix de Feu sequence that indicated the source of the organization's funds. Graham Greene, in the November 8 issue of *Spectator,* felt that this deletion imparted a fascist tone to the picture that was not otherwise intended by the film's producers. Alistair Cooke, writing in the November 20 issue of *The Listener,* called the deletion ". . . a serious act. . . . Delete one incident, suppress one comment and the whole balance is disturbed. The film becomes, by what it omits . . . a vehicle for the most pernicious kind of propaganda—propaganda by implication. 'The March of Time' must be left as it was composed."

The hostile reaction of left-wing critics appears to have astonished the producers of the *March of Time,* for they had considered the thrust of this film to be unmistakably *anti*Fascist. Mary Losey, an outspoken liberal then on the staff of the *March of Time,* recalled her enthusiasm for this issue:

> . . . we did one on the Fascist movement in France which was very "anti" the Fascist movement. . . . That definitely was a good example of a liberal or at least anti-Fascist position that the film took. . . . I remember . . . the fantastic march [of the Croix de Feu] down Champs Élysées which has been used by every newsreel on earth. I was 24 years old, and extremely excited about the changing world, and that particular scene was to me one of the most moving things I've ever seen.

No one was more astonished by the scattered charges of right-wing bias than Richard de Rochemont, Louis's brother, who had directed the film's production in Europe and was responsible for securing the remarkable footage that went into it. Richard was the most politically moderate of men—an urbane, reasonable, and courageous newsman who had covered the story so successfully that he managed to talk Col. de la Rocque out of some of his organization's own footage for the *March of Time*'s release. Indeed, the dramatic torch-lit meeting of the Croix de Feu in a field near Chartres was Dick's idea—an instructive example of "real-life" events being shaped by the news media—what historian Daniel Boorstin has referred to as a "pseudo-event." In a July 11, 1935, memo to his brother, Dick wrote: "This is the first night meeting

the Croix have ever had, and they owe me the idea." Some other
shots in the film were either inspired by Dick or simply staged by
him. These included a shot that purported to show an automobile
in which fascist leaders sat reviewing the ceremonies. Richard
wrote, in a note to the New York office that he must have thought
would get a laugh: "Another shot shows March of Time car with
two prominent fascists seated in it. The first one is G. Ward Price
of the *Daily Mail*. In the rumble seat, Mr. Daniel Longwell [then
editor] of Time, Inc."

Taken as a whole, this August 1935 issue became one of the
March of Time's most controversial films. No group was more unhappy with it than the Hollywood motion picture industry. The
Hays Office, watchdog of the film industry's morals, began a careful consideration of the *March of Time*, hesitant to place it in the
same classification as regular newsreels, which did not come under
their production code control.

Completely in line with Hays Office concerns was an editorial
in the November 2 issue of the *Motion Picture Herald*, the film
industry's leading trade paper, which concluded:

> Now with "The March of Time" leading a trend toward the pres-
> entation of screen material of viewpoint, if not opinion, a whole
> set of problems looms. The problem is not what the pictures may
> stand for, but that they may stand for anything. The motion pic-
> ture theatre as the servant of the millions has never been able to
> afford opinion, attitude, ideas—anything but sheer entertainment
> pabulum.

In September 1935 the *March of Time* released its sixth issue,
covering the Ethiopian crisis (employing a *March of Time* office
boy named Hugh Fettis as a double for Haile Selassie); malcon-
tents and undesirables in the New Deal's Civilian Conservation
Corps; and a coalminers' strike against management in Pennsylvania which resulted in the digging and "bootlegging" of coal by
the miners. By now, partisan viewers and politically inclined
critics were reading whatever they liked into *MOT* releases as a
kind of cinematic Rorschach test. Although this sixth issue was
generally praised as a worthwhile release, some groups found the

September issue on Ethiopia included a nicely executed impersonation of Haile Selassie, played by a *March of Time* office boy. (Courtesy Time, Inc.)

"bootleg coal" sequence unduly sympathetic to the union workers while others deplored its support for management.

With the release of Issue No. 7 in October, the number of individual sequences rose again to four, including a dramatic staging of Joseph Furnas's shocking article in the *Reader's Digest* on automobile accidents, entitled ". . . And Sudden Death"; a discussion of neutrality and the refusal of an American barbed-wire manufacturer to sell his product to belligerent countries; a description of the summer theater movement; and a provocative, prophetic sequence on Palestine.

The Palestine footage was particularly well designed, painting a background of oppression of the Jews in Nazi Germany, their flight to Palestine, and the rebuilding of Haifa, Tel Aviv, the Valley of Israel, and other locations into a new home for the refugees. On October 23 *Variety* called the edition, "possibly the best to date. It is smooth in direction and editing and timely in subject matter . . . all in all, maturer showmanship is evident."

Apparently the "maturer showmanship" was not evident to censor boards in Ohio and Chicago, both of which deleted sections of the film. The Ohio action followed protests by both Jewish and German community leaders in that state. E. L. Bowsher, Ohio's Director of Education, ordered the deletions on grounds that the scenes depicting Nazi attacks on Jews would provoke bitter class feeling between Germans and Jews in Ohio. These cuts involved scenes of Nazi storm troopers raiding stores operated by Jews (staged by *March of Time* crews in New London, Connecticut), and the burning of books of Jewish authorship, as well as the narrator's statement: "Hitler is the man who has brought more evil on the Jews than any man in his generation." In Chicago, Police Lieutenant Harry M. Costello, Chicago's one-man Board of Censors, ordered a cut of 150 feet of footage depicting street riots in Germany on grounds that these scenes might excite the public.

The *March of Time*'s first year of production was now drawing to a close. Issue No. 8 covered the coming presidential election and the efforts of the Republicans to wrest control from the Democrats; a review of the work of the U.S. Biological Survey in preserving migratory wildfowl; and an account of the expulsion of professional strike-breaker Pearl Louis Bergoff from Georgia by Governor Eugene Talmadge.

In December 1935 the ninth and last issue of the first volume was released, covering the Japanese occupation of China and the formation of the puppet state of Manchukuo; the coast guard and secret service's fight against narcotics smugglers; and the economic panaceas then currently offered by senior-citizen-organizer Dr. Francis Townsend.

With completion of *Time*'s first volume of film publications, bewildered film critics and political observers paused to gain perspective and to evaluate this new and unpredictable motion picture phenomenon.

The Time of Their Lives: First Year

In his August 19, 1936, article in the *New Republic,* George Dangerfield, most articulate of the *March of Time*'s early critics, found fault with the producer's apparent attempt to achieve objectivity:

> There is a lot of money involved in The March of Time, and how can it afford to risk offending anyone by telling a deliberate truth? . . . I wish that the editors of The March of Time, since they have at their disposal these fictions which excite and enrage people, would use them to some purpose. I wish they wouldn't float above the clamor they create, like a god or a Zeppelin, indifferently; but would take off some divinity, or take on some ballast, and sink to earth. I wish they would say—outright, beyond question—that somebody was right or wrong. . . . Then we could attack them or defend them, and they would be exciting their audiences honestly.

Alistair Cooke prophetically outlined the danger of "witless" imitation of the series by other film companies in *The Listener* of November 20, 1935:

> Let no other film company, which is a film company simply, imagine that by adding a picture of Mrs. Smith at her mid-day meal to the pictures of Thursday's electioneering, they will be adding a small, but crucial, comment. They will be adding nothing less dangerous than whimsy. And whimsy, however droll in fiction or occasional essays, is immoral when mixed with fact. . . . "The March of Time" is not the result of bright inspiration. Behind it is ten years' experience with a magazine of the same style; an army of correspondents and cameramen scattered throughout the world; an historical film library it took two years to prepare; a newspaper cutting library as exhaustive as anything extant; and in New York and Chicago a vast research staff alert to trace the origins of any family, war, author, statesman, treaty, or breath or rumour. With no less than this should any other film company irresponsibly compete.

C. A. Lejeune of the London *Observer* offered one of the more sober evaluations of the film's potential:

> The whole value of a publication of this kind depends, as you will see, on the integrity of the men behind it. In the wrong hands it

might conceivably be the most dangerous organ of sedition that modern pulpitry has yet evolved. In the present instance the reputation of TIME magazine for truth and fearlessness must be its guarantee.

In the end, no one was more fearful of the capacity of the series for mischief than the *March of Time*'s own distribution and promotion head, Albert Sindlinger. Speaking years later, with more than thirty years of audience opinion research behind him, he voiced the fears with which he had originally viewed this creature of Louis de Rochemont's:

The thing that fascinated me about the *March of Time* was the power of pictorial journalism. What scared me about the *March of Time* was that we had this power and the guy that was running it didn't understand it.

4

Time and the Documentary Tradition

"To us, the word 'documentary' was a dirty word."

Louis de Rochemont

No one knows for sure what "documentary" film is, but this has never bothered the more than three generations of film makers throughout the world who have spent their lives making it. As with pornography, most people think that they can recognize "documentary" when they see it. Nonetheless, the documentary form, or style, or approach to film making, after more than half a century's practice, still defies description. The only thing that everyone seems to agree upon is that "documentary" film is supposed to be "true" and seems to have something to do with "reality."

It was apparently British film critic and producer John Grierson who first used the term "documentary" in referring to the early work of the American film maker, Robert Flaherty. The term is an unfortunate one, for what Grierson had in mind was not a "document" at all, in the sense that the word is used in either legal or historical fields. Flaherty's films portrayed primitive peoples in exotic locales, superimposing upon their cultures a kind of Rousseauian philosophy to which he was committed. Employing dramatic re-creation and the staging of events, Flaherty simulated reality and "celebrated" the lives of his subjects, producing sensitive and compassionate portraits of them in a style that has sometimes been called "romantic naturalism." What emerged were not documents, however. They were anthropological hypotheses.

As for Grierson, when he turned from film criticism to film making, the kinds of films he made were even less "documentary" than Flaherty's. A teacher, critic, theorist, and lifelong social activist, Grierson regarded the motion picture as a pulpit from which he could most effectively proselitize for reform. He aimed to change men's minds, and the films he made had clear attitudinal and behavioral objectives. They were also artistically exciting and stylistically innovative, thanks to the talented young directors he attracted to his organization. More than anybody else, he created and sustained the British documentary film movement, and is remembered as the father of the so-called propaganda tradition in documentary film making. But the films he made were not documents. They were political and economic arguments.

Grierson subsequently defined "documentary" as "the creative treatment of actuality." From a rhetorical point of view, it was an inspired definition, for its vagueness defied criticism, and its scope encompassed virtually every kind of film including animation.

The American film director Willard Van Dyke defined the documentary more narrowly, as "a film in which the elements of dramatic conflict represent social or political forces rather than individual ones." This definition speaks well to the kind of film that both Grierson and de Rochemont made, but it does not work so well with either Flaherty's work or that of the "city symphony" directors (such as Cavalcanti and Ruttmann) or the naturalist film makers (such as Sucksdorff or the Oxford group).

Some purists argue that the documentary must not use professional actors or reconstructed sets. Yet, Pare Lorentz's *Fight for Life* fell into the first of these excluded categories, and some of both Flaherty's and Sucksdorff's into the second, and critics agree that theirs are documentary films. In a 1950 lecture at U.C.L.A. "B-film" producer Sol Lesser defined a documentary as "a film with narration." Still another Hollywood producer, Columbia's Harry Cohn, is alleged to have defined a documentary as ". . . a picture without women. If there's one woman in it, then it's a semi-documentary." Neither of these requires comment, but they do suggest the confusion that the word involves.

Within the last fifteen years or so, an entirely different kind of film has appeared that many critics also consider a form of documentary. This school of film making capitalizes upon the miniaturized cameras and sound recorders, the light-weight portable lighting units and battery packs, and the high-speed, finer-grained emulsions that manufacturers have recently provided the trade. This equipment and technology allows for the intimate photography of human beings in their natural habitats to an extent that was not previously possible. These films seek to catch human beings unawares, with their private faces exposed, as did still photographers during the "candid camera" craze of the 1930's and 40's. Unlike the candid camera "fiends" of the past, however, who were having mischievous fun with their cameras, today's voyeuristic film makers take themselves very seriously indeed. Methodologically doctrinaire and artistically inflexible, they have advanced a superficially complicated philosophy that alleges to provide a unique and exclusive access to truth. "This is the way it is," they say, without bothering to tell us what *it* is. In the end, as with revealed religion, one either believes or one doesn't, and any rational analysis of these beliefs will usually prove unrewarding.

A number of generic terms have attached themselves to the voyeuristic approach, most of which are intellectually offensive. These range from *"cinéma vérité"* (which is presumptuous and condescending) to "the living camera" (which is preposterous). The technique seems to work best when recording human beings in moments of great stress—responding irrationally, speaking emotionally, and moving convulsively, as at an exciting football game, or during a political debate, or in a family quarrel, or amongst the wretched victims of an ill-managed mental institution. As with other kinds of voyeuristic experience, the results are sometimes titilating, though, for some, subsequently guilt-provoking. From a cinematic point of view, this kind of film making seems to generate its most interesting images and sounds either when its subjects are profoundly grotesque or when it photographs celebrated personalities whose lives and destinies move rapidly towards a spectacular and visibly dramatic climax. In the first instance, films such as *Titicut Follies* and *Gray Gardens* come to mind. In the second, convicted murderer Paul Crump faces death in the electric chair (*The Chair*); the will of antisegregationists in Alabama is pitted against those of politicians John and Robert Kennedy as the deadline for the integration of a university approaches (*Crisis: Behind a Presidential Commitment*); professional pianist Susan Starr competes for first prize at an international concert competition (*Susan Starr*).

By contrast, this "candid camera" approach seems least effective when used to address what Grierson considered one of the most important tasks of documentary: the dramatization of the common man and woman to other common men and women.

Grierson's point was that the business of dramatizing common people requires the artistic talents of uncommon film makers. Actually, Grierson was not much of a film maker himself, but he was a brilliant leader who attracted to his shop a number of talented directors who invested his films with humanistic themes, a poetic treatment, and a profound respect for individual human dignity. The voyeuristic cinema, by contrast, offers little poetry and precious little humanistic perspective. Its practitioners typically refuse to take a stand on controversial issues. They retreat behind their cameras, shoot enormous amounts of film, and hope that their subjects will say something minimally intelligent. What is more serious, they nearly always eschew responsibility for the artistic and thematic integrity of their product. "I am a journalist, not an artist," one of them once told me with pride.

It follows, then, that if the voyeurist film lacks flair and style, and if its creators refuse to make statements with which we can take issue, then, in the absence of scintillating personalities, sensational action, or an entertaining freak show, the resulting film will probably be dull.

Our discussion of the documentary mode here is by no means gratuitous, for many critics, both contemporary and revisionist, have appraised the *March of Time*'s sixteen-year output with reference to the documentary tradition.

A younger generation of Americans, which has grown up enjoying the variety of news, public affairs, and documentary programming that television networks offer, must be reminded that, with the exception of the newsreel, the motion picture that was seen by 95 per cent of the American public prior to the introduction of the *March of Time* was fictional/entertainment feature fare. If you wanted melodrama, adventure, comedy, or fantasy, you went to the movies. If, on the other hand, you wanted information, you got it from books, magazines, newspapers, and radio— and that was that. Until the coming of the *March of Time,* there was no documentary film movement in the United States in so far as the mass theatrical audience was concerned. Two or three of Flaherty's feature films had proved economically viable and had been seen widely by 1935, as had those of Merian C. Cooper and Ernest B. Schoedsack, but these did not a movement make. The early documentary impulse and the films that resulted from it may have had considerable influence on film makers around the world, but hardly any of the many independently produced documentary features and shorts that were made during the 1920's and early 1930's (and which, in retrospect, have assumed a critical reputation far out of proportion to their social impact) were ever seen by mass audiences in America. Neither were they widely seen in schools or film societies in those days, for the widespread use of audio-visual equipment and product did not occur in the United States until the post-World War II period. It was the *March of Time* alone which successfully introduced and established the documentary format for film audiences in the United States. And all of this occurred before the films of Pare Lorentz, Joris Ivens, Willard Van Dyke, and Herbert Kline, or the wartime indoctrination films of Frank Capra and Anatole Litvak, or the appearance of postwar television public affairs programs. As John Grierson, an admirer of the *March of Time,* wrote in 1937:

. . . something more intelligent has already arrived. It has crashed through from the America that succeeded the slump and learned with Roosevelt the simple braveries of the public forum. It is called

73

The March of Time to-day, but to-morrow, so strong is the growth, so strong the need and so different the younger generation which handles cinema, it will be called by a dozen names— Window on the World, World Eye, Brave New World, and what not. . . .

Only three years old, it has swept through the country, answering the thin glitter of the newsreels with nothing on the face of it more dramatic than the story of cancer research, the organisation of peace, the state of Britain's health, the tithe war in the English shires, the rural economy of Ireland, with here and there a bright and ironic excursion into Texas centennials and the lunatic fringe of politics. In no deep sense conscious of the higher cinematic qualities, it merely carries over from journalism into cinema, after thirty-eight years, something of that bright and easy tradition of free-born comment which the newspaper has won and the cinema has been too abject even to ask for.

It can be argued, of course, that the *March of Time* was not a documentary at all. What textbooks call motion picture "documentaries" have nearly always been produced as isolated, one-shot films. Generally made on a modest budget, each tended to be the product of a single director's style and vision, on which production might extend for more than a year.

By contrast, the *March of Time* was a corporate product, whose title did not even carry the names of the people who made it, fashioned by scores of people over a sixteen-year period during which time more than 200 issues were produced and almost 300 subjects explored. The budget was substantial by conventional documentary standards, but the length of time allowed for the completion of any single issue was minimal. As for a political and social point of view, the *March of Time*'s staff did indeed have one, and during the 1930's it was predominantly liberal. Nevertheless, the expression of that point of view was not the central thrust of the film's production. Released within the context of commercial, theatrical exhibition, the *March of Time* was designed to vend information and to provoke public discussion on current issues.

De Rochemont *never* considered the *March of Time* a documentary. "For us," he said on a 1974 CBS television broadcast, "the word 'documentary' was a dirty word." I asked de Rochemont what he meant by the remark. "I mean you couldn't get any box office," he said. "People didn't go out for [documentaries]. You'd never say [to the exhibitors]: 'A beautiful documentary.' You'd be crazy if you did. . . . [The exhibitors would reply] 'Oh, Jesus, don't send us any more of those documentaries.' "

Louis's commercial disdain for the term "documentary" was shared by others at the organization. Musical director Jack Shaindlin came in to work one morning to find Jack Glenn slumped down in an office chair, just returned from an exhausting assignment on location. Glenn had a three-day beard, his voice was hoarse, and he was bleary-eyed from lack of sleep. "Jack!" said Shaindlin, cheerfully, "You sound so 'documentary' today—so scratched and grainy." (Such anecdotes should not obscure the fact that though the *March of Time* staff recognized that documentaries were not popular at the box office, many of its members were intimately familiar with the international documentary film movement and sympathetic to its thematic and artistic aims).

If the *March of Time* wasn't a documentary, then what was it? De Rochemont and Larsen coined the term "pictorial journalism" to refer to it. This expression seemed fresh in 1935, although, in fact, it had been used as early as July 29, 1911, by a trade publication, *The Moving Picture World,* in a review of the first motion picture newsreel series (Pathé) to be released in the U.S. Be that as it may, the *March of Time* was not a newsreel. The distinctions between the two seem worth describing here:

1. The *March of Time* made no attempt to report up-to-the-minute news. It was released only once a month. The regular newsreel was released twice weekly.

2. The *March of Time* dealt with a limited number of subjects in each issue; after May 1938, with only one subject in each issue. The newsreel dealt with as many as eight or ten different topics in each release.

3. Each *March of Time* issue ran as long as twenty minutes, allowing a fairly leisurely and detailed exposition of subject matter. The American newsreel rarely ran more than ten minutes, often less.

4. The *March of Time* was an interpretive, discursive reel that

elaborated with titles, maps, narration, and supplementary archival footage upon the subjects it treated. The newsreel, with rare exceptions, treated only the superficialities of day-to-day events.

5. The *March of Time* spent from $25,000 to $75,000 on each issue. During the same period of release, the newsreel spent $8,000 to $12,000 on each of its releases.

6. Both the *March of Time* and the newsreel staged and re-created events, but the *March of Time* did so to a far greater extent—sometimes, in the early years, to the almost complete exclusion of spontaneously photographed footage. Moreover, it frequently used impersonators of celebrities when it was found that actual footage was not available. The *March of Time* admitted and even publicized its use of reenacted scenes. The newsreel never admitted publicly to its own similar practices.

7. The intention of the *March of Time* was to create and exploit controversy and to provoke discussion of politically, economically, racially, socially, and militarily touchy subjects. Newsreel producers tried to avoid controversial subject matter whenever possible.

8. The *March of Time* was sometimes openly partisan; the newsreel rarely so.

Was the *March of Time* a "dramatic" production? After all, the radio version of the *March of Time* was classified in broadcasting circles as a dramatic show rather than a news broadcast, and the film version sometimes also employed dramatically staged reenactments with actors. Nonetheless, the emphasis in the film, unlike the radio version, was clearly on journalistic rather than dramatic interpretation of the news. De Rochemont's re-creations were integrated continuously with bona fide newsreel footage, and what with the maps, diagrams, and frequent title inserts that were used, the resulting style was as much didactic as dramatic. Furthermore, as time passed and the film version of the *March of Time* gained in prestige and popularity, it became feasible to replace the professional "impersonators" who had been used in the early issues with the actual celebrities they featured, playing themselves on the screen. Certainly film reviewers of the day never regarded the *March of Time* as a dramatic product. Entertaining as it was, a

March of Time issue was not likely to be confused with heavy-weight contemporary drama. Indeed, some of the more sophisticated critics referred to the series derisively as *"Time*'s amateur theatricals," a reference to Louis's ham-handed attempts at dramatic dialogue. Jimmy Shute recalled that the late Robert Richards, one of de Rochemont's writers, said that the dialogue Louis and his staff wrote for the famous people who appeared in the film made them sound like characters in the comics, as though word-filled balloons were coming out of their heads. The *March of Time* was neither documentary, nor newsreel, nor dramatic product, and yet it had elements of each.

Perhaps the closest anyone ever came to classifying the *March of Time* properly was British director Paul Rotha, who used the term "newsreel tradition" (with emphasis on the word *tradition*) to refer to both the *March of Time* and an earlier silent-film series made by the Soviet director Dziga Vertov that had the unfortunate title *Kino Pravda*. Surviving on very low budgets and produced under difficult circumstances, Vertov's *Kino Pravda* was both eccentric and crude by professional standards, but those few examples that have been seen, more-or-less intact, in the United States suggest a stylistic kinship with the *March of Time*. Apparently neither de Rochemont nor Larsen was familiar with *Kino Pravda,* the only available example of which, in this country, appears to be an anthologized mélange of different issues in the collection of New York's Museum of Modern Art, which was not accessioned by the Museum until sometime between 1935 and 1939, well after the introduction of the *March of Time*.

The *March of Time*'s distinctive style was an amalgam of many features and stylistic touches—fresh in their day, unique in their combination, and imitated in the years that followed. The cutting was quite rapid. According to the final continuity scripts (which indicate the precise footage for each shot in a finished reel to the nearest foot) individual shots were often cut as short as 2-3 feet in length ($1\frac{1}{3}$ to 2 seconds), while an occasional shot ran only one foot in length ($\frac{2}{3}$ second). An examination of the scripts reveals that during the 1930's an average issue ran 19.39 minutes, and contained 288 shots, the average length of each shot being 6.04 feet, and the average duration of each shot being four seconds. Following World War II the cutting rate slowed slightly. An examination of scripts released between January 1949 and August 1951 shows that an average issue ran 18 minutes and contained 211 shots, the average length of each shot being 7.65 feet and the average duration of each shot being 5 seconds.

Shots within scenes, as well as scenes within sequences, were almost always connected by straight cuts, in a fashion that is widely used today. "Wipes" and "dissolves," favorite devices of lazy news-film editors, were rarely seen in *March of Time* issues.

It was Louis's rule that camera movements (dolly shots, trucking shots, pans, and tilts) were never to be allowed except under the most extraordinary circumstances. Panning, tilting, or dollying shots are almost impossible to cut into or out of without jarring the audience. The editor must wait until the camera movement comes to a complete stop before making the cut. What this means is that if a moving camera shot is used, then, for the period of time when the shot is on the screen, the control of the film has passed out of the editor's hands and into those of the directors in the field. With Louis de Rochemont sitting at the editing bench in New York, that would never do.

Scenes were *always* photographed with the camera mounted on a tripod. Rock-steady shots such as these were undeniably static, but that was exactly what Louis wanted. The rapid editing which he favored more than compensated for the static quality of the shots. Indeed, *without* static shots, he could not have cut rapidly at all. So-called "dynamic" or "montage" cutting only works when each of the individual camera shots is made from a steady platform.

The angle-of-view Louis required was straightforward and conventional—nothing tricky like a bird's eye or worm's eye view, which might distract the audience from the journalistic or dramatic point being made in the sequence. Peter Hopkinson, a cameraman in *Time*'s London office, recalled being instructed in these matters by head cameraman Jimmy Hodgson. "No post-office angles," said Hodgson, referring obliquely to the arty compositions that the Grierson crowd at the British Post Office film unit sometimes went in for.

Steady cameras and the absence of zoom lenses in the 1930's meant that Louis was spared the "water-hose" and "zoom-mooz" camera movements that have become so fashionable in recent television-news coverage—the kind of shot in which the camera's optical system begins drawing the audience closer and closer to the subject until the audience can no longer tell whom they are looking at. Back in the *March of Time*'s day, if any such footage had ever found its way back from the field to the editing rooms, it would have been the end for the cameraman involved, for Louis's standards were high and uncompromising.

The *March of Time*'s photographic style was simple and austere. "Anything that's honest is O.K.," said director Jack Glenn. "Don't strive for an effect." Much of the footage was photographed in authentic locations—in apartments, offices, factories and the like. Photographing in such places meant that working space was limited and camera angles cramped. In order to photograph the widest possible angle and to secure their establishing shots under these conditions, and also produce a substantial depth-of-field at large apertures, wide-angle lenses as short as 25mm were frequently used. These often produced optical distortion around the edges of the frame, which meant that the "actors" had to be positioned toward the middle of the picture lest they appear grossly inflated, and out of shape. Props that appeared at the edges of the frame, such as cups, saucers, dishes, and ash trays, would have to be propped up with invisible wooden blocks and adhesive, at strange angles, in order to come out "on even keel" in the finished picture.

It was also standard *March of Time* procedure to place the camera at the height of a sitting person's eyes. The idea behind this, according to Tom Orchard, was: "the audience is sitting in a seat, so we look at things from the angle of the audience. Also, it gave us an 'opening up' quality." Camera positions such as this tended to dramatize the individuals who appeared in the frame, making them appear slightly larger than life when they were standing.

One of the unintended, unwanted, but inevitable consequences of this combination of short-focus lenses and lower-than-normal camera angles was the frequent inclusion of ceilings in the shots. Although not unknown in theatrical feature films, Hollywood film makers usually kept the appearance of ceilings in scenes to a minimum. In 1941, Orson Welles attracted a good deal of attention by purposely emphasizing ceiling shots throughout the whole of his feature film, *Citizen Kane,* the plot of which involved the operation of a thinly disguised version of the *March of Time* organization.

Because of the speed with which *MOT* camera crews worked, the cramped space in which they operated, and the limited amount of electrical power available to them, the lighting used was ultra-realistic. Although always well composed and properly exposed, scenes were lit flatly, without the theatrical backlighting, accent lights, and lovely atmospheric shadings Hollywood's audiences had become accustomed to. This never bothered Larsen or de Rochemont, as it fitted perfectly into their concept of "pictorial journalism," and helped to make the images more believable. Ironically, in time some of Hollywood's film makers began to imitate the *March of Time*'s lighting, especially after the war when, due largely to de Rochemont's innovational feature-film productions for Twentieth-Century-Fox (*Boomerang, The House on 92nd Street*), a so-called "semi-documentary" style of film making was introduced into theatrical features. This amused many of the *MOT* staff, since the lighting that they used had been dictated by journalistic and economic constraints, not by aesthetic choice.

Louis never allowed the use of "talking heads"—a kind of shot familiar to television-news audiences of today in which a person is discovered "in limbo," photographed in close-up, speaking extemporaneously toward the camera, and addressing his remarks principally to the audience. "The talking head," said Dick de Rochemont, "is like a rewrite man on a newspaper. He's repeating what somebody has told him or has been dug up, so there isn't any great progress." By contrast, in a *March of Time* shot, there was always enough set detail around the subject so that the audience knew where he or she was located—at a table, at a podium, in front of a piece of machinery, in a kitchen, and so forth. The subject didn't talk to the audience; he or she talked to someone *else.* "We didn't even have an off-screen interviewer," said associate producer Arthur Tourtellot. "If we wanted to talk about the effects of mobilization on the national economy in 1942, we would have two fictional businessmen meeting in a club car on a train, and Jimmy

Shute would write the dialogue, and this was the way we put the point across. We didn't have either an on-stage or an off-stage voice saying, 'Mr. Jones, what do you think about this?' "

Time's "amateur theatricals" and the dialogue that went along with them may have been trite, but the narration which was read by Westbrook Van Voorhis was beautifully and meticulously crafted, without a spare word or phrase. "Stylistically," said Lothar Wolff, "what makes the *March of Time* different from everything else is in many instances the script dominated the picture, rather than the other way around. . . . [Louis] was the first man, in my opinion, who gave words and image the same value. There is a documentary maxim that the picture should tell the story. I never subscribed to it. I think it's an oversimplification, just like *cinéma vérité*." Morrie Roizman added, "If the script didn't fit the pictures, we'd make the pictures fit the script, and we'd work until we had a happy marriage."

Nearly always, the narration was indirect, in the sense that it amplified rather than repeated the information provided on the screen. Louis de Rochemont's first rule of editing was, "Never call your shots." That is, first try to tell the story with pictures alone. If narration must be used, never allow it to repeat what the picture itself tells us. For example, given a scene of a man seated at his breakfast table buttering a piece of toast, direct commentary would tell us that this is Mr. Jones, sitting at his breakfast table, buttering his toast—an event which is patently clear. Indirect commentary might explain that he will leave shortly for his job in the city, where, still part of a depressed economy, he earns a salary which remains inadequate for his family's needs. It would comment upon the growing size of his food bills during the last quarter-year, the result of drought and a poor harvest in the midwest, and then (as the picture changes to a graph which shows statistical data), goes on to explain why the price of dairy products has risen so high.

An example of indirect narration is an early *March of Time* issue describing the affairs of wealthy, elderly munitions manufacturer Sir Basil Zaharoff. The following narration concludes over shots of tombstones in a cemetery:

VOICE OF TIME

For close as he is to making his final peace with his Maker, he is still, today, the chief adviser, the wisest and richest of the dealers in death. [Vol. 1, No. 3]

Every now and then, Van Voorhis's powerful narration would stop abruptly and an informational sub-title would flash across the screen, backed up with dramatic music. Like chapter headings in a book, these provided for a change in subject matter, locale, time, or point of view. They were also useful in filling gaps in the visual continuity. The following title examples are taken from several different issues:

GAY WAS THE VIENNA INTO WHICH OTTO OF HABSBURG WAS BORN TWENTY-FOUR YEARS AGO. [Vol. 2, No. 6]

OLD DEIBLER'S LIFE HAS BEEN SPENT IN THE SERVICE OF THE GUILLOTINE, BUT YEARS AGO HE SOUGHT TO ESCAPE HIS GRUESOME CAREER. [Vol. 2, No. 1]

LUSTY AND GLAMOROUS WAS THE THEATER OF YESTERDAY. [Vol. 3, No. 4]

CHIEF CHARACTER IN ANY MEDITERRANEAN CRISIS OF 1939 WILL BE EUROPE'S NO. 2 SWORD-RATTLER—BENITO MUSSOLINI. [Vol. 5, No. 8]

The relationship of narration, sub-titles, and staged live-action sequences was always intimate and carefully designed. The following sound and picture elements are taken from the *same* episode.

TITLE:

THOUGH THE BOOTLEG COAL INDUSTRY IS LAWLESS, ITS BEGINNINGS ARE SIMPLE, UNDER-STANDABLY HUMAN.

VOICE OF TIME

Today, the business of stealing coal has become a community enterprise.

LIVE-ACTION *(staged):*

MINER-SPOKESMAN: Men, we're going to fight this injunction to a finish! We're organized now! Our lawyers are as good as theirs. And so's our cause! Our grandfathers worked these hills and so do we. If they try to put us off, we'll show them.

[Vol. 1, No. 6]

In other cases, insert scenes such as newspaper or magazine headlines took the place of titles. Sometimes, a series of these would appear in rapid succession, the juxtaposition of one headline after another telling a story of its own and making an unmistakable editorial comment. For example:

Magazine Title: WHAT IS HITLER GOING TO DO NEXT?

Magazine Title: DESTROY, DESTROY, DESTROY!

Magazine Article: Photograph of Hitler and Mussolini shaking hands. [Vol. 4, No. 9]

In the early years of the series the literary construction of the narration was identical to that of *Time* magazine—that is to say, grammatically eccentric. This was entirely intentional, a great effort having been made by John Martin and others to adapt "Timespeak" to the motion picture series. Examples follow:

VOICE OF TIME

"Bright is the prospect for renting agents during Coronation time . . ." [Vol. 3, No. 8]

"Great fun has the self-styled Kingfish in running Louisiana . . ." [Vol. 1, No. 3]

"Soon, than Captain Trujillo no young officer was more diligent and alert." [Vol. 2, No. 7]

As they say in the trade, it was a "high-density" narration, and faithful *March of Time* patrons never let their attention wander very far. If they did, how could they ever have made sense out of this last example of "Time-speak"—surely one of the most convoluted and impenetrable sentences ever written for an information film:

VOICE OF TIME

Arrested, this bogus Ethiopian is unmasked as a lovesick Japanese college boy, trading on Ethiopia's current popularity to make an impression on a waitress. [Vol. 1, No. 7]

Henry Luce had a passion for facts, and he mandated lavish display of them in all the company's publications. Larsen carried this passion to the *March of Time,* illuminating abstract ideas and concepts with concrete statistical data whenever possible:

VOICE OF TIME

6,000 men dig in to build a ditch designed to be twice the length of the Suez—four times the length of the Panama. [Vol. 2, No. 4]

and in this title:

TODAY, THERE ARE FEWER PRIESTS IN MEXICO THAN THERE ARE GENERALS IN THE MEXICAN ARMY—ONLY 300 AUTHORIZED PRIESTS TO SERVE 14,000,000 MEXICANS.   [Vol. 1, No. 3]

Narration was compressed, as in *Time* magazine, by coupling powerful adjectives with the first mention of each personality's name, often with obvious editorial intent:

VOICE OF TIME

. . . crafty little Benes of Czechoslovakia . . . [Vol. 2, No. 6]

. . . shrewd, Russian-born Sidney Hillman . . . [Vol. 7, No. 5]

. . . young and able lawyer, Thomas E. Dewey . . . [Vol. 4, No. 2]

Foxy little Max Weygand . . . [Vol. 1, No. 5]

Handsome braintruster Doctor Tugwell . . . [Vol. 1, No. 4]

France's swarthy little Pierre Laval . . . [Vol. 1, No. 2]

As was the case with *Time* magazine, if one appeared in a *March of Time* issue, the resulting image largely depended upon whether one emerged as "handsome, able, Mr. Smith," or "shrewd, foxy, crafty Mr. Jones."

In less than a couple dozen words, the Voice of Time provided a transition from one scene to the next, set the stage for the action that followed, and told the audience exactly what the *March of Time* thought of the people appearing on the screen:

VOICE OF TIME

Publisher Randolph Hearst, keen student of mob psychology, calls Father Coughlin to his ranch to look him over. [Vol. 1, No. 5]

Bitterest opponent of American aid to the embattled democracies is the number one appeaser—ex-hero, ex-colonel, Charles Augustus Lindbergh . . . [Vol. 7, No. 10]

By contrast, when it did not suit the *March of Time*'s interests to commit itself openly to a particular point of view, potentially hazardous judgments were put into the mouths of "thoughtful observers," "serious commentators," or "some there are who say":

VOICE OF TIME

Thoughtful observers realize that here is a scene close to anarchy . . . [Vol. 2, No. 5]

Today, with U.S. labor split in two, some there are who say that miner [John L.] Lewis is seeking power in steel because his grip on coal is slipping. [Vol. 3, No. 2]

But as Japan's militarists march on behind their Emperor, observers may well wonder what a nation whose war dogs go mad at home might do if allowed to run loose throughout the world. [Vol. 2, No. 3]

The tone of the Voice of Time was frequently ironic, in a decade in which irony may have been the only sensible response to economic disaster and political demagoguery. Sometimes, too, there was a trace of big-city, smart-aleck snobbery. Here, the *March of Time* interviews the American winner of the 1937 Irish sweepstakes:

MAN   I just come home from woik and mamma tells me the news. You could have knocked me over wid a fedder.

OFF-SCREEN CAMERAMAN   Say that again, slower.

MAN   You could have knocked me over wid a fedder. [Vol. 3, No. 10]

And sometimes, the combination of dramatically fashioned language, and Van Voorhis's powerful reading of it, was electrifying:

VOICE OF TIME

THEN CAME MADRID! The air squadrons he sent to bomb the city should theoretically have demoralized its people, destroyed their will to resistance. Instead, an outraged populace rushed to volunteer, began drilling in the streets. Loyalist morale ran high when, from friendly Russia, came vital weapons for defense—Soviet armaments as effective as any from Italy or Germany. [Vol. 3, No. 13]

Was the *March of Time* propagandistic? Not in the usual sense of the word; certainly not in the Griersonian sense; not in the sense of its existing principally to realize a political or economic end; not in the sense that its producers possessed an ideologically coherent and consistent point of view.

Lothar Wolff denies *any* editorial intent.

"You said that it consciously editorialized," he told this author. "I think if we look back now, it may give that impression, but when I was around I only noticed a great striving for impartiality. That they didn't quite succeed we see better now than we did then."

According to Richard de Rochemont:

To say that we had a "philosophy" seems to me to exaggerate a journalistic attitude. . . . If we could beat the newsreel with a subject, if we could get a laugh or a round of applause in the theaters, and if people we liked and respected spoke well of us, we felt a tremor of success.

The men who made the *March of Time* were not political theorists they were journalists. For them, fascism, communism, and native demagogues seemed foreign to the American ethic, and they exposed and attacked them accordingly. "In those days," said director Jack Glenn, "patriotism was a thing accepted. It was one of the starting points of objectivity, as far as we were concerned. It was a platform for objectivity, because if freedom isn't an objectivity, what the hell is?"

Implicit in all *March of Time* issues was a kind of uncomplicated American liberalism—general good intentions, a healthy journalistic skepticism, faith in enlightened self-interest, and substantial pride in American progress and potential. "It was not partisan in a small way," said associate producer Arthur Tourtellot, "it was partisan in a big way. It was against the Nazis and the petty exploitation of people which was represented by various adventurers in this country during the depression."

A cinematic *agent provocateur*, the *March of Time* turned over a lot of rocks, both at home and abroad, and illuminated the creatures it found beneath them. The demagogues and quacks whom they attacked in the 1930's may seem like obvious targets now, but they didn't seem so then. They were popular, powerful, frightening people, and the *March of Time* stood entirely alone in theatrical motion picture circles as a muckraker.

Believing that
the responsibility of
the motion picture
is to inform
as well as entertain
...this theatre shows
THE MARCH OF TIME
regularly

5

Louis's Boys: The Men Who Made Time March

Most arts are practiced individually, the composer at the piano, the painter at the easel, the novelist at the typewriter. But the motion picture is a corporate art, requiring the services of dozens of energetic, well-trained collaborators to realize the intention of the producer or director. As at a great Continental restaurant the chef requires the help of many assistants, with the quality and consistency of their work, as much as the art and taste of their leader, determining whether the group produces a *Ballotine de Canetone*, or garbage.

De Rochemont may not have been much of an administrator, but he picked his subordinates with care and skill. Like British film producer and critic John Grierson, whose single-mindedness and egocentricity he shared, he found his best film makers in a variety of places, some likely, some not. A few of them, mostly film cutters, he brought with him to the *March of Time* from Fox Movietone News. Other professionals he brought into the organization as they became available and came to his attention. But many of his best people began their careers quite ignorant of film technique. For one reason or another, they wandered accidentally into the *March of Time* organization, where Louis tested them, indoctrinated them, and finally trained them to be professional film makers. Reminiscing years later, many of Louis's boys may have wondered whether another line of work might not have been better for their wallets, their indigestions, and their nervous systems, but none who came to the *March of Time* innocent of film-making experience ever doubted who it was who had taught them how to put a film together.

It worked both ways, of course, for Louis needed them as much as they needed him, although he seemed less aware of the fact than they. "Louis was a bright guy," recalled one of his associates, "but he succeeded and survived because he was surrounded by very able people." "Louis was always the guy up in the tower, thinking, away from the people . . . ," added another. "He didn't like the smell of people. He liked to be 'up there,' observing, selecting."

De Rochemont enjoyed playing commander of the organization, but he depended absolutely upon his subordinates to realize the ideas he conceived for the *March of Time*. It was a psychologically complicated symbiosis, the general in the front office, providing the will, the energy, and the central idea which propelled the *March of Time* to success and prominence; his loyal, harassed "soldiers" finding ways, however exotic and ingenious, to get him the footage he required.

So many talented individuals played such crucial roles in the history of the *March of Time* that it is difficult to rank them or to differentiate their relative contributions, especially since everyone doubled and tripled in brass—writing today, directing tomorrow, editing the third day, and carrying film cans up and down stairways on the fourth. Nonetheless, one has to begin somewhere, and it seems appropriate to do so with Louis's brother, Richard. No one after Louis played a greater variety of roles than he, or had more impact over a longer period of time upon the *March of Time* and its development.

Richard Guertis de Rochemont, like his brother, was a product of New England, born almost five years after Louis, on December 13, 1903, in Chelsea, Massachusetts. His early education was acquired at the Cambridge Latin School. Unlike his brother, he went to college, graduating from Harvard, *cum laude*, in 1928. While Dick was still in college, Louis got him a job as an editor and general helper for the New England edition of the Pathé News. Dick also worked part-time, during the same period, for the *Boston Advertiser* as a reporter.

Following graduation, Dick went to work in 1928 for the *New York American,* got fired, and moved on in 1929 to the *New York Sun,* both newspapers now long defunct. By that time, Louis had become active in the affairs of Fox Movietone News which, together with the Hearst Metrotone Newsreel, was being produced at 54th Street and 10th Avenue in New York. "I had reached a point on the *Sun,*" said Dick, "where, as a reporter, I wasn't going to get any more money unless I stayed on it for a good many years, so I fired up my job on the *Sun* and went up to work on the editorial staff of Movietone."

At the Fox/Hearst shop, Dick worked with veteran newsreel editors Mike Clofine and Ed Harvey, both former newspapermen.

Clofine told me, "Come in here and keep your mouth shut for a month. We don't want to hear from you until you've been sitting here every day for a month." I don't think I managed to keep quiet that long, but it was good advice because I did pick up a lot and it saved me from making a fool of myself.

The transition from silence to sound was under way in films. Dick was put to work first as a title writer and then as foreign editor. Fox Movietone, the world's largest newsreel, was then putting out thirteen different editions throughout the world, each translated into appropriate language, first with titles and then, as sound was added, with foreign-language narration. Early in 1931 the people at Fox asked Dick if he would like to go to Paris to edit the French edition, replacing Harry Lawrenson who had been sent to Australia. Dick accepted quickly, began polishing his French, and, with his wife Helen, headed for Paris where he served as editor and later manager for France of Fox Movietone's *Actualité Parlant* until 1934.

By 1934 Louis and Roy were at work planning the *March of Time.* Louis had succeeded in going over the head of Truman Talley, his former boss in New York, and gaining from Fox Movietone the right to use its vast film library for *March of Time* productions. This arrangement upset Talley immensely, and on his next trip to Europe he raised the matter at once with Dick de Rochemont. "I had not been a party to any of this going on," said Dick, "although I knew about it. And Talley said, 'I assume you're immediately going to join Louis and be one of my competitors?' I said, 'Frankly, I hadn't discussed it.' I had never worked side by side with Louis—I didn't know how that would go." Talley decided to take no chances, and fired Dick de Rochemont at once.

Dick returned to New York to speak to Louis and Roy Larsen about their new venture. Hedging his bets, he also began talking to the people at Paramount News about joining their organization. "I hung around," said Dick. "My wife was in France, living in a big house we had rented outside Paris, and so I waited, and I thought, well, maybe this [*March of Time*] thing is never going to happen." In the end, Larsen decided to take a chance and sent Dick back to Paris as European head of operations, despite the fact that the new series had not yet been introduced to the public. "I was given a ticket for Europe and a $500 expense check," Dick recalled, "and Larsen said, 'Be sure not to start opening any offices.' Within a year I had an office opened in Paris, another one opened in London, and, I think, twenty people on the payroll."

Richard de Rochemont became *Time*'s first full-time salaried employee to be permanently stationed overseas. In Paris he first secured space in the Twentieth Century Fox building at 27 Champs-Élysées. Subsequently, *Time* marched to the *New York Herald* building at 21 rue de Berri, and finally settled down at 52 Champs-Élysées. The London office was located at 4 Dean Street, in Soho. These offices also became the first overseas bureaus for *Time, Life,* and *Fortune* magazines.

For several years thereafter, Dick de Rochemont ran an efficient, aggressive European operation for the *March of Time*. Like his brother, he was a first-rate journalist with a nose for news and the energy to pursue his subjects to a successful conclusion. He loved to get "scoops" on the competition, and many of his memoranda of the 1930's describe with relish how he stole a march on Fox, Paramount, or Pathé newsreelers. An urbane, cultured, well-educated man, he made good and lasting friends in political, cultural, and military circles in England and on the continent.

Important staff members at his Paris office were French editor

Richard de Rochemont, head of *MOT*'s European operations, photographed in his London office with staff members. (l. to r.) Rita André (secretary), Edgar Anstey, Richard de Rochemont, Humphrey Swingler, Maurice Lancaster, John Mansfield. (Courtesy Time, Inc.)

Gilbert Comte, whom he had acquired from Fox Movietone News; cameramen Marcel Rebière and Paul Martelliere; and contact man (later, director) Jean Pagès. In addition, a mobile *MOT* unit, headed by cameraman S. R. Sozio (formerly with Paramount News), roamed throughout Europe as needed.

One of Dick's first and smartest moves in England was to acquire the services of influential documentary film producer John Grierson, whom he put on the *March of Time* payroll as consultant. Grierson admired the *March of Time* for its aggressiveness, and is remembered by Dick as being consistently supportive. Typically, Grierson began at once to ease many of his own people onto de Rochemont's staff, which was all right with Dick because they were very good film makers. These included directors Edgar Anstey (who also worked as foreign editor on the *March of Time* in New York from 1937 to 1938), Harry Watt, Len Lye, and Maurice

British director Edgar Anstey (seated) discusses a shot with cameraman Jimmy Hodgson (left) before filming a scene in England. Soundman Dennis Scanlan stands between Hodgson and Anstey. Renacre adjusts the microphone and Humphrey Swingler stands at far right. (Courtesy Time, Inc.)

Lancaster, the latter of whom became manager of the London office a few years later when Richard returned to the United States. Richard also had occasional dealings with Arthur Elton. All of these men were in the process of building a dynamic and influential documentary film movement in England.

Len Lye, in addition to being a competent film director, is also remembered by film historians for his graphic arts experiments. He pioneered the technique of painting abstract colored images on clear motion picture film, producing a series of charming experimental short subjects for the British Post Office. It was a technique that was later adopted and refined by the talented Canadian animator Norman McLaren. According to his *March of Time* col-

leagues, Lye was bitter over the subsequent publicity that Mc-
Laren erroneously received as the "originator" of this new technique. During the Second World War, Lye was one of the European
employees whom Dick brought over to the United States, where
he continued to work as an *MOT* director. He also did some
graphic arts work for the organization, including the redesign of
the *March of Time* logo at the time the company began releasing
through Twentieth Century-Fox. As Dick said, looking back on
his acquisition of this interesting film maker, "It's a poor company
can't afford one artist," which, if memory serves, is a variation on
Grierson's remark about McLaren, that "I can only afford one
artist."

Harry Watt, another of Dick's British directors, recalled the
good salaries that *MOT* paid the Grierson people. "I was getting,
I think, eight pounds a week, which was an enormous salary from
what I was getting at the GPO [General Post Office], something in
the region of three or four pounds then. I found working with
them fascinating because there was a lot of money available, and
you could actually stay in decent hotels and things like that."

Dick's senior cameraman was Jimmy Hodgson, who was the first
film maker he employed full time in London, and who remained
with the *March of Time* for many years thereafter. Other important London film makers were Jack Cotter and Robert Alonso
Navarro on camera, Dennis Scanlan on sound, and (later) Peter
Hopkinson on camera. As with Louis's North American operation, Dick empolyed numerous freelance cameramen throughout
Europe as the need arose, on a per-job basis. He also bought footage regularly, both from commercial film libraries and from private owners.

The *March of Time* was a cosmopolitan series, whose producers
brought an international perspective to bear upon all of the news
stories they treated. Louis, with his "Admiral Mahan" view of the
role navies played in geopolitical matters, and Richard, with his
sophisticated, Francophile sensitivity to European political and
military affairs, were well suited to their jobs. And it was Dick and
his staff who acquired, regularly and dependably, the remarkable
footage that made the *March of Time*'s treatment of international

One of Dick de Rochemont's British crew on location near Westminster Abbey. Soundman Dennis Scanlan operates out of the automobile's back seat. (Courtesy Time, Inc.)

affairs during the 1930's not only exciting but intelligent and comprehensive. Dick de Rochemont's influence on the evolution of the *March of Time* grew with the passing of years, and will be treated in much greater detail in the chapters to come.

Louis de Rochemont's New York staff included several "field directors." Publicly, even within the trade, they were *never* referred to as "directors." There were no credit titles on any of the *March of Time*'s monthly films, and in the flood of promotion materials which were generated by the parent corporation during the early years decision-making personnel were always referred to, generically, as "editors." It was felt, as a matter of policy, that the term "editor" was more appropriate to a news-gathering enterprise, although in view of the *March of Time*'s well-known practice of dramatically re-creating events, the term "director" would have been particularly appropriate.

Whatever *Time* called them, they were, in fact, directors, and the *March of Time* had several of them working in the field, generating footage of the American scene. Over the years, these included Jack Glenn, George Black, William Zubiller, Victor Jurgens, Gray Lockwood, Alan Brown, Len Lye, Peter Hopkinson, Beverly Jones, Gunther von Fritsch, and (occasionally) Tom Orchard and Lothar Wolff; and assistant directors G. B. Buscemi, D. Corbit Curtis, Bob Daly and Franklin Schaffner. Of all these men, Jack Glenn was senior and unquestionably the most important. Like Dick de Rochemont, he was one of the few *MOT* staffers to remain with the series from beginning to end.

One of *Time*'s publicity releases estimated that Jack Glenn had directed more than 121 of the 290 episodes released during the sixteen-year history of the series. What is more important is that the issues he directed included the best and most exciting of the lot. In the *auteur* sense, it may have been Louis who determined the character and direction of the *March of Time,* but it was Jack Glenn who realized the scenes that Louis needed.

Adventurous, likable, amusing, and insatiably gregarious, Glenn was a professional, with journalistic instincts and great energy. Born in Terrell, Texas, in 1904, he attended Rice University where he graduated with the class of 1926. A well-educated and well-read man, he was fluent both in French and Spanish, and a connoisseur of good conversation and good cooking. He was fully as aggressive and tenacious as Louis in attacking and completing the assignments given him, and was just as inventive and devious as the boss in getting his "scoops." He was also one of the few staff members capable of standing up to Louis and answering him back.

Glenn was passionately antifascist and anticommunist, and took special pleasure in exposing the political extremists and assorted nitwits who made America the divided country that it was in the 1930's. In the best professional sense of the word, he was a "con man," capable of talking this country's most intractable and suspicious political figures into appearing before *March of Time* cameras, oftentimes against their own best interests.

He was never happier than when he was traveling around the country, trying to actualize de Rochemont's impossible ideas. He referred to himself as Louis's "shovel man." "I was one of the happy slaves . . ." said Glenn. "I'd go out and get the characters, who were the little people back of the news. . . . We were never bored. It wasn't going into the office every morning. You were out in the world. . . . The *March of Time* was something new in the world; it was something exciting. . . . It put you in contact with the heart and mind of everybody in sight."

Glenn had begun his career in the newspaper business. By the late 1920's he was working in France as a correspondent for the *New York Herald* (published in Paris), which he described as "the sweetest newspaper job in the world—a small-town newspaper in a metropolis." While there, he was assigned to cover the story of Charles Lindbergh's 1927 trans-Atlantic air flight.

According to Glenn, the *New York Times* had bought exclusive rights to a story from Lindbergh and it was Glenn's job to break that exclusive for the *New York Herald.* Glenn was at Le Bourget Airport when Lindbergh landed, and was one of the first men to reach the plane when it came to a stop, propeller still turning. Some newspapers subsequently reported that the aviator's first words were, "I am Charles Lindbergh." Glenn recalled that his first words were, "Are there any mechanics around?"

Glenn decided to sail with Lindbergh on the *Memphis* for the flier's triumphal return to the United States. Since only wire service and New York Times reporters were officially on board, Glenn couldn't travel as a newspaperman, so he had Pathé Newsman Harry Harde teach him how to operate a 35mm Eyemo hand camera, and then signed on board the *Memphis* as a Pathé cameraman.

No sooner had the ship set sail than Glenn's columns began to appear in the Paris *Herald* under his by-line, describing the voyage, a copy of which was immediately wired to the ship at sea. Neither Lindbergh nor Admiral Burrage was pleased. Glenn was called into their presence and asked if he were filing stories from on board.

"How could I, sir?" said Glenn. "I have no wireless under my hat."

"When did you join Pathé, Mr. Glenn?" asked the admiral.

"The morning we sailed, sir," said Glenn.

"And when did you quit the *Herald?*"

"The night before we sailed, sir."

Most important of the *March of Time*'s directors was Jack Glenn (right) photographed here in one of his rare visits to the editing room. A film maker of
great energy and tenacity, he directed more than 121 of the *MOT*'s 290 episodes. (Courtesy Jack Glenn)

Lindbergh laughed, and that was that. What Glenn had done,
of course, was to write all of his daily dispatches, on more or less
predictable topics, the day before the ship sailed. These were
printed daily with his by-line, as if they were bona fide dispatches
from sea. It was good preparation for the kind of re-creations he
would do later for the *March of Time,* but this was 1927, and all
of that was well in the future.

Between the time the ship sailed and the time it arrived in
Washington, D.C., Glenn learned how to operate his camera. The
shots he took of Lindbergh and his party were widely used by
both Pathé News and King Features newspaper syndicate; the
latter also published several of Glenn's cartoons.

When the ship arrived in Washington, D.C., it was Louis de
Rochemont, then associate editor of Pathé News, who picked up

the film from Glenn. It was an historic meeting for the two of them, but it didn't last more than a moment. There was a twenty-one-gun salute under way, and neither could hear the other talk. "We didn't finish our conversation," said Glenn. "That's the way it was all our lives together—we never finished a conversation."

Before Louis left with Glenn's footage he told Glenn to meet him for dinner that evening at the Mayflower Hotel. "That night I saw him," said Glenn. "Typical de Rochemont—I saw him this way for the next thousand years: hand up, waving, 'Hi, boy, come in, come in.' So I went to work for Pathé."

Glenn's stay with Pathé was brief, and then he was off again, first for a trip home to Texas, then back to Paris. Before Jack left, Louis told him about his plans to travel around the world shooting enlistment comedies for the U.S. Navy as an independent contractor. "I'll tell you all about it next fall, and you'll come with me," said de Rochemont. Glenn figured it was just one of Louis's pipe dreams, but several months later Louis showed up in Paris as he had promised, and the two of them set off at once on their round-the-world trip, with Louis operating the camera and Glenn writing, directing, and acting in the films. "I had long hair in those days," said Glenn, "and I was a sailor in the film." It was great fun while it lasted. Louis was a good deal more easy-going and more convivial then, and the two men's personalities meshed nicely.

Some months later, Glenn introduced Louis to a pretty young lady named Virginia Shaler. Not too long after, on September 12, 1929, Louis married Virginia, beginning what was for both of them a long and happy marriage that lasts to the present day.

After Glenn and Louis completed their filming in Asia, they returned to the United States by way of Canada. Back in the U.S., Glenn entered into a theatrical adventure with Christopher Morley, appearing as an actor in a historical melodrama which they produced in Hoboken, New Jersey. Glenn played the villain, Lloyd Nolan the hero. The depression hit hard, and their adventure came to an end. Glenn headed off to Texas, where he became a sports editor and married Althea Jones Hill of Houston. In time, he and his wife found their way back to New York. His wife worked at Macy's for $8 a week, and Glenn spent his time looking for employment. Things were getting grim when Louis reappeared in New York with a job for Glenn as an actor in his new Columbia Pictures series, *The March of the Years*. Glenn joined de Rochemont in production. In time, as Glenn recalled, Louis began to lose interest in the series and turned much of its direction and production over to him. Louis, by then, was already at work planning the *March of Time* with Roy Larsen.

In 1934 Louis put Glenn to work as an actor in one of *Time's* experimental reels. A few weeks later Glenn was hired as a director. It was the first permanent job he had had for a long time. It would be his for eighteen years.

Glenn's experience as both a newspaperman and an actor prepared him nicely for his new career. His great talent lay in his ability to identify with the people he photographed and to ingratiate himself into their confidence. "Hell, I became a sharecropper," he recalled: "I became a Negro in Harlem, I became a Park Avenue hoity-toity, I became a Bowery bum—I had to drink 'smoke,' which damn near killed me. I would dress the way the people did—farmers, longshoremen, New Englanders. I put on a lot of accents."

Operationally, Jack's ethical code was complicated but inflexible. In the absence of an understanding, anything went. On the other hand, once he gave his word to an individual, on any particular point, he stuck to the understanding even if it meant losing a shot, an interview, or a "scoop." "I tried never to mislead anybody," said Glenn piously. "I would try to get on one subject that we could agree on and never let them change the subject." Glenn found that there was hardly a person with whom he couldn't agree on some matter or other—even if it was only the weather. As a consequence, political, social, and economic extremists of all persuasions usually thought that they were talking to someone who shared their most bizarre notions. It was only when they saw the finished sequence on the screen that they were disabused of the notion.

Glenn spoke of his handling of an American Nazi who appeared in one of the *March of Time's* antifascist issues. "I'm not going to betray anybody, and besides, I'm compassionate in this feeling. Everybody has his virtues as well as his faults. Especially in journalism, you cannot just make it all black and white. . . . He's a son of a bitch, I agree, but you can't say he's a son of a bitch; not properly. Just show what he does; it'll speak for itself."

A resourceful director, Glenn's only peculiarity was an inclination to overshoot footage at very high ratios. Whether he was unsure of himself or just a perfectionist is not clear. Back at the *March of Time*'s editing rooms, nobody cared what the reason was. Whenever Glenn was on assignment, thousands of feet of 35mm negative would pour into the place from his cameras. "Shoot, shoot, shoot, shot," recalled associate producer Tom Orchard. "Not one take, but ten takes. And after all, as production manager, I was responsible to the business manager for holding down the footage. This was Jack's problem. . . . However, once this footage was edited down, it was elegant."

Although never credited as a writer, Glenn actually wrote most of the dialogue that his performers spoke. *MOT* directors usually were given only an outline to work from and were expected to generate dialogue and "actor's business" on location. Narration, on the other hand, was written by Louis and his staff back in New York.

During his long career, Glenn became an important creative figure in east coast documentary, theatrical, and television production. Along the way, he served a fifteen-year term as president of the Screen Directors' Guild. But it was the *March of Time* he loved, and to which he devoted almost two decades of his life.

The powerful and unusually compelling voice that narrated the *March of Time* was that of (Cornelius) Westbrook Van Voorhis, billed as The Voice of Time. Cultured, precise, fast-paced, ominous, the voice quickly guided the audience from shot to shot and sequence to sequence, now directing their attention to supplementary facts not illustrated on the screen, then posing a thought-provoking question and pausing, appropriately, while the audience answered it. Curiously, Van Voorhis's voice had no distinct personality characteristics with which members of the audience could identify. Like some of *Time* magazine's pronouncements, it appeared to speak *ex cathedra,* with the weight of some omniscient power behind it. Critic George Dangerfield felt sure that "Just such a voice . . . would have been hired to speak the lines of one

"Time Marches On!" intones Westbrook Van Voorhis, who narrated the *March of Time* during its entire history. Although he was not seen by audiences, his powerful, authoritative voice was said to be even more familiar than that of President Roosevelt. (Courtesy Time, Inc.)

of Euripides' suave male gods—those gods who appeared so opportunely at the end of a tragedy when everything was going up in flames and agnosticism, and explained matters away. Nobody has ever been quite sure what those gods believed in or whether they even believed in themselves; and this gives them a real affinity with the voice that does the talking for the March of Time [*New Republic,* August 19, 1936]."

Other critics, less kind, called it the "Voice of the Tomb." Roy Larsen had originally intended to use Harry Von Zell (the Voice of Time for the radio version of the series) as narrator for the film, but just about the time the screen version was introduced, Von Zell was offered a splendid opportunity to go with one of the major New York advertising agencies as their principal radio announcer, and he asked *Time* and CBS to release him from his *March of Time* commitment. Reluctantly, they agreed, fearful that Von Zell's distinctive voice and talents might be indispensable to the show. Von Zell went on to an immensely successful career as a radio, film, and television announcer and actor. The man they picked to replace him, thirty-four-year-old Westbrook Van Voorhis, had also been with the radio version of the show for some time.

> He was the "Voice of Fate" [recalled Von Zell]. He was used in the program frequently when a catastrophe had happened—earthquake, floods, or . . . the passing of some great person. And then it would be the "Voice of Fate." And Van, of course, had the perfect voice. He *was* fate [Imitating him]. "And today, as it must to all men, death came to so-and-so." Or: "Today, as it will from time to time, the elements ran rampant in Japan. An earthquake of monstrous intensity—lives snuffed out by the thousands." This was his job.

Initially, not everyone on the staff was pleased with Van Voorhis's voice. "I objected when I first heard him," said writer Jimmy Shute. "I said, Oh, my God, this portentous voice will kill me. But then it turned out that he was such a marvelous technician; he could take a line and give it a twist and a validity that you wouldn't have believed anybody else could read into it. It was great."

A New Yorker by birth, Van Voorhis had led a varied and interesting early life, attending the U.S. Naval Academy at Annapolis, then inheriting $100,000 from his grandmother, spending every cent of it in his early twenties, and finally turning to the professional stage and radio for a career. In time, after his success on both the radio and film versions of the *March of Time*, his services were acquired exclusively by Time, Inc. Hired at $50 a week for the radio show in 1931, he was making $25,000 a year by 1937. In addition to his work as narrator on the two shows, he traveled widely and continuously throughout the country on behalf of the corporation, giving lectures and participating in *Time-Life*'s various sales programs.

Certainly no one on the *March of Time* staff was more popular than Van, who remained unspoiled by the enormous celebrity that his career brought him. "He was an absolutely lovable man," recalled Lothar Wolff. As with Dick de Rochemont and Jack Glenn, Van Voorhis was one of the few staff members who remained with the *March of Time* film series from beginning to end.

Louis's right-hand man during the 1930's was Thomas Orchard. He had come to the *March of Time* in 1934 at the age of twenty-three, without any film-making experience, and within a relatively short period of time rose to successive positions of increasing responsibility. In those days, Time, Incorporated, ran a so-called "CBOB" program—"College Boys, Office Boys." Promising young college graduates were brought into the various divisions of the corporation and put to work as lowly office boys. If they showed journalistic or administrative potential, they were moved up rapidly; if not, they were shipped out. The position was similar to that of page in network radio and television studios, and to clerical worker in the mail rooms of the Hollywood film studios. In each case, the initial job was menial in character, but it opened onto routes upward for bright and energetic young men.

Having graduated from Hobart College in 1931, Orchard had tried a variety of unrewarding depression-decade jobs, first as a reader for D. Appleton Company, then as an editorial assistant at the Haley M. O. Company, then as stock boy at the J. J. Newberry Company, and finally as a Wall Street runner, earning $14 a week in 1934. Later that same year, Orchard was hired onto the *Time* staff by business manager Bill Commons at $18 a week, and worked as a general office boy for three or four months before being offered a chance to go with the new group being put together by Roy Larsen. It had something to do with motion pictures, he was told, and Orchard said he thought that sounded fine. The day finally came, in August 1934, when he got a call from the *March of Time*'s studios on West 54th Street. Larsen and de Rochemont were then in the midst of producing the first *MOT* experimental reels, and they sent a call over to the parent company for four or five CBOB's to be used as actors in one of the issues. Tom hustled over to the studios and was outfitted by the Eaves Costume Company as a midshipman. The sequence in which they appeared re-created a recent visit by U.S. Navy personnel to the Vatican, at which an audience had been granted by the Pope.

Tom Orchard came to the *March of Time* as an office boy, quickly became a director, then production manager, assistant producer, and associate producer of the series. (Courtesy Tom Orchard)

At a certain signal from Louis [recalled Tom] we were to say "Hip, Hip, Hooray for the Pope." So we did this three or four times, and took our hats off and waved. . . . This, then, was my introduction to the technique of re-enactment, and subsequently that little shot of these Annapolis midshipmen on a cruise was cut in with newsreel shots of the guys who went to call on the Pope.

Intense, introspective, and conscientious, Orchard impressed Louis with his hard work and selfless enthusiasm, and was given a permanent assignment on the *March of Time* staff.

My duties were to work around the clock if Roy and Louis were working around the clock, which they frequently did. . . . My job was to brew coffee for them, to run errands, get sandwiches, the usual office boy, and I think I impressed them because I kept everything very neat and clean, everything was swept up, pencils freshly sharpened for them, and all that sort of nonsense. That was my start.

Orchard's rise within the organization was swift.

I was the first office boy, and I was practically the first everything else. I was the first director of the *March of Time*. I was the first production manager of the *March of Time*. . . . I was the first assistant producer, and then I became the first associate producer and subsequently the senior associate producer.

Over the years, no one served Louis as faithfully and loyally as Tom Orchard. De Rochemont expected him to be available twenty-four hours a day, and he nearly always was. It was a difficult and generally thankless job, but one that Orchard filled continuously until shortly before the outbreak of World War II, when he left the *March of Time* to activate his commission in the navy.

Louis always had ambivalent feelings toward the numerous college graduates he had brought into the organization. He needed their skills, but resented their college backgrounds. "You college boys," Tom recalled Louis snarling, "you think you're so damned smart."

Sometime around 1937 Orchard attempted to arrange for Louis to receive an honorary degree from his alma mater, Hobart College. Orchard wrote to one of Hobart's trustees outlining Louis's qualifications and achievements and suggesting the nature of the degree. In due time, Hobart's president wrote back. They had decided to award the degree not to Louis, but to Orchard! Hobart had instituted an honorary degree for recent graduates who had gone off into the world and had shown promise in their careers. Hobart was proud of Tom, and it was he who got the degree. Louis was not amused. Indeed, not until the University of New Hampshire made Louis an honorary Doctor of Humane Letters in 1944 did his resentment of college men finally disappear.

Music played an important part in the production of the *March of Time,* and issues were always heavily scored, "wall-to-wall," from beginning to end. Over its sixteen-year existence, background music was fashioned by three different musical directors, the first of whom was John Rochetti, who had worked previously with Louis as musical director on the *March of the Years* series. Rochetti retired in 1940 because of illness and was replaced by Louis De Francesco. De Francesco, in addition to scoring the monthly series, also scored *MOT*'s first feature, *The Ramparts We Watch,* in 1940. De Francesco departed in 1942 and was replaced by Jack Shaindlin, who remained with the series until its end. Shaindlin was born in 1909 in the Crimea, where he studied music at the Rimsky-Korsakov Conservatory. With his mother and brother he emigrated to the United States in 1922, becoming an American citizen in 1937. In America, Shaindlin continued his musical studies, while a teen-ager, at the Glenn Dillard Gunn Conservatory in Chicago and the Brooklyn Conservatory in New York, while simultaneously earning a precarious living as a pit pianist in burlesque and vaudeville houses. By 1933, at the age of 24, he was at work at R.K.O. Pictures in New York as composer and orchestrator. In 1936, he also began scoring shorts for Universal Pictures.

Shaindlin was recruited to the *March of Time* in 1941 by chief film editor Lothar Wolff, who was impressed by the score for a short subject called *The Eagle and the Dragon* which Shaindlin had done for Universal. Shaindlin was first hired by Wolff to score some of the *March of Time*'s nontheatrical "industrial-film" productions. In 1942, he replaced De Francesco as *MOT*'s regular musical director. A popular, funny, irreverent man, a talented and prolific worker, Shaindlin scored numerous feature films, including *MOT*'s *We Are the Marines* and *The Golden Twenties,* and also served as musical director for both Fox Movietone News and Universal Newsreel.

The *March of Time*'s head of distribution and promotion during the early years was Albert Sindlinger. Born in Tuscarawas, Ohio, in 1907, Sindlinger developed a teen-ager's interest in wireless communication. In the process of acquiring a professional broadcasting license in the early 1920's, he became acquainted with then Secretary of Commerce Herbert Hoover, thus beginning a

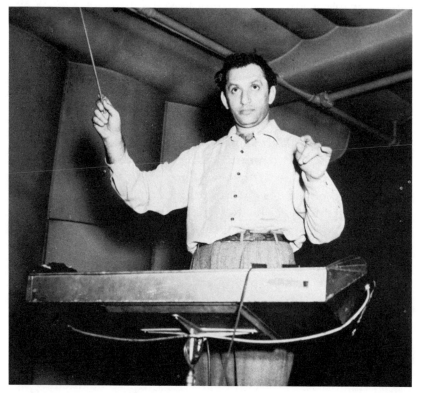

Jack Shaindlin was the third and longest-lasting of the *March of Time*'s musical directors, scoring and conducting the film's background music from 1942 onward. (Courtesy Jack Shaindlin)

long-lasting and valuable friendship with the future President. While attending Ohio University, where his father was a professor, Sindlinger operated both the campus radio station and the local motion picture theater. With his background in electronics and theater operation, he found his services in great demand when sound was introduced to films in the late 1920's. He eventually managed several theaters and installed sound systems in many more on the east coast and throughout midwestern parts of the country.

As a theater manager he went to great lengths to develop audience opinion surveys, which he conducted much of the time in the lobbies of his theaters. These were intended to guide him in the booking of films. In his search for audience response data, he even bugged the rest rooms of his theaters!

In July 1935, by which time the *March of Time* had just been introduced to the public, Sindlinger was invited by former President Hoover to dinner at his apartment in New York's Waldorf Astoria Hotel, at which both Albert Lasker of the Lord and Thomas advertising agency and Henry Luce were present. Hoover described Sindlinger's attempts at audience opinion analysis and his concept of consumer confidence. Luce ended up asking Sindlinger to set up a research department at Time, Incorporated. Sindlinger accepted, and on his first day at work at *Time,* in September 1935, he was invited to lunch by Roy Larsen. There, joined by R.K.O. executive Ned Depinet and financier Joseph P. Kennedy, Sindlinger found himself in the midst of negotiations that were under way between *Time* and R.K.O. Pictures for the latter's distribution of the film series. According to Sindlinger, he discovered to his astonishment that Luce, innocent of motion picture economics, was prepared to give R.K.O. up to 40 per cent of the gross for distributing the series. Sindlinger managed to get Larsen outside long enough to tell him that 12-13 per cent would be more appropriate. Larsen delayed negotiations long enough to correct the matter, and, impressed with Sindlinger's expertise, instantly appointed him head of the *March of Time's* distribution and promotion program. By 3:00 p.m. on his first day at work, Sindlinger had a new job and a new title. He stayed with the *March of Time* from 1935 through the end of 1942, building a substantial market for the series. By early 1939 the *March of Time* had reached its peak distribution, booked into 9800 theaters in the United States. At that time, when the total domestic American film audience represented approximately 84 million paid admissions each week, Sindlinger estimated that an average *March of Time* issue was seen by between 22 million and 26 million people. Sindlinger never forgot whom he was working for. He even managed to peddle copies of *Time* magazine in theaters where the *March of Time* was running.

De Rochemont and Sindlinger disliked each other intensely, which was ironic considering that one of Sindlinger's jobs was to publicize de Rochemont. According to Sindlinger, Louis fired him repeatedly, usually after completing each issue. Then, within a day or two, he would hire him back again. Theirs was a thoroughly unpleasant relationship which ended when Sindlinger left to join Dr. George Gallup's audience-opinion research organization. More than thirty-five years later, they obviously still feel the same way about each other. "He hated my guts," concluded Sindlinger. It was clear that the feeling was mutual.

A pivotal figure in *March of Time* operations was chief film editor (later assistant producer) Lothar Wolff. A talented film maker and effective administrator, Wolff is remembered by his colleagues as the man who made things work. More than one veteran *March of Time* staffer regarded Wolff as the most important man in the organization after Louis de Rochemont. Modest, urbane, whimsical, humane, and unfailingly diplomatic, Wolff, more than anyone else on the staff, was able to cope with Louis, de-fuse him, and direct his energies into constructive channels.

Louis's ego being what it was, ideas that originated manifestly with other individuals were nearly always unacceptable to him. According to de Rochemont's subordinates, the key to working with him was to introduce important, desirable, and necessary ideas into Louis's mind gradually without his becoming aware of the process. This kind of operation is an art in itself, as administrative assistants all over the world have discovered. Lothar Wolff was especially adept at it.

Wolff had come to the *March of Time* with considerable film-making experience. Born in Bromberg, Germany, in 1909, he had worked in European film studios for many years as a publicity director, production assistant, and film editor with outstanding directors, including G. W. Pabst, Fritz Lang, Rex Ingram, and Abel Gance. It was Wolff who edited the French version of Lang's last German film, *The Testament of Dr. Mabuse,* and it was Wolff who, at considerable personal risk, helped to smuggle the work print out of Germany and into France where postproduction work was completed after propaganda minister Joseph Goebbels had ordered the film destroyed. Wolff fled from Germany in 1933, at the same time that Lang and many other German film makers did, ultimately arriving in the United States in 1936 with no job. One of his friends, actress Maggie Mullen (who had played parts for de

111

Rochemont in his *March of the Years* series), brought Wolff to de Rochemont's attention. In a letter dated March 10, 1936, de Rochemont advised Wolff that he would be happy to try him out as a cutter at $25 a week. Lothar reported the following Monday to Beverly Jones, then a supervisor in Louis's cutting department, and began what became a productive and rewarding association with de Rochemont that was to last for more than twenty years.

In film circles, the distinction between a cutter and an editor is that a cutter is a technician, responsible for mechanical assembly of film clips and the filing of footage, upon the instructions of the editor, who makes creative decisions regarding the order in which images appear on the screen, the rhythms that their various lengths produce, the juxtaposition of sound and picture, and the general meaning of the various sequences. Although Wolff had had long experience as a supervising editor, he was happy, under the circumstances, to be put to work by de Rochemont as a lowly film cutter. Ironically, he had to be shown how to splice and assemble film by a fellow cutter, Morrie Roizman. In Wolff's European experience this kind of work had always been done for him by his assistants, and he had never taken the time to learn how to do it himself.

After he got the hang of things, Wolff rose rapidly in the *March of Time* organization, ultimately becoming chief film editor and an assistant producer. Still later, he produced feature films for de Rochemont. Most important for everyone else at the Lexington Avenue sprocket factory, Wolff was able to deal effectively with Louis.

Arthur Tourtellot, *March of Time* associate producer (later CBS executive), provided an insight:

> Lothar is a sophisticated man. First of all, he'd been through, in his life, as a human being, enough, so that he wasn't going to be undone by Louis de Rochemont having a tantrum over nought. Some bitterly resented [de Rochemont]. Lothar just kind of rose above it, and was, I think, a pacifying influence. Lothar, as you know, is himself a very gifted man . . . one of the few people that Louis respected who never felt required to agree with Louis about everything, and as a matter of fact, didn't. But he never came into conflict. Lothar has discretion. He knew when there was a point to

Lothar Wolff, a central figure in *March of Time* operations, was an experienced European film maker who fled Nazi Germany in 1933, joined the *March of Time* in 1936 at $25 a week. He rose quickly in the ranks to become chief film editor and assistant producer of the series. (Courtesy Lothar Wolff)

raise some hell and when there was no point to it, when it would be self-defeating.

Musical director Jack Shaindlin recalled a typical instance in which Lothar would softly inquire of Louis whether he had meant, perhaps, to do so-and-so, and such-and-such. Louis would mumble something, and Lothar would exclaim: "You're right, Louis. *That*'s the way to do it. Just like you said."

Did this mean that Lothar Wolff's regard for de Rochemont's abilities was in any way diminished? Not at all. "The end result," said Wolff, "was still that Louis was the genius. It was Louis's vision. It was frequently a groping process. It was not an intellectual process, but he had innate good sense and good taste—good news sense, and he had the willingness and desire to experiment."

Writers came and went at the *March of Time*. At any one time there might be as many as five or six writers on the payroll. Over the years these included Jimmy Shute, Robert Richards, John Martin, Dwight Cook, Sam Bryant, Arthur Tourtellot, Tom Everitt, Donald Higgins, Robert Wetzel, Carl Norcross, Fred Feldkamp, Ted Wear, and Martin Plissner. Of these, Jimmy Shute and John Martin had the most impact. Born in 1900, James Shute, like de Rochemont, was a New England boy. Educated at Gloucester High School in Massachusetts, he headed for a career in theater, then wandered into film production, working briefly with Ben Hecht and Charles MacArthur at the time they were producing their own films at the Paramount Studios in Astoria, New York. "They were delightful people," said Shute. "I had a wonderful time with them. But I was nothing. I got $35 a week as secretary. They hired me chiefly because I forgot their engagements regularly."

In June 1935 a friend of Shute's sent him around to meet Roy Larsen and before Jimmy knew what had happened, he was working as a writer for the *March of Time*. "I never thought I'd last," said Shute. "I thought I was going to be fired. This was work I didn't know anything about. I just fell into it." Shute had something to worry about, for Louis would hire and fire people as the mood hit him. "Louis was always meeting people in Pullman cars and saying, 'Come to work for me,' " said Shute. "[They] came in under the wing of Louis and bounced out from under the wing of Louis about two weeks later. And that was the way that things always went there. It was a highly personal organization with Louis at the top." Ironically, Shute lasted from 1935 until he resigned in 1949 to join the Marshall Plan's film unit, having become one of the *March of Time*'s longest-lasting staff members.

How did a script idea originate at the *March of Time?* All *ideas* originated with de Rochemont. Nonetheless, his colleagues appear to agree that Louis found it difficult to create a script outline himself. He had to have something to begin with, something to react against. One of Shute's principal functions was to develop both script outlines and narrations that Louis could then attack, demolish, and rebuild into something more to his liking.

It would begin with Louis and me . . . [recalled Shute]. Louis would simply issue the order, "We're going to do this." And then I'd start in to try to get an outline of it. And sometimes he'd reject my outline *in toto,* with scorn. . . .

He knew at least what he didn't want after he saw my thing. Whatever anyone else had written, he didn't want. He had to do it his own way. . . .

Other times, he'd think it was great. I remember, "Rehearsal for War" [in Spain] was the first one that really he thought was great. I was so pleased. It's been one of my favorites ever since. . . .

A self-effacing man, Jimmy Shute ultimately became senior writer at the *March of Time*. In later years, the organization set up its own editorial board, and Shute became its head, although, as he recalled, "It didn't mean a bloody damned thing. I was supposed to remind everybody we had a meeting, and don't go away."

Self-criticism within the editorial board was always professional and severe. Shute recalled:

I was supposedly the head of it, but actually by the time they got [through] trampling over my script, I could hardly sit up and face it. It was a rigorous, rigorous scrutiny of everything. They would just take every sentence and scrutinize it, and challenge it . . . ; it was quite a to-do, and we'd usually finish about seven or eight in the morning.

"I enjoyed it and was proud of what we were doing," said Shute. Still, he had few sentimental illusions about his years with the organization. Unlike Glenn, Orchard, and some others, for whom the *March of Time* was a great adventure, Shute suffered Louis's eccentricities stoically, performed his work with great professionalism, and then, after fourteen years' service, headed off to film-making assignments elsewhere.

Even before Shute had arrived, in 1935, however, the *March of Time*'s distinctive style of narration had been created and set by others. The man frequently credited with this was John Martin. Born in Winnetka, Illinois, in 1900, a graduate of Princeton University, he, together with his cousin Briton Hadden, had been most responsible for creating the literary style of *Time* magazine

Senior writer Jimmy Shute (at end of table) supervises an editorial board meeting. Left to right: Robert Wetzel, Jim Wolcott, Arthur Tourtellot, Jimmy Shute, Sam Bryant, and (in rear) Yancy Bradshaw. (Courtesy Time, Inc.)

years earlier. By the late 1920's, he had become *Time*'s first managing editor and a major stockholder in the corporation.

A brilliant writer and literary perfectionist, Martin is remembered by his colleagues as a remarkable and powerful personality. He had lost his left arm in a hunting accident as a boy but never let the disability slow him down. Variously remembered by former staffers as the *March of Time*'s "style setter," "literary Plimsoll mark," "custodian of the *Time* style," and "the ultimate word man," he endowed the film series with the same lively, eccentric syntax that had characterized the magazine.

A brilliant man [said Lothar Wolff]. Absolutely brilliant. One of the best writers I've ever seen. One-armed, terribly powerful, strong-minded, strong-willed writer . . . , he used to appear on the scene and when there were script problems he would take the

John Martin, *Time* magazine's first managing editor, also played an important role in designing the narration style of the *March of Time*. A brilliant writer, he is remembered as a creator of "Time-speak." (Courtesy Time, Inc.)

script under one arm and disappear somewhere to write, and he had a wonderful, clear, concise, dramatic, straight-forward style.

Martin also frequently reviewed the historical and descriptive accuracy of *MOT*'s film scripts, providing extensive, scholarly criticisms of the preliminary drafts. Finally, he played an occasional role both as a director and as a high-level "contact man" for *March of Time* productions. It was he who is remembered as the man who talked Senator Huey Long into appearing in the classic 1935 issue that ridiculed the Louisiana dictator.

The backbone of the *March of Time*'s permanent domestic staff was provided by the cameramen and sound recordists who worked both in the field and in the company's New York studios. In the early years, the regular staff of first cameramen included Dick Maedler, Charles Gilson, John Geisel, Charles Herbert, and Nick Cavaliere. A bit later, cameraman Frank Follette also became a member of the full-time staff. Principal sound recordists on the domestic crews were David Y. Bradshaw (later associate producer of the series) and Ken Hawk.

Victor Jurgens, an office-boy-turned-cameraman/director, joined the *March of Time* in 1935 at the same time as Tom Orchard, and, like Orchard, moved up rapidly in the organization. While head office boy, Jurgens had shown some talent for finding the impersonators that Louis needed for his re-creations. He had found an excellent Lindbergh so Louis sent him out to find a Huey Long:

> I said, "Jesus, there must be someone around town who looks like him," so I said, "Victor, you go over to the 54th Street police station and talk to the sergeant or lieutenant who is on the desk and please just ask him to tell you if there's anyone he knows in the bars or elsewhere who looks like Huey Long."

Jurgens did as he was told. It was some time before he was seen again. By coincidence, the New York police had been alerted that day to an alleged conspiracy to assassinate Senator Long. The moment Jurgens wandered into precinct headquarters asking where he could find someone who looked like Huey Long, the police seized him and began a lengthy and unpleasant interrogation. It was hours before they finally called de Rochemont to check out Jurgens's crazy story.

Happily, Jurgens's luck improved. Louis encouraged him to develop both as a cameraman and a director. Jurgens had an urge to travel, so Louis sent him abroad as a roving staff cameraman/director. Much of the *March of Time*'s footage of Chinese, Japanese, and Pacific subjects in the late 1930's came from Jurgens. Another cameraman/director, Britisher Peter Hopkinson, signed on to the *March of Time* staff after the Second World War and provided much of the company's footage from the Middle East and Far East.

De Rochemont dealt with numerous freelance cameramen, both in the United States and throughout the world, either buying footage that they had already shot, or commissioning them to photograph a particular subject that he needed. Within the continental United States, cameraman Carl ("Cap") Pryer was used with great frequency, as were Roy Phelps and Jack Haeseler, the latter of whom had played an important role in the early educational film business as head of a Carnegie Foundation-sponsored film unit at Harvard University in the late 1920's. Haeseler was remembered by his colleagues as the "gentleman's cameraman." The most important of the international freelance cameramen who supplied footage was Julien Bryan, a well-known photographer of documentary and travel films, who ranged throughout Europe, Asia, Russia, and the Middle East. Harrison Forman also provided some footage during the 1930's from the Far East.

For one brief period the distinguished still photographer Dr. Eric Salomon was hired by the *March of Time* as a motion picture cameraman. Salomon had pioneered the use of early Ermanox and Leica cameras for unposed, "available light" still photography in the late 1920's. He was one of the first photographers to call himself a "photojournalist," and he delighted in photographing people unawares—yawning, eating, laughing, talking. Because so many of his friends were international celebrities and highly placed political figures, his pictures were journalistically important, and his skill with this new kind of miniature camera helped popularize "candid" photography and the 35mm format.

In an attempt to stimulate photojournalism in the U.S., *Time* magazine brought Salomon to the United States in 1931 to accompany and photograph Premier Pierre Laval of France on his visit to President Hoover. During his stay, Salomon secretly managed to take the only known photograph of the Supreme Court in session. A few years later, following his example, *March of Time* personnel constructed a phony brief case that held a miniature motion picture camera with an ultrafast lens. The case had an aperture at one end through which the lens could shoot. According to Tom Orchard, it was their plan to duplicate the Salomon coup with motion pictures for the *March of Time*'s 1938 issue on the Supreme Court; but in the end the *March of Time*'s *paparazzi* got cold feet and the idea was abandoned.

In the late 1930's, Dick de Rochemont brought Salomon to England, outfitted him with a specially built, miniature motion picture camera, and sent him up to Scotland to pursue and photograph his friend, Ramsay MacDonald. In due time, Salomon's first footage came back.

> He decided he was going to make a 360° pan [said Dick], which he did. And so we sent the 360° pan of the highland landscape back to New York, where they called off the experiment. . . . I don't know, he was a nice old boy.

War broke out soon after. Salomon never got a second chance; he died in a gas chamber at Auschwitz.

The *March of Time*'s cameramen and sound recordists worked regularly under the most difficult conditions, hauling hundreds of pounds of 35mm cameras, tripods, batteries, generators, temperamental sound recorders, and incandescent lights back and forth across the country. It was an array of equipment that today's generation of television newsmen, brought up on lightweight, miniature, portable apparatus, could neither believe nor cope with.

The sound camera that was almost universally used by *March of Time* cameramen was the Wall. The silent equipment included Akeley, Debrie, and Eyemo cameras, and a curious French make that the French crews were fond of, called the LeBlay. Because of Louis's strongly held opinions about image quality, these cameras were *always* operated on tripods, except under the most extraordinary circumstances. The sound equipment employed consisted of vacuum-tube amplifiers and the RCA Photophone variable-area optical recording system. Crews, whether in the field or in the cutting rooms, never enjoyed the convenience of magnetic sound recording technique, as it was not widely introduced into commercial use until 1950-51, by which time the *March of Time* was going out of business.

Most of the cameramen and recordists had newsreel backgrounds, which was a good preparation for the problems they encountered. Like all newsreelmen, they were a hearty, irreverent, no-nonsense group of professionals whose pride was to "get the shot" for Louis, no matter what obstacles arose. "I shot alongside these guys for 18 years," recalled Jack Glenn. "These guys, the crew, were willing to work 24 hours a day, 365 days a year, even sometimes against union regulations, because they felt they were

Cameramen and sound recordists were the backbone of *March of Time* production. A few of them are shown here with their heavy, awkward 35mm equipment. Left to right, standing: Bill Gerrity, Bill Shaw, Frank Calabria, Johnny Geisel (behind camera), Jack Glenn, unidentified. Seated: Al Shaw and Tony Girolami.

creating something. *March of Time* directors always solicited the advice of everybody [on the crew]. Everybody was creating the *March of Time*."

Enthusiastic though they may have been, newsreel cameramen were often short on tact. Well-meaning barbarians, they were a constant hazard on diplomatically delicate assignments and a frequent mortification to the directors with whom they worked. Lothar Wolff recalled the *March of Time*'s coverage of the opening of the first regular ship communication between the U.S.A. and South America—a by-product of Roosevelt's Good-Neighbor policy. For this occasion, on the maiden voyage, a number of high-ranking ambassadors, admirals, consul-generals, and government

March of Time cameramen dressed to suit the occasion. Burt Pike had to wear top hat and tails when he photographed a performance of the Metropolitan Opera. (Courtesy Time, Inc.)

officials from both the United States and South American countries had been assembled. Cameramen Charles Gilson and Burt Pike were there with Wolff to photograph it all.

. . . Charlie Gilson and Burt Pike's origins were the newsreels [said Wolff]. They were used to the most informal way of operating that you can imagine. Names meant nothing [to them]. So we arrived in Rio de Janeiro, and then president of Brazil, Vargas, came aboard. That was all meticulously worked out—how people would be dressed, brass bands, the Brazilian foreign minister, the American ambassador, really all done up in a very punctilious manner. . . . So the camera was set up there, with Charlie Gilson and Burt Pike and George [Black, the director] there, and I was there. . . .

The president came up and stopped where he was supposed to stop and talked to the foreign ministers, the American ambassador, Roosevelt's envoy . . . and the president was standing with his back to the camera.

Suddenly, I see Burt Pike dash out, taking the president, who is very small, by the shoulders, turning him around and pointing with his finger toward the camera, walking back, and Charlie Gilson shot it. And I thought the earth would drop from under me. And I'm standing there full of embarrassment. The president was nonplussed for a while, then he faced the camera and they got the shot.

Other necessary members of the field crews included electricians Artie Jones, Al Shaw, and Bill Shaw; stage mechanic Bill Gerrity; and property man George Dangerfield (no relation to the critic).

Dangerfield is remembered with great affection by his fellow workers as a man who could talk anybody out of anything, anytime. His services were invaluable. Whenever feasible, *March of Time* scenes were shot in authentic locations, with on-site locations. Much of the time, however, it was necessary to stage or re-create the set in the company's "studios." In fact, the *March of Time* never enjoyed decent studio facilities. It had some office space and hallways in its Lexington Avenue building that it could use if needed. If more space were required, the company could shoot at the Fox Movietone News building, or would rent a garage or a hotel suite in town for the day and shoot there. Costumes for such re-creations were usually rented from the Eaves Costume Company of New York, but it was Dangerfield's job to get the props and the furnishings. Most of these he borrowed, and often from perfect strangers. Dangerfield would appear on the doorstep of a New York housewife's apartment, and explain to her that the *March of Time* was shooting a new film and needed certain kinds of furnishings for its scenes. ("The *March of Time*, ma'am. I'll bet you see it every month, right down the street at the Bijou, don't you?") Looking beyond her into the apartment, he would exclaim over the things he saw within—the rug in the foyer, the sofa in the parlor, the pictures on the wall, the bric-a-brac covering the mantlepiece. Dangerfield would wonder aloud whether the *March of Time* might borrow a couple pieces for a few hours to use in the movies. If necessary, he would offer a modest rental fee. Talking continuously, soothingly, seductively, hypnotically, he would move through the apartment, followed by an assistant, and, as in a dream, would scoop up the furnishings he needed and transfer them to his truck in the street below. "What an exquisite rug that is, madam," he would say, and before the bewildered woman could thank him for the compliment, he already would have rolled it up. A few minutes later, Dangerfield would depart, leaving a dazed, psychologically immobilized housewife standing in the middle of her denuded living room, listening to Dangerfield's truck accelerating off into the distance.

In Louis's shop, it was always the *men* who made *Time* march. There were women on the payroll, of course, but with a couple exceptions, none of them occupied decision-making positions in those days. Almost all of the researchers (called "checkers") were women. The *March of Time* had access, of course, to the vast research resources of Time, Inc., and it was the researchers' job to acquire the statistical and factual information that staffers needed for their work.

Publisher Henry Luce had a passion for facts, and it was a passion that was carried forward into each of the various divisions of the corporation. Within the *March of Time* it was the job of the "checkers" to scrutinize for accuracy every film script, especially the narration, prior to release. Each word was examined minutely, and if it passed muster, was rewarded with a dot above the word. Even articles, participles, possessives and the like got their dots. By the time the script had been researched thoroughly, it was fly-specked with dots.

Throughout most of the corporation the work of these "checkers" was routine, but within the *March of Time* shop they had to contend with Louis de Rochemont. Sometimes Louis listened to his researchers, sometimes not. Jimmy Shute remembered an occasion when one of the research women told de Rochemont that he had inaccurately quoted the burial verse ("ashes to ashes, dust to dust") from the Book of Common Prayer. "This isn't the way it is," she said. Louis stared at her. She showed him the quotation in the prayer book itself. Then she read the text in the prayer book. Then she read Louis's version. Then she waited. Louis thought it over. Then he said he liked his version better, and told her to buzz off. That's the way it went between Louis and the "checkers."

According to Jack Glenn, Louis actually would try to alter the names of real people in his films if he thought it would produce a better effect. On one occasion, so Glenn recalled, while editing a sequence on the Women's Christian Temperance Union, Louis tried to change the name of the Union's head, Mrs. Ida B. Wise Smith, because he thought the name sounded odd. "Louis, the woman's name is Ida B. Wise Smith," said Glenn. "Yeah, I know," said Louis, "but it sounds like a gag." "Well, isn't that too God-damned bad," said Glenn. "That's her name. She'll sue you." "Oh, she wouldn't do that," said Louis. "She likes to be in the movies too much." "The hell she wouldn't," said Glenn. "You check with the legal department." And so, apparently he did, for it was rendered accurately in the finished film (Vol. 3, No. 7).

Other women on the *March of Time*'s staff included film librarian Connie Greco, negative cutter Louise Logue, researchers Leona Carney, Elly Aron, and Maria Sermolino, and numerous secretaries and assistants.

Of all the women, however, only two of them—Mary Losey and Celia Sugarman—had any real influence. Mary Losey (later Mary Losey Field) had joined the *Time* magazine staff in February 1935. Twenty-four years old, a graduate of Wellesley, she had responded

to an advertisement that *Time* circulated to recruit recent graduates in political science, history, and related fields.

> So I went around and had an interview. . . . And they wanted
> me to be a researcher. And I didn't want to be a researcher, be-
> cause I didn't see why if I had a good enough education to be
> selected to work for *Time*, I shouldn't be a writer, like some Har-
> vard or Yale boy with the same qualifications. After quite a lot of
> backing and forthing, they said, "Well, if you wouldn't like to be
> a researcher for *Time* or *Fortune*, we're starting a new enterprise.

The new enterprise was the *March of Time*, and it was there
that they sent her, perhaps with some relief, for she was a feisty
young lady with notions of the role of women in American society
that were several decades ahead of their time. Had she lived a few
decades earlier, she would certainly have been a suffragette.

The suffragette point of view was no more welcome in Louis's
shop than it was at the magazine, but that was where Losey went
to work just as the *March of Time*'s first issue was released to the
public. In the beginning she worked under the supervision of
Maria Sermolino, who was then in charge of *MOT* promotion.
Later, she worked for Al Sindlinger, who took Sermolino's place as
head of both promotion and distribution.

Losey knew the eastern-seaboard college scene intimately, and
was assigned to develop educational promotion. She launched, and
subsequently edited, a promotional magazine named *The Photo
Reporter*, which was intended principally for high school students.
The size of a tabloid, with typography which was almost identical
to that of *Life* magazine, it was heavily illustrated and included
a variety of information, both on general topics of interest and on
the particular subject matter of recent *March of Time* issues. "People were just beginning to get interested in teaching young people
something about the real world outside the ivy halls," recalled
Losey. The *Photo Reporter* was intended to serve those interests
and, specifically, to stimulate attendance by young people at *March
of Time* screenings.

> The idea [said Losey] was to sell these things in bulk to high
> schools and the high school teachers to use as current events texts,
> and send their students to see the *March of Time*. At the same

time, we lined up a bunch of teachers from New York University to write what were called study guides [entitled *The March of Time Scholastic News,* the first issue of which appeared in April 1935, and *A Teacher's Manual for Class Study of the Monthly Newsmagazine of the Screen: The March of Time,* which appeared around the same time]. So, a school would buy 100 copies of *Photo Reporter* [@ 5¢ a copy or 50¢ a year subscription price] and would then get, say, five copies of the study guide which had suggestions about classroom exercises which could be built around seeing the film or reading the paper or both, and this had a very large distribution.

The first *March of Time* Club was founded in the fall of 1935 at West High School, Salt Lake City, and by March 1936 the *Photo Reporter* was advertising the sale of *March of Time* Club buttons for 10¢ each, featuring the drum major that appeared on the *MOT*'s film logo.

Among the features of the *Reporter* was a series of articles on the art and technique of the motion picture, some of them written by film historian Jay Leyda. After the *March of Time* had signed its distribution contract with R.K.O. Pictures, the *Reporter* began promoting numerous other R.K.O. releases, including the films of Walt Disney, Richard Dix, and Frank Buck.

During this period, Losey worked as chief researcher, reporting to John Martin. She collected statistical data, interviewed prominent people in fields that the *March of Time* was exploring, assembled biographical profiles, and generated background summaries which Jimmy Shute and the other writers could develop into script outlines for Louis. "If there was a big gaffe in it," she said, "I was the one who got the blame."

"It was also the point," Losey continued, "at which I came into serious conflict with the editors because they didn't like some of the information I collected for them." Before long, according to Losey, she had managed to acquire a reputation at *Time* as a "dangerous radical." Quite possibly she exaggerates. She had strong opinions about political and social issues, and her attempts to introduce these opinions into her research reports were resisted by both de Rochemont and Larsen. In her research for the issue on American medicine, for example, she became quite enthusiastic

Mary Losey was one of the few women to play an important part in *March of Time* affairs, in charge of educational promotion from 1935. She helped the Newspaper Guild organize the company in 1937, departed in 1938. (Courtesy Mary Losey Field)

about a particular advocate's campaign to promote group medical practice. "I was very convinced what he was talking about made sense," she said, "and I was very strong on pushing his point of view about what was needed in the medical world."

Losey acknowledged that Time, Incorporated, had every color of the political rainbow present in the rank and file of its employees. Talking to this author forty years after the fact, she still sounded indignant and surprised to discover that film makers at the *March of Time* had not had complete freedom to say and do what they liked:

> You know, I wasn't close enough to the policy level to be absolutely certain about this, but I would say that there was not total freedom. For one thing, Larsen was in both organizations. For another, the promotional end of *March of Time* was controlled by *Time* itself, so any idea that they were just romping around doing what they felt like doing is totally unrealistic.

Whatever ideological problems may have arisen, it is clear that she and Louis de Rochemont never hit it off very well. They disliked each other, there were frequent confrontations, and she played an important role in the organization of the *March of Time*'s workers by the Newspaper Guild in 1937-38. Louis must have sighed with relief when she departed, in 1938.

Because of her relatively short stay at the organization, she is not remembered by *March of Time* veterans as a member of their production "family." In the years that followed, she worked with documentary film makers in both England and Canada with whose ideological bias she apparently felt more at home. "For me," she concluded, "the *March of Time* was the *beginning* of my existence, and it's like another time and world."

Celia Sugarman would never have described herself as having any power at all. Still, if knowledge is power, she had as much of that kind of power as anyone else, for Sugarman was Roy Larsen's executive secretary.

"Celia knew more about the inside of *March of Time* and its growth than practically anybody else," said Tom Orchard, "because she typed all of Roy's letters." As Larsen's secretary, she was obliged to spend a great deal of time in the early years at *March of Time* headquarters. Sugarman loved the *March of Time* and the "boys" who made it, and they loved her in return. Tom Orchard recalled working with her:

> She was a young girl . . . recruited by Roy . . . when *Time* was published in Cleveland, and she came here to New York with him. . . . She was a rather plain little woman, about the same age as we were. . . . I was always crazy about her, and everyone else was, because she mothered us, we the "College Boys, Office Boys."

. . . She had to come over there to 460 West 54th Street, which is part of "Hell's Kitchen," and she would work there sometimes until one, two, or three o'clock in the morning, and then, of course, we would have to go out and get her a cab and get in the cab with her and take her back east.

The last important group of specialists at the *March of Time* were the editors and cutters, many of whom had been brought over from Fox Movietone News by Louis in 1934-35. During the early years, the group included Jack Bradford (one of the first supervisors of the editing department); Morrie Roizman, Johnny Dullaghan, Beverly Jones, and Charles Morrison (all four of whom had worked with Louis on the "March of the Years" series); Joe Trimarco, Sam Bryant (later, an *MOT* writer); Ken Cofod, John McManus, Leo Zochling, Howard Head, George Johnson, and Jack Bush. Of this group, Bradford and Roizman were especially important.

Jack Bradford, born in St. Paul in 1904, had come east to Princeton University, where he majored in English literature and graduated in the class of 1928. Shortly thereafter he went to work for cameraman Jack Haeseler, making early educational films at the University Film Foundation in Cambridge, Mass. Still later, he traveled throughout the world shooting footage for the Fitzpatrick travelogues which were released into neighborhood theaters during the 1930's. Bradford had met de Rochemont shortly before leaving on one of Fitzpatrick's cruises, and when Jack returned, Louis hired him to work on the new *March of Time* series —not as a cameraman but as a cutter. By late 1936 or early 1937 Bradford had become administrative head of the editing department. Remembered as a hard-working and conscientious man, he trained many of the company's beginning cutters (some of them newly recruited office boys), supervised and coordinated the cutters' work, and generally represented their interests to the management. It was Bradford who designed the excellent indexing, classification, and retrieval system for the *March of Time*'s film library—a library which, by 1951, held more than 10 million feet of film. Bradford remained with the *March of Time* until 1940, when he left to enter the armed forces.

Morrie Roizman had spent his childhood growing up in New

Jack Bradford had begun his career as a cameraman but was hired by Louis as a cutter. By 1937 he was supervisor of *MOT*'s cutting department. (Courtesy Jack Bradford)

York's tough East Side and Brooklyn's Brownsville section. Born in Berditchev, Russia, a refugee from both Bolshevism and anti-Semitism, he emigrated to the United States with his parents in 1920. Completing eight years in New York's public schools, he went to work as an office boy in the summer of 1928 for Courtland Smith at Fox Movietone News. Roizman did such a good job that Smith moved him up to the cutting department, and Morrie decided to stay on with Fox rather than finish high school. In 1929-30, he was assigned to work as Louis de Rochemont's cutter on the *Magic Carpet* series, and when Louis left Fox to produce the *March of Time* he brought Roizman with him. With the passing of years, he advanced within the company and was finally appointed chief film editor of the series after World War II, remaining with the organization until 1949.

Like everyone else in the organization, the cutters put in impossible hours. They were never paid for overtime, and the total work week sometimes ran from 80 to 100 hours. "You worked very hard on the *March of Time*," said Bradford. "We had no social life. Nothing else. You *had* to be there, and if you weren't there when he [Louis] wanted you, you were disloyal. . . . We were all caught in the web . . . because of the feeling of pride we had in the *March of Time*. And we'd write our families about it. . . . We loved it so much."

One night, staggering out of the *March of Time* studios at two in the morning, exhausted after twenty hours' work, the cutters came across a "do-it-yourself" recording booth in an all-night arcade. They had recently completed a *March of Time* issue on the black ex-convict folk singer Huddie Ledbetter. The group crammed themselves into the booth and recorded an off-key rendition of one of Ledbetter's most popular songs, "Good Night, Irene." Forty years later, in 1976, Jack Bradford found the record and brought it to New York to play for an informal reunion of old *March of Time* hands. It was typical of the memorabilia and bric-a-brac which nearly all of Louis's boys saved to remember the 20-hour work days, the crushing schedules, the frustrations, and communal indignities they had shared. The good old days.

These were the men who made *Time* march—not all of them, but the ones who counted most. They were a young crowd, with

Editors Johnny Dullaghan (left) and Morrie Roizman (right) had worked with Louis at Fox Movietone News, were brought by him to work on the new *March of Time*. Roizman remained for many years, became chief film editor after World War II. Lothar Wolff at center. (Courtesy Lothar Wolff)

an average age, at the time they joined the organization, of thirty years. They never knew what they'd be called upon to do, and that, together with the camaraderie, was one of the features of the job that kept them going. Over the years, office boys and sound record-ists became production managers, cutters became writers, writers became directors, and directors, associate producers. The *March of Time* never enjoyed the luxury of a really coherent table of organization, and today many of the old hands cannot say for sure who did what or what their titles were.

Have we forgotten anyone important? At different times John Wood, Jr., John Wintgerter, and Brandt Enos were business man-agers and Bob Carr was assistant business manager. Jim Wolcott and Bob Schofield were production managers and John Savage was assistant production manager. Phil DeLacy and Allan Raymond were production supervisors. Ralph Rolan, Albert Sindlinger, and P. A. Williams were heads of advertising and promotion.

What of Henry Luce, the founder of the firm, the chairman of the board, without whom no study of twentieth century journalism is complete?

Everyone agrees that he had nothing to do with the *March of Time*. Once every thirty-sixty days, Luce would stop by to look at a recent release, to watch, uncomprehendingly, the chaos of professional film production, and to chat with de Rochemont and Larsen. "He never bothered me until the very end," said Louis, contemptuously. "He used to come over once in a while to 460 West 54th, which was Movietonews, with his girl friend Clare Boothe."

What of the corporation's political point of view? Assistant producer Lothar Wolff recalled, "It was really Louis de Rochemont who set his own policy as long as he ran it, and later, Richard. And Time, Inc., had, to my knowledge, no influence on the editorial approach at all." Editor Jack Bradford agreed. "I hardly saw anyone from the corporation coming over. When they did, it was more out of curiosity. I don't think we knew the word censorship then." Added associate producer Tom Orchard, "I, myself, never felt any editorial control. . . . There was no censorship in the modern corporate sense. We were always looked upon by the magazine writers as a sort of strange lot. They didn't know our métier, and we didn't know theirs."

The only meddling that subordinates recall Luce indulging in occurred during those few times in the history of the series when the releases dealt principally with China, India, or Formosa, on which subjects Luce held strong and inflexible points of view. Said Richard de Rochemont, "We felt we were on the side of the angels in most cases, with the possible exception of Chiang Kaishek, whom we regarded as a protégé of Mr. Luce, and who was the only sacred cow we admitted . . . I don't recall ever hearing Luce dictate to *March of Time*, but I usually managed to be on vacation the month we tackled that subject."

Astonishingly, the rest of the time Luce allowed film subjects to be released which regularly contradicted the political positions

134

enunciated in the newsstand issues of *Time* magazine. Either he failed to recognize the disparity between film and magazine points of view, or he considered the film too unimportant to worry about, or—quite possibly—he considered the film to be Larsen's turf and decided not to walk on it any more than necessary. Larsen told me emphatically, "Nothing was ever carried downward to the *March of Time!*"

There is even some reason to suspect that Luce resented the film's great popularity and success and found it convenient to ignore the whole messy business of its production. Director Jack Glenn, who admired Luce, recalled the one occasion on which the publisher formally addressed the *March of Time* staff. No transcript of this late 1930's pep talk exists, but Glenn recalls its substance:

Harry told us a story. He said, "In a way, I hate you people. But I don't, really, cause you're contributing a lot of Time, Inc. I'm just old-fashioned and pig-headed enough to admit that I don't like everything that's happening. For example, I'm in London. I said to a passerby, "Can you direct me to the office of Time, Inc.?"

"What, sir?"

"Time, Incorporated."

"I never heard of it, sir."

The next person: "Are you familiar with *Time* magazine?"

"Oh, yes."

"Can you tell me where their office is?"

"I'm sorry, no."

Next one: "Can you tell me where *Life* magazine's offices are?"

"I'm sorry, what's the name? *Life* magazine? I'm sorry."

Finally, I asked somebody, "Can you direct me to the *March of Time* offices?"

"Oh, yes, sir. *The March of Time* is right down the street."

"Now, that makes me mad," concluded Luce.

6

The Big Time: Censured, Censored, and Sued

The *March of Time,* celebrating its first year in February 1936, was still in its experimental stage. During the next few years, the film's production techniques, format, and style were all to vary from time to time. The quality of photography, editing, and direction was gradually improving. Reviewing the first issue in February 1935, one critic had held that the new feature was somewhat below the level of both the ordinary newsreel and the regular Hollywood film. By February 1936, however, the quality of the photography alone had risen sufficiently to elicit frequent praise from film reviewers.

The staging and re-creation of scenes continued, especially to fill gaps in a film's continuity. With the passing of time, however, impersonators and professional actors were used less and less frequently, and "real" people, whether ordinary citizens or celebrities, were enlisted to play themselves. According to a gee-whiz publicity piece:

While THE MARCH OF TIME was still young, the Editors stumbled into a big discovery that changed the course of THE MARCH OF TIME. The unimportant town of York, Pa. was the locale of that discovery. THE MARCH OF TIME cameramen had gone there to photograph Fred Perkins, the hard-working battery-maker who went to jail in challenge to NRA. Almost before they knew it, they had him acting out his own role, in his own person. When the film was developed Pa Perkins washing his hands was real. Ma Perkins preparing supper, the Perkins kids, the simple men who worked for Pa Perkins in his battery shed—they were all real. From the Perkineses THE MARCH OF TIME discovered that real people can be photographed doing naturally that which it is their nature to do.

Only the cinematically uninformed will have to be told that Robert Flaherty and a whole generation of earlier film makers had discovered the same thing several years before.

Although the overall length of the *March of Time* remained the same, the number of episodes in each issue steadily decreased: from six subjects in the first issue, to three in the fourth issue, to two in the fifth issue, and finally, as we shall see later, to only one featured subject. Such a reduction in the number of episodes allowed a more complete treatment of each subject. Roy Larsen, who was intimately associated with the production of these issues, said that he much preferred the earlier format, and regretted the necessity of reducing the number of subjects in each reel. The decision, according to Larsen, was an economic rather than artistic or journalistic one. It simply became too expensive, to present many different subjects in the same reel. Larsen admits that his recollection of the matter is self-serving—that he is inclined to recall those earliest issues with special affection because he played such an important role in their production. Later, at about the time that the single-subject issue became standardized by the group, Larsen was obliged to leave his day-to-day work with the film people to devote all his time to the design and publication of the corporation's new magazine, *Life*. As for Louis and the other members of the *March of Time* staff, they were delighted to move toward a single-subject format, running 15 to 20 minutes in length, as it gave them time to develop subjects more fully, from both cinematic and journalistic points of view.

Despite the short time allotted each subject in those early issues, writers and directors made every effort to present each subject as

137

a polished, coherent, dramatic unit. Edgar Anstey, a film critic and foreign editor of the *March of Time,* wrote in the May 1949 volume of *Penguin Film Review:* ". . . the creation of character by script analysis and screen synthesis was not regarded as the exclusive prerogative of the feature fiction film . . . leading personalities of America were re-created on the screen with understanding and often with delightful humour. These were tiny screen biographies; they were full of the life and warmth of real people."

Commercially, the series was a qualified success. Although it wasn't making a profit, it wasn't losing much either, and with a suitable interpretation of the corporation's books, could usually be made to appear to be breaking even. Although the foreign distribution program was still in its formative stages, domestic release had jumped from 417 theaters in February 1935 to 5236 theaters by April 1936. The *March of Time* had shown that at least one type of documentary could more or less pay its own way. Whether the film industry was pleased with the prospect of a financially viable "idea film" is not clear. As Richard de Rochemont wryly suggested several years later, when his brother successfully popularized feature-length documentary dramas, "Documentaries became known as *semi*-documentaries . . . when they started to make money."

Motion picture patrons were dazzled by the wide variety and apparently inexhaustible supply of subjects. The first issue of the second year featured a screen biography of Pierre Deibler, France's chief executioner—"The Outcast of Paris." In a lively piece of cinematic *Grand Guignol,* the *March of Time* cameras followed this untouchable through the streets of Paris at dawn, watched him set up his quillotine, described the grisly occupation that he had inherited from his father, and returned with him to his tomb-like house in the Paris suburbs to speculate on rumors that this lonely man planned retirement, fearing that he, like his father, might go mad. Only a couple shots of Deibler, made with hidden cameras and telephoto lenses, were authentic. The rest used a double, photographed in the *March of Time*'s studios. The blend was quite effective.

The second issue, released in February, examined the role of black "prophet," Father Divine, and described at length his reli-

By 1936 the *March of Time* was being seen by 12 million people in 5236 theaters each month in the United States alone. (Courtesy Smithsonian Institution)

gious organization and theories. An enormously entertaining issue, the film is of interest to both black and white audiences today, after the passing of three decades of growing sensitivity to racial issues in American society.

From any political point of view, Divine was a bizarre figure, but he was an endearing personality. He was regarded by many of his followers as God incarnate, the theological likelihood of which this shrewd, fifty-year-old religious leader neither affirmed nor denied. The financial holdings and extent of Divine's organization were considerable; the fiscal and legal arrangements under which it functioned were mysterious. Divine himself claimed to own no property whatsoever. Some of his associates were white, and at least one of them, Paul Christian, aspired to put Divine in the White House.

139

This is an authentic shot of French executioner Pierre Deibler, "stolen" by a hidden *March of Time* camera in Paris. (Courtesy Time, Inc.)

PAUL CHRISTIAN: Peace, everybody!
Hoover could not straighten out this country.
President Roosevelt has failed to straighten out this country.
But God Almighty, Father Divine will straighten it out!

Illuminating the twilight zone between religion and politics, Divine's organization provided food, lodging, support, and encouragement to the demoralized black men and women who became his disciples, at a time in our history when both white and black men were selling apples on street corners.

Jack Glenn, who directed the issue for the *March of Time,* liked Father Divine immensely, both as a person and as a subject. Less than five feet tall, the diminutive Divine was noisy, brash, funny,

This is the impersonator whom Louis found to play Deibler in New York City. Both authentic and re-created shots were blended to tell the story of this secretive man and his grisly occupation. (Courtesy Time, Inc.)

devious, exotic, and surprising—an ideal subject for cameras and microphones. Divine had wired his Harlem headquarters with a network of loudspeakers and intercoms with which he periodically greeted, addressed, and conversed with his loyal followers. "Peace, everyone!" the loudspeakers sang. "Thank you, father," replied his disciples, as hundreds of hands reached toward the speakers scattered throughout the building, addressing the boxes that carried his voice as if each were Divine himself. These and many other curious but fascinating scenes appeared throughout the film, some staged by Divine for *MOT* cameras, others "stolen" by the cameramen and sound recordists without the participants' knowledge.

Religious leader Father Divine collaborated with *MOT* director Jack Glenn (right) in producing a fascinating account of the black prophet, his flock, and his activities. (Courtesy Jack Glenn)

Interviewed nearly forty years later, Glenn recalled that he had insisted on treating Divine and his movement seriously. He respected Divine and found him energetic, constructive, and fun:

> Father was a very dear friend of mine. He was a little man. . . . He was sincere. It was a socialist movement, where you'd have a meal for 10¢ and the restaurant would go broke.

Divine had a "heavenly" name for all his angels: "Hot Sunshine," "Bright Star," "Tree of Life," "Gracious Lamb." He christened Jack Glenn "Humble Hope," making Jack feel like one of the flock. Divine trusted Glenn's handling of the film and cooperated fully in its making. Glenn said:

> When I went to get this story, I told Louis and Roy, I'm not going to shoot this as a minstrel show. I'm going to shoot it exactly as it is and you must use it that way. . . . no shots of Negros with watermelons. I wasn't out to ridicule them. . . . Well, when

finally cut, it was [originally] called "Little Black Messiah." Well, he wasn't black, he was Mulatto. And they didn't like the word "black" in those days—that's a modern word. . . . in fact, we had an awful time getting "black" out of the script. . . . So I went to Roy and said, this is not right. You promised me you wouldn't treat it as a minstrel show. Well, last day of mixing, he said, "Jack, I was able to get all the "blacks" out [of the script] but one. [The title was subsequently changed to read, simply, "Father Divine."]

In the theater, when they saw these pictures in the movie hall— [Father] let his people come to the movies for the first time because he was in it. . . . it was a riot at the [Radio City] Music Hall.

The film that resulted is as fascinating to see today as it was then. Jack Glenn and Father Divine had established a good rapport, which was to bring them together again on another film the following year.

The same issue also included a study of life in the Soviet Union which was even more simple-minded than the issue on the U.S.S.R. which had been released in May of the previous year. The Soviet Union has never enjoyed a reputation as a consumer's paradise, and the 1930's were especially difficult for its people. At a time of extreme austerity, when Russians were experiencing grave shortages of food, clothing, and nondurable household goods, Julien Bryan's footage showed grocery, clothing, and department store shelves piled high with pastries, meats, canned goods, dry goods, and shoes, while the Voice of Time burbled on about "Moscow's glittering shops":

VOICE OF TIME

Like her capitalist sister, the Soviet woman finds a lift to her morale in shopping. In well-stocked stores, today she can buy to her heart's content.

Everyone makes mistakes, and this was one time when Louis was certainly off target, not only in his analysis of Soviet economic conditions, but of the character of Soviet life in 1936. In 1932, an estimated three million people had died of starvation in the

Ukraine alone, while an additional half million people were either executed or jailed during the Stalinist purges of 1935 and 1936. A special kind of foolishness must have operated at *March of Time* headquarters when the commentary for this issue was finally put together and handed to Van Voorhis:

VOICE OF TIME

Into government-owned shops, for all manner of beauty treatments, Moscow women flock, cheerfully submitting to new government edicts urging them to keep up appearances. . . .

In touch with the capitals of fashion, Soviet designers hunt for ideas to please the Soviet woman. Today, she looks over the new styles at frequent shows.

Somewhat more realistically, the film concluded with a description of Russia's second "five-year plan" and the efforts of labor supervisor Alexei Stakhanov (played by an impersonator) to increase production among Russian workers. The episode ends with a mad, staged scene of Stahkanov and his friends at a drunken revel, celebrating his achievements with champagne, a new automobile, and other lavish gifts from the Soviet government, all to the tune of Walt Disney's "Who's Afraid of the Big Bad Wolf?"

The third issue, released in March, featured an analysis of the political revolt and the murder of government officials by army officers in Tokyo. The episode outlined the course of rising militarism in Japan and the resistance to it by democratic leaders. Included in the film was another of de Rochemont's *Grand Guignol* "illuminations"—a re-created suicide, by hari-kiri.

Critic George Dangerfield, in reviewing this issue, again questioned *Time*'s efforts at impartiality:

It wanted to be fair to both the murderers and the corpses. To achieve this dialectical feat it produced an argument that was really very difficult to follow: that murder was horrid . . . that this was patriotic murder, mistaken patriotism of course, and while it wouldn't want the cadets at West Point to go in for murder, still it had to admit that the Tokyo officers did what they did because they wanted to help the peasants. The episode had apparently taken no sides; it had praised the butchers and the butchered. But what did it really mean? . . . was it a polite way of saying that dog had bitten dog?

Ambassador Hiroshi Saito, appearing in the episode, explained that "The insurgent subalterns were—misguided."

The fourth issue, released in April, featured a hilarious but thought-provoking account of the founding of the Veterans of Future Wars at Princeton University. This student group, concluding that war was inevitable within the next couple years and that they were certain to be obliged to fight in it, reasoned that they were entitled, ahead of time, to the military bonus traditionally given to veterans at the conclusion of a war. That way, they argued, they could all enjoy it while they were still alive. It was a lark, of course, but an inspired one, and the group worked up a manifesto which they published in the *Daily Princetonian*. To their surprise, it attracted widespread attention and good-natured support. Their next step, they decided, was to petition Congress officially. The *March of Time* was glad to help them. Tom Orchard spent two days at Princeton, directing the students in a re-creation of the steps that had led up to the organization of their group.

TITLE: AT PRINCETON UNIVERSITY, THREE LIKELY
PIECES OF CANNON FODDER GENERATE AN IDEA
(Medium shot of students in lounge)
RUSHTON: Well, how long do you give us before we have the 1914 business all over again?
TURNER: (Snaps fingers) About that long!
GORIN: Will you go?
RUSHTON: Like it or not, we'll all go. Just as they went into the last one.
GORIN: I guess there'll be parades and speeches, and when we come back, if we do come back, we'll ask Congress for a bonus.
RUSHTON: Suppose we don't come back? Why shouldn't we get our bonus now?
TURNER: Sure, cash in advance.
GORIN: Why not? Patriotism prepaid. Wait a minute—I have an idea. Listen, give me a pencil.

145

In Washington, congressmen and senators were happy to speak for the *March of Time*'s sound cameras, either in support of, or opposition to, the petition.

CONGRESSMAN MAVERICK OF TEXAS   I think you boys have the right idea. If we have to pay for wars in advance, it will make wars ridiculous, if not impossible, and I'm with you on it.

VOICE OF TIME

Sharply to their bait rises Congressman Fuller of Arkansas.

CONGRESSMAN FULLER   There's no danger of any of these so-called veterans ever volunteering to defend America. Their actions clearly show that they are yellow.

A sober-looking group of American Legionnaires at Pawtucket, Rhode Island, also commented upon the proposal, clearly taking it all very seriously:

LEGIONNAIRES   Veterans of Future Wars! Nuts! *(Cheers, applause, etc.)*

The Veterans of Future Wars even had a salute. At first glance, it appeared to be fascist, but on closer examination in the film was shown to differ significantly:

VOICE OF TIME

Undergraduates pack into a mass meeting, roar their approval of "The Veterans of Future Wars," give the official salute—the outstretched itching palm!

The film that resulted was entertaining and provocative screen journalism—unsentimental, sardonic, and curiously frightening. The film was one of Roy Larsen's favorites, and, in the rare instances in which it is screened today, still plays well with college-age audiences.

In the years that followed, *March of Time* staffers were often asked whatever happened to the "Veterans of Future Wars" who had appeared in the film. With the exception of one individual, who had been injured in an auto accident, all of them were in military service during World War II. And, as they had predicted, several were killed in action and never did get to enjoy their postwar bonus.

Another subject in this issue explored the angry debate then under way over the construction of the Florida Canal, for which the Roosevelt administration had allocated $5,000,000. Within Florida, as between the northern and southern parts of the state, citizens and political leaders were split over the project's relative advantages and disadvantages.

For this issue, director Jack Glenn went about as far, ethically speaking, as one can go—perhaps farther than one ought to go—to dramatize a story that would illuminate the issues. He not only *pre*enacted and *re*enacted events; he actually *brought about* incidents that probably would not have happened had he not been present. Said Glenn:

> We would go into a place where there were simmering hosilities and we'd bring it to the surface. It was not a case of having our nose on the news. No, we were *creating* the news! . . .
>
> We were *creating* news—bringing it to the surface. Sometimes, we'd shoot stuff and have it in the can when the thing would suddenly break open. We'd be prepared. . . .
>
> I went to Jacksonville—Mayor Alsop was there. . . . I told him I wanted to make a film on the canal. The mayor said the council would rather not go into this with you. I said, "Mr. Mayor, I must say this in fairness, you should defend yourself. I've got to get this thing on the screen in a hurry."
>
> "Defend myself?"
>
> I said, "Yeah. Do you know what they're saying about you in south Florida?"
>
> "What's that?"
>
> "That you don't care what happens to Florida so long as you get the business the canal will bring to Jacksonville and Tampa and so forth."
>
> "That's a God-damned lie!"

I said, "Now's your chance to say it for the cameras."

He said, "Sure. Bring your cameras in."

I got my story. I did the same thing with the south Floridians [to whom he showed the north Florida footage]. . . . It wasn't really dishonest. . . . But now it's all changed. The literal interpretation . . . has become the norm.

Glenn said he had thousands of circulars made up, half of which said "Save the Canal"; the other half, "Stop the Canal." These were widely circulated throughout the state, many of them posted on telephone poles and trees, to be photographed by *MOT* cameras. Glenn was especially pleased when the *New York Times* published a photograph of one of his fake circulars, having assumed it was authentic. The techniques Glenn employed here are by no means unknown in news-gathering circles, although in general they are considered marginally ethical, and in television news circles theoretically taboo. The techniques are substantially identical with those allegedly employed by some network cameramen during the student riots of the late 1960's and early 70's when they brought with them pre-printed placards with "appropriate" inflammatory slogans to give to students who had neglected to bring their own. Glenn concluded, "It was the first time in my career I felt as though I were working for a yellow sheet, but I had only ten days to get it in the can. . . . The show had to go on, and did, although a bit soiled, I'll admit, but accurate as hell measured in terms of what was happening down there."

Nearly six months had passed since the Ohio Board of Censors had clipped scenes from *MOT*'s controversial "Palestine" issue. With the release of the fifth issue, in April 1936, the producers met with censor action abroad. The issue featured a comprehensive, bitter look at the impotent League of Nations and at the progressive worsening of international relations throughout the world. It was an issue that staff liberals remembered with special affection.

The *March of Time* labeled the League a "hollow mockery" and concluded with the thought: "What will England do to strengthen the League and preserve peace in Europe?" They soon found out.

In London, sixty-one feet were deleted from the reel by British censors Lord Tyrrell and J. Brooke Wilkinson, including shots of British troopships steaming to the Mediterranean and the Voice of Time's pronouncement: "British troops follow the fleet to the garrisons of Malta and Egypt. There is even talk of closing the Suez Canal. . . ." Also deleted was a shot of Mussolini and British ex-Prime Minister Ramsay MacDonald in friendly conversation, and a discussion of the British-based League of Nations Union and its poll that showed massive popular support among British citizens for the exercise of League of Nations economic and military sanctions. "This tremendous new political fact," said the censored Voice of Time, "sends England's Prime Minister into speedy consultation with his Cabinet."

Edgar Anstey, the British director whom Dick de Rochemont had assigned to get the footage for this issue, had already been arrested by British police during its production. Anstey and his crew had positioned their truck in the midst of a political demonstration in London's Trafalgar Square, with the *March of Time* camera mounted on the truck's top. Arresting officers claimed that Anstey's "presence" had incited the crowd to demonstrate.

The film was never seen in England. Following its suppression in that country, Anstey screened it privately for Winston Churchill, then out of power, seemingly at the end of his career, and yet to be called by his country to assume the Prime Minister's role. Anstey recalled the occasion:

> Winston said, "Mr. Anstey, this film should be seen by everybody in the world; certainly, everybody in Great Britain. But I cannot help you. I am out of power now. I'm an old man. My time is over," he said. And he tottered out on a walking stick, escorted by Randolph [his son]. Little did he know!

If, as censor Wilkinson explained, the object of the cuts was to avoid ruffling "the customary calm of a cinema audience," he should have left well enough alone, for the action provoked a storm of protest. According to the June 1 issue of *Time*, Viscount Cecil of Chelwood, a founding member of the League of Nations Union, complained: "It seems to me utterly ridiculous because everything that has happened in the past few months has been recorded in the press, and I fail to see why it should not be shown in the films." Most London editors agreed with him. The *Daily Herald* proclaimed: "This time the film censorship has really passed all bounds. Such dictatorship possesses a quality which can only be described as impertinence." The *News Chronicle* published photographs from the film and headlined "CENSOR HAS DELETED WHAT THE WHOLE WORLD KNOWS." The only major London papers sympathetic to the censor's action were the conservative *Morning Post* and *The Times*. The latter solemnly concluded: "Most impartial critics will agree the Censor has improved the film."

In New York the producers of the *March of Time* stated, according to the May 23 edition of the *New York Times,* that they "could not understand the censorship of its film in London. The film was made in England with Lord Cecil . . . and others re-enacting parts they took in the League of Nations Union peace ballot in England." If Larsen and de Rochemont were not secretly pleased with the controversy, they should have been, for all the furor ultimately boiled down into the publicity pot and ensured a successful run for the film at over 7000 theaters within the United States.

In New York City the *March of Time* ordinarily opened at the Centre Theater in midtown Manhattan. In June 1936, the Centre closed its doors, and *Time* moved up the street to the Radio City Music Hall. *Variety* called the change "a prestige first run for the film and a colorful addition to the Music Hall's screen where the editing of the newsreel stuff is often too addicted to brevity. The fuller treatment of selected themes which 'March' provides ought to please the Music Hall's high-type clientele [June 24]."

The first *March of Time* film to be shown at the Music Hall following this change was Issue No. 6, which featured one of the earlier "case histories" of crime, showing the progression of a fictional "Joseph Krutz" from a sordid childhood in New York's tenement district to petty larceny, to grand larceny, and finally to the penitentiary. Melodramatic and simplistic, the film plays like a parody of itself today, but at the time of its release it was widely acclaimed by critics and law enforcement authorities. Also included in the reel was a satirical study of the Texas Centennial celebration, directed by Texan Jack Glenn. Picturing the $8,000,-

000 Centennial Fair, Glenn's cameras emphasized the carnival and vaudeville atmosphere (staged, in large part, by showman Billy Rose), and the film concluded with the remarks of an elderly Texan, a descendant of Sam Houston: "I don't know whether they're celebrating the birth of the Republic of Texas or the birth of musical comedy."

In July the *March of Time* again made front-page headlines with an exposé of the Dominican Republic's dictator-president, Rafael Leonidas Trujillo, termed by the Voice of Time: "sometime informer to the U.S. Marines and scourge of all liberal Dominicans." Intercut with authentic newsreel shots of Trujillo was an elaborate banquet scene, directed by Tom Orchard, in which the dictator and his associates were impersonated by performers in speaking parts, photographed at the *March of Time*'s New York studios in the Fox Movietone News building. Also staged was a shot of an assassinated political rival of Trujillo's which followed the banquet scene in which Trujillo was seen toasting the health of the man. Additional shots in the film of jails and government offices were also staged.

The film's treatment was distinctly unfriendly to Trujillo, called by the Voice of Time "the dictatingest dictator who ever dictated." It reviewed the fate of many of his political rivals, either dead or exiled, and described the political corruption that he had introduced in the course of his stewardship:

VOICE OF TIME

The Army's dirty linen went to a laundry owned by his shrewd second wife, also his business agent. And to please her, Trujillo commissioned their six-year-old son a colonel in the Army with full pay.

The film was well and widely reviewed in the United States. E. V. R. Wyatt wrote in *Catholic World* in August:

For a long time we have meant to say something about *The March of Time* for we find that if we miss the monthly issue we have decidedly a gap in our current education. Do you know anything about the Dictator of San Domingo? Did you know that he had

151

.

For its July 1936 issue the *March of Time* staged an elaborate impersonation of Dominican Republic dictator Rafael Trujillo. Shots such as this banquet scene, played by a double, were intercut with authentic newsreel footage provoking an international incident between the United States and the Trujillo government. (Courtesy Time. Inc.)

changed the name of the capital—where Columbus lies buried—to his own name, Trujillo? That in fact almost everything that has a name in San Domingo, banks, theatres, parks, restaurants, beaches are all being named Trujillo? That "Trujillo" has begun to have a general, pervasive connotation? This instructive and rather terrifying historical résumé of one of our neighboring republics is in the latest issue of *The March of Time*. . . .

Critic John T. McManus called the film "a courageously outspoken film discussion on the political technique of President Leonidas Trujillo y Molina. . . . It makes no secret of its opinion that the executive in question has held sway with the aid of profiteering and assassination and predicts that this regime is about over [*New York Times*, July 19]."

The Big Time: Censured, Censored, and Sued

The reaction of the Trujillo government was swift. In Washington, Dominican Minister Andreas Pastoriza filed a formal protest with the State Department. According to the *Motion Picture Herald* (July 25), he charged that the film was "devoted exclusively to attacking the personality of President Trujillo Molina in a disrespectful and unjust manner and to give a completely false impression of the Dominican nation and the political situation prevailing therein." Señor Pastoriza further deplored the "improper manner in which certain American journalists, in a strange alliance with Dominican revolutionaries residing here, are devoting themselves to the task of defaming with impunity a friendly ruler and a country which has always striven to maintain relations of sincere cordiality with the United States. . . ." It was about this time, in the streets of Ciudad Trujillo, that Louis de Rochemont was burned in effigy.

An international incident, perhaps the first ever provoked by an American motion picture, now existed. Secretary of State Cordull Hull, without referring directly to the *March of Time,* replied to the Dominican minister in a diplomatic note:

> There is no one more than I who deprecates the publication of any article or the exhibition of any film which causes offense to any foreign government. It is the policy of this government to strengthen friendly ties between this and other countries. . . .

> My government, therefore, deplores any actions of private citizens that are in discord with this policy and that cause offense to the peoples of other countries. Such actions sometimes occur, however, for the reason that in this country, unlike many other countries, freedom of speech and of the press is deeply imbedded in our tradition; is cherished by every citizen as part of the national heritage, and is guaranteed under our Constitution.

> Although appreciating your desire to prevent any occurrences which might reflect upon your country's name, I am sure you understand that for the reasons just explained this government is not in a position to prevent the matters complained of by you [Motion Picture Herald, July 25].

The ever cautious management of the Radio City Music Hall eliminated the episode when informed of the protest, explaining that "it had no wish to affront any of its patrons." *Motion Picture Herald* reminded its readers that the Music Hall Theater was controlled by the Rockefellers, "who have considerable oil markets in the Dominican Republic, . . ." while *New York Times* columnist John T. McManus observed, "You could probably count off the patrons of the Music Hall from the Dominican Republic on a book of matches, but that's the way they are over there."

In the summer of 1936 the *March of Time* celebrated its first birthday with a beautifully printed, seventy-page sales promotion "picture book," entitled *Four Hours a Year*. It has been suggested within the trade (confirmed years later by Roy Larsen and other *Time* staffers) that this book was a prepublication, experimental version of *Life* magazine, which officially appeared for the first time in November of the same year. Liberally sprinkled with laudatory reviews, complimentary quotes, and congratulations from film industry leaders, the book outlined the progress of the *March of Time* film series during its first year. Of particular interest was *Time*'s disclosure of its film budgets and exhibition grosses:

> More than $900,000 was invested in THE MARCH OF TIME in its first year. It is now grossing nearly $1,000,000 a year and should soon be earning a satisfactory profit. . . .

> A typical short [produced by a Hollywood studio] costs about $8,000 to make and is intended to gross about $25,000, netting a small profit. . . . But the publishers of THE MARCH OF TIME saw clearly that a monthly gross of $25,000 was a totally inadequate sum out of which to publish and distribute to millions of people a significant journal of events. They had no alternative except to shoot boldly for a $100,000 gross per issue. Such figures to the trade were nonsense. . . .

> The goal of a monthly $100,000 gross still remains only a goal, true. But a gross of $75,000 monthly is already a reality—with THE MARCH OF TIME but recently past its first birthday.

Also of interest was a breakdown of domestic and foreign distribution. As of April 15, 1936, each issue played to an audience of 12 million people at 331 first-run, 701 second-run and 4204 subsequent-run theaters in 3215 cities throughout the United States—a total of 5236 theaters. The approximate length of time required for an issue to complete its U.S. circuit run was 90 days.

Abroad, the *March of Time* was released to 709 houses throughout England, Scotland, and Ireland, while in South America the film series, with a Spanish narration, was released in seven Spanish-speaking countries. In France the film was at first banned by the government. The publishers of *Time* diplomatically observed: "Frenchmen, aware of their low boiling points, have imposed upon themselves some of the world's strictest censorship laws. Result: though THE MARCH OF TIME's headquarters for Europe are in Paris, the film is not yet released in a French-speaking edition. But with THE MARCH OF TIME now reaching audiences from China to Guatemala, from Spain to Chile, it is believed that French cinemaddicts, from Paris to Saigon, will eventually become familiar with the name, 'La Marche du Temps.' " In time, Dick de Rochemont succeeded in securing a censorship permit for the release of the series in France, but, both officially and unofficially, the heavy hand of French censorship was frequently brought to bear upon both its production and release in that country.

The plight of both black and white sharecropper farmers in the South was starkly rendered in the *March of Time*'s August issue. Predicting the breakdown of the South's single-crop system, the issue revealed the economically brutal conditions under which indigent Americans, owning no land but farming 70 per cent of the cotton-crop acreage, were forced to live in 1936. The finished film is said to have gone through more than the usual number of rewrites and re-editings, and several different titles ("Sharecroppers," "King Cotton's Slaves," "Land of Cotton"). Sympathetic to southern strikers, the film included a re-creation of the murder of a union member and the flogging of social worker Sue Blagden and the Reverend Claude Williams, who were investigating the union member's death. Jack Glenn, who seemed to get all the "hot" subjects to direct, never doubted how touchy this subject was and how hazardous his job might become. "I was shooting the sharecropper story," he recalled, "and got a wire from John Wood [*MOT* business manager] the first day of shooting across the Mississippi from Memphis. The wire said: 'We are taking an extra $10,000 life insurance policy on you.' "

THE MARCH OF TIME

RADIO PICTURES

NEW BRITISH EDITION

No. 3
SECOND YEAR

FOOTBALL POOLS

UNEMPLOYMENT— AMERICA'S BIG POLITICAL ISSUE

MUSSOLINI'S DIPLOMATIC CONQUEST

Beginning in November 1935, a British edition of the *March of Time* was released in England, containing episodes from the American issues and material specially produced for British audiences. Sequences were occasionally removed by British censors. (Courtesy British Film Institute)

After a while, justifiably or not, a mild but permanent paranoia settled into the consciousness of many *March of Time* staffers. Louis de Rochemont and Tom Orchard kept their telephones unlisted for years to keep the pests off their backs. Jack Glenn had bigger worries on his mind:

A Spanish-narrated version was released throughout seven Spanish-speaking countries, but was banned in Spain itself. (Courtesy Time, Inc.)

Audiences in Holland saw a Dutch-narrated version. After the German invasion, Nazi officials banned it. (Courtesy Time, Inc.)

It took more than a year before Dick de Rochemont could get a license for release of a French version of the series. Sequences were frequently censored by French officials. (Courtesy Time, Inc.)

GLENN: God, after the Nazi story, nobody would admit that I worked at the *March of Time*. . . . I had controversial films on every subject—I had the sharecroppers, I had the Nazis, I had the communists. . . . I wouldn't have an office with a window in it until the closing days of the *March of Time*. . . .

FIELDING: You were afraid someone might take a pot shot at you?

GLENN: Oh, they would, too. I was threatened many times.

Hazards of a different sort worried other *March of Time* workers. Despite the relative autonomy of the film group, there was always an outside chance one might displease someone in the corporation. Mary Losey recalled an instance:

> I remember one letter which very nearly got me fired, because for some reason we did an issue on Albania—now don't ask me why. But I left in the script a phrase that one of the writers had written about Zog [Albania's king], characterizing him as a "musical comedy monarch," and a letter was written to Luce himself saying that whoever allowed that insulting misrepresentation of this great man should immediately be thrown from the top of the Chrysler building. . . . I remember it seemed very threatening to me at the time.

Most such incidents seemed amusing to *MOT* staffers when recollected years later, but they didn't always seem funny at the time. Musical director Jack Shaindlin recalled an issue the group did in March 1942, called "The Argentine Question," in which Shaindlin's orchestra played that country's national anthem. At the last minute, Louis pulled out six seconds of footage from the anthem sequence and told Shaindlin to cut the music accordingly. Jack told Louis there was no way in which he could cut six seconds from that particular piece of music, so Louis told him to play the thing faster. The rendition that resulted sounded a little peculiar, played at double-time as it was, but Shaindlin did as he was told and thought no more of the matter until, some weeks after the issue had been shown in South America, there appeared at Time, Incorporated, a letter from an Argentinian, violently protesting the insult that had been laid upon his country by the parodic, high-speed rendition of the anthem. The gentleman explained that he would be in the United States in the near future—

158

he even gave the exact dates—and that he would deal personally with the musical director responsible for the outrage. Shaindlin took it seriously enough at the time to make sure he was out of town during the man's visit.

The *March of Time*'s September issue featured a devastating attack on the then current crop of political soothsayers—Gerald L. K. Smith, Father Divine, Francis Townsend, and Father Charles Coughlin—termed by the Voice of Time "self-styled Messiahs of the U.S. Lunatic Fringe." Most of the episode was devoted to the political machinations of Gerald L. K. Smith, disciple and heir-apparent to the late Huey Long. The film was unequivocal in its condemnation of him:

VOICE OF TIME

Exhorting the lunatic fringe today is one of Huey Long's henchmen, who, little more than a year ago, was unknown outside the red clay parishes of Louisiana. . . . Today this ambitious, churchless clergyman is determined that Gerald Smith shall be ready, as men have been ready in other lands, when the chaos, then the communism he believes inevitable for the United States, engulfs this country. . . . With Huey Long in his grave, Gerald Smith proclaims himself political and spiritual heir to the dead dictator.

Astonishingly, all of the shots of Smith were authentic. Somehow, director Jack Glenn had talked him into playing himself in every self-parodying sequence. These included a scene of Smith standing in front of a mirror, practicing to be a rabble-rouser:

VOICE OF TIME

Disowned and discredited by Huey Long's successors, Gerald Smith decides to forsake Louisiana. Practicing at his mirror, he schools his booming voice in the gospel of discontent.
(Series of brief, separate shots of Smith)
SMITH: God, let me be a rabble rouser . . .
SMITH: I see chaos approaching . . .
SMITH: And our people are hungry . . .

159

SMITH: Why shouldn't the cream of the population enjoy the cream of the nation's wealth?

SMITH: Then communism. . . .

SMITH: There shall be no Spanish, Russian, Mexican church-burning in America. . . .

SMITH: I get my inspiration from the sky.

Years later, Larsen told me that he had always suspected that the Hearst organization had supported the Gerald L. K. Smith group—a suspicion that presumably made Larsen's work on this reel especially enjoyable. The *March of Time* wasted few circumlocutions in labeling Smith a demagogue. Readers will wish to contrast the following narration with that of today's cautious television newscasters:

(Long shot of crowd giving Fascist salute)

VOICE OF TIME

For Gerald Smith, the Fascist salute makes its first appearance in America.

(Smith, shown in a variety of brief shots, generally haranguing people—in hotel lobby, shaving in front of mirror, sticking his head out of the shower, etc.)

VOICE OF TIME

Today, as this mighty demagogue swings from town to town, impressing his personality upon millions of puzzled Americans, thoughtful observers wonder if Gerald Smith is a man of destiny— or merely a political windbag temporarily disturbing the peace of the nation.

On September 9 *Variety* found the issue "quite graphic," and "representing obvious ingenuity and deft camera work. . . . Plenty of this last subject in the 'Time' release is staged but never lacks lustre both because Smith is a good actor and because there was an alert cameraman on duty."

The Big Time: Censured, Censored, and Sued

The *New York Times* reported on March 19, 1939, that Smith sued Time, Inc., Roy Larsen, Louis de Rochemont, Westbrook Van Voorhis, Rockefeller Center, R.K.O. Pictures, Inc., Radio-Keith Orpheum Corp., Newsreel Theaters, Inc., and Jack Glenn, individually and collectively, asking compensatory, exemplary, punitive, and aggravated damages in the amount of $5 million and claiming that the issue pictured him as a person who was "insane, crazy, a crackpot, a lunatic, mentally unbalanced" and as one who was "dangerous to the political institutions of the United States of America." (Jack Glenn, seizing the opportunity, asked Roy Larsen for a raise on the grounds that if he was going to be sued for sums like that, he ought to get a little more take-home pay.) The *March of Time,* in answering the complaint, pointed out that Smith had consented to being photographed by the *March of Time* and that "Mr. Smith is a nationally-known citizen and subject to news comment."

One of the stickiest legal problems that *Time*'s lawyers had to handle in this case was the appearance of a shot (already cited) in which a crowd of individuals was shown giving the fascist salute, ostensibly for Gerald Smith, who was not seen in the shot. Smith's lawyers argued that, considering the *March of Time*'s well-known way of doing things, a member of the crew probably asked the crowd: "How many of you want coffee?" and set the cameras running as the people raised their arms. In the end, Smith's suit was settled out of court on May 4, 1939, for one dollar. Smith, who apparently had a sense of humor, met Jack Glenn again at a later date and said, introducing him to an associate, "This is Mr. Glenn. He doesn't fight for causes, he causes fights."

In November 1936, the *March of Time*'s staff moved to new quarters on the second and third floors of a new building constructed for *Time*'s motion picture and radio divisions at 369 Lexington Avenue. The new quarters provided over 10,000 square feet of library, laboratory, editing, and office space.

About this time, Roy Larsen reluctantly concluded his intimate, daily association with the *March of Time* in order to serve as publisher of *Life.* The vacillation and hesitation that *Time*'s executives had experienced in trying to launch *Parade* magazine a few years earlier had finally been overcome following the brilliant success of the *March of Time's* experiments in "pictorial journalism." According to many *Time* veterans, had it not been for the success of the *March of Time* the corporation's board of directors would never have had the courage to proceed with publication of *Life*. The new magazine was, as we now know, a great success. Brilliantly conceived and executed, *Life* exerted a profound influence upon the practice of photojournalism throughout the world during its thirty-six-year history, ironically disappearing from newsstands and subscription lists at the height of its success in December 1972, after increased printing, paper, and postage costs rendered its continued publication economically impossible.

The planning and preparation of *Life* had extended over a period of many months, of course, during which time Larsen was still devoting a considerable amount of attention to the production of the *March of Time*. Interestingly, according to *Time* historian Robert Elson, Larsen at one point proposed to name the new picture magazine, *The March of Time,* but wiser heads prevailed and the name *Life,* which was purchased from the owners of an older, declining magazine, was adopted.

Time's investment in *Life* was hazardous, representing an investment by late 1937 of $5 million. Even during its planning stages, however, as the deadline for its introduction approached, Larsen still spent an inordinate amount of time at the *March of Time* studios. Larsen told me that during the formative stages of the film series he quit everything he was doing in the corporation to work with Louis. "I just gave up *Life* magazine," he said. "I didn't even appear [in the corporation's editorial and executive offices]."

On December 10, 1936, Larsen announced to the *MOT* staff that Louis de Rochemont (who had formerly served as vice president of the March of Time, Inc.) would become its producer. In March 1937, Time, Inc., officially announced the organization's new "publisher system," at which time Larsen was designated publisher of *Life* magazine. On behalf of the corporation, Larsen continued to supervise *March of Time* operations during the rest of its history, but he was never again able to give the film series the loving care, time, and attention that had brought him so much pleasure during its formative years.

The Big Time: Censured, Censored, and Sued

1936 marched quickly to an end. An issue released early in November was entitled "The Presidency" and purported to review Franklin Roosevelt's four years in office. Actually, the film's subject was not so much Roosevelt but the White House. For the first time, *MOT* publicists announced, cameras had been allowed to roam throughout the White House, given free movement through bedrooms, dining rooms, hallways, and offices. In the years that have followed, the communications media have taken American audiences on similar tours through the president's mansion, but this was apparently the first occasion, and it was quite a novelty. All of the footage was shot while Mr. Roosevelt and his family were at Hyde Park. As with all good journalism, personal details built the story. *MOT* cameras detailed the interesting clutter of memorabilia and bric-a-brac on F.D.R.'s desk, the ship models on the mantle, the dining room table being set, shirts being put into bureau drawers, the pictures on the walls, and the efficient housekeeping staff at work.

VOICE OF TIME

Here, their privacy is guarded by old White House retainers, who have served many presidents. In this upstairs living room, amidst surroundings rich in memories and historic associations, the president may entertain an after-dinner coffee, preview new motion pictures. Here, his guests may have the thrill of writing their notes on White House stationery.

Direction of the White House film had been assigned to Tom Orchard, but permission to photograph there had been arranged by Louis de Rochemont through Tommy ("The Cork") Corcoran, a member of Roosevelt's "kitchen cabinet." According to Orchard, Louis discovered that Corcoran was quite musical and loved to play the piano and sing. Louis had a grand piano installed in his suite at the Carlton Hotel in Washington, D.C., arranged for an introduction to Corcoran through *Time* correspondent Harold Horan, and then invited Tommy the Cork up for drinks and some good singing. "Louis is a great host," recalled Orchard. "We had everything to drink there. Louis very interesting. Tom very interesting. He

163

The White House and its occupant (photographed here with his mother) were featured in one of the last issues of 1936. For the first time motion picture cameras were allowed to roam through the personal quarters of the President and his family. (Courtesy Time, Inc.)

had a couple of drinks. Finally, Tom got over to the piano. We ended up we were pals."

> The idea which Louis propounded to him [continued Orchard]— the theme of the picture—was that the White House is simply no more than an American house. It has a parlor, bedroom, and bath. It has a kitchen, a toilet, and the rest. Sure, it's a big house in Washington and has history and everything, but it's just a house. Tom said, "Oh, that's a great idea. The president's going to love this. He doesn't live in the *White* House, he lives in a *house!*"

Apparently the president *did* love it, for Orchard and his crew obtained permission to photograph whatever they wished. Subsequently, Tom and Louis went to Hyde Park to shoot some footage of the Roosevelts "at home." While there, a curious incident occurred. Roy Larsen had given Louis a copy of one of the prepublication "dummies" of *Life* magazine (which at that point was tentatively called *Parade*). One of the experiments involved in the dummy's production was a color-printed insert, for the purpose of which a tasteful but fairly explicit photograph of a nude woman had been included as a Playboy-style centerfold. This was more for the enjoyment of the staff than anything else—it certainly was not intended for inclusion in the finished magazine. Larsen, without thinking much about the centerfold, suggested to Louis that he bring the dummy along and show it to Roosevelt for a reaction.

> So we carried this around [said Orchard]. One day, Mrs. Roosevelt [the elder] was there and Louis said, "I wonder if you'd like to see this new *Time* publication," and as luck would have it, she opened it up at the centerfold, and was shocked. She gave it to Louis and said, "Mr. de Rochemont, I don't think a magazine like that is going to be in *my* house."

In putting the finished film together, *MOT* editors added newsreel material of Roosevelt, former President Hoover, and Republican candidate Alf Landon to provide continuity and balance for the film. Eleanor Roosevelt's voice (impersonated by either Agnes Moorhead, Jeanette Nolan, or Marion Adair, all of whom did this part for the *March of Time* at different times), was laid over the 1933 inauguration footage.

The film that resulted was scheduled for release immediately after election day, 1936. Some of the polls had given Roosevelt's opponent, Alf Landon, a good chance of winning, and the *March of Time* staff decided to hedge their bets by making up two endings for the film, one of which was shelved, of course, as soon as the outcome of the election became known:

Ending No. 1 (shelved):

VOICE OF TIME

To the White House, where a job which in the next four years of troubled world politics may well prove to be not only the highest position within the bestowal of the American people, but a focal

165

point of world affairs, goes the 33rd U.S. President, Alfred Moss-man Landon.

TIME MARCHES ON!

Ending No. 2 (used in film):

VOICE OF TIME

Back to the White House, as the nation endorses the New Deal, back to the familiar desk, which in the next four years of troubled world politics may well prove to be not only the highest position within the bestowal of the American people, but the focal point of world affairs—goes Franklin Delano Roosevelt.

TIME MARCHES ON!

A second November issue, released later in the month, featured an entertaining description of the Federal Theater Project, entitled, "An Uncle Sam Production." *Variety,* the weekly show-biz chronicle, was pleased with the issue (December 2):

> Nice ingenuity incorporated in the subject of Uncle Sam's entrance into theatrical production with the opening depicting a dress rehearsal of a musical production and fade-out showing same cast in finished stage show. In between, editors have given a quickie close-up of traveling troupes, typical vaudeville acts of bygone days and the decision of the Federal Government to bring the stage out of the doldrums and put actors back to work. . . .

This particular piece was directed by *March of Time* writer Jimmy Shute. Shute recalled:

> One day, Louis sent me up to Boston and I had two days in which to get together a production on the WPA Theater. And what I had to get was an old-time theater with vaudeville acts going on, and an audience all in costume—the whole damned thing! I had to get a turn-of-century hotel with palm trees, spittoons, and everything. Then I had to find a turn-of-the-century railroad station, with the girls from the traveling shows getting off and the boys in the town looking at their ankles appreciatively. . . . So I went to the Howard Theater [a Boston's burlesque house]. Well, it was a

166

dump, of course, with all these girls with nothing on at all, and I tried to pay attention to business. So, I finally thought that place would do. We could fix it up so that you'd see the two opera signs. And then somehow I found a vaudeville act of the 1905 period—old people, but they had all the style and spirit of that period. And then we had to have an audience, so I went to a costumer and I got lots of boas and hats and feathers and things like that, and you couldn't tell from the back whether the men [in the audience] were dressed as today or yesterday, but the feather boas and the strange hats and everything [provided] the style. And then I went to the Boston and Maine Railroad and they had a scarcely used station somewhere out in the suburbs, and they had an old-time locomotive, and they made the train up for us—all free! And we got people to dress up in these costumes. I never did succeed in finding the old-time hotel, but that wasn't terribly important. Louis was absolutely delighted. I was terrified, because he'd raise hell if he didn't like it.

The last issue of the year included episodes on the kidnapping of Generalissimo Chiang Kai-shek by Manchurian war-lord Marshal Chang Hsueh-liang, and the role of "Business Girls in the Big City." The latter subject highlighted the part that women played in business, industry, the professions, and government. Although Time, Incorporated, discriminated openly against women in its hiring practices, it paid lip service in this film to the notion of economic and professional equality for women—provided it occurred in someone else's business. The *March of Time* managed to be both hypocritical and progressive.

VOICE OF TIME

Throughout the nation, women hold a majority of office jobs. In many fields, they are far more efficient than men. In most, they are indispensable. Without women, today, the nation's work could not be carried on. More and more women are moving to top flight executive jobs—women like MARY VAIL ANDRESS, an officer of Manhattan's Chase Bank; MARY ELIZABETH DILLON, president of a big New York utilities company; EDNA WOOLMAN CHASE, editor-in-chief of smart *Vogue*, ERMA PROETZ, high ranking advertising director.

167

7

The Best of Times:
Maturity and Recognition

By the start of its third year, the *March of Time* was firmly established as a successful journalistic phenomenon. Unlike the newsreel, it was billed as a kind of second feature. Its name was featured on theater marquees, and audiences looked forward with enthusiasm to each month's issue. Reviewers alternately praised and criticized it. Rival news organizations attacked it. Politicians and other public figures both courted and condemned it, and *Time*'s busy corporation lawyers were kept hard at work defending the producers against numerous court suits for libel and defamation.

The first issue of 1937 featured an episode that Louis de Rochemont in later years regarded as one of his favorites. Entitled "Conquering Cancer," the film described the history and nature of the disease and traced the progress being made to combat it. Included in the episode was an attack on Norman Baker, who had previously been convicted of practicing medicine without a license in Muscatine, Iowa, and who had made broadcasting history of a sort by advertising alleged cancer cures over radio. The Voice of Time called him a "notorious quack" and the film incorporated studiomade shots of "Baker," using an impersonator. Baker filed suit against R.K.O. Radio Pictures, Inc., and Time, Inc., charging, according to *Variety*, on January 26, 1938, that "he was libeled, confidence in his work was destroyed, his reputation damaged and he was presented as one foisting fraudulent cures upon the public to enrich himself." Like most such law suits, Baker's proved unsuccessful, but a description of the action is useful for our purposes in illustrating the way these cases often went. According to a memorandum prepared for me by *Time* executive Arthur Murphy on November 3, 1955:

> The Baker case was not one action, but several—actions having been filed in the United States District Court for the District of Columbia, in the Circuit Court of Cook County, Illinois, in the Hennepin County Court, Minnesota, and in the Scott County District Court, Iowa. In each action Baker sought $550,000. When THE MARCH OF TIME procured a copy of Baker's hospital treatment book showing that dandelion juice was the principal ingredient of his famous cancer treatment, and took the testimony of a former employee of Baker's—a Doctor Potter—Baker signed a general release in return for (1) return of the hospital treatment book, (2) agreement on the part of THE MARCH OF TIME not to file the testimony of Dr. Potter, and (3) a general release from THE MARCH OF TIME relative to a counter claim for libel which had been filed.

The reel was well received by critics and audiences. Subsequently, the first *Clement Cleveland Award* was made to the *March of Time* for "conspicuous aid in the educational campaign to conquer cancer." Louis de Rochemont was especially proud of a letter he received from U.S. Surgeon General Parran crediting the film with providing a crucial influence in securing a federal appropriation for the National Cancer Institute.

Issue 7, released in February 1937, featured an account of the Westernization of Turkey by dictator Mustapha Kemal, which involved the outlawing of Arabic writing, the adoption of European dress and architecture, and the Westernization of social and industrial institutions. On March 10, *Variety* called it "a blatant piece of tom-toming in the Ataturk's behalf [which] reveals some neat skirting of the issue. The other side of the case is not even hinted. The bit glorifies the dictator's efforts of forcing the Turks into the latest models from Hart, Schaffner and Marx, and into cramming themselves with a Latinized version of their language." Much of the footage in the film had been photographed by Julien Bryan. Louis de Rochemont also incorporated into this issue the combat footage he had photographed years earlier as a newsreel cameraman in Turkey.

On the night of March 4, 1937, the film industry paid tribute to the producers of the *March of Time* with the presentation of a Special Academy Award for the film's ". . . significance to motion pictures and for having revolutionized one of the most important branches in the industry—the newsreel." This special award—presented at the ceremonies by seven-year-old Shirley Temple and accepted by Roy Larsen—had been given only four times previously by the Academy for outstanding contributions to the art of the motion picture. Despite the award's citation, however, the *March of Time* had not had the slightest effect on the form, style, or content of the newsreel. In fact, the granting of the award to the *March of Time* was bitterly protested within the film industry as an insult to the quality of the regular newsreel service. Executives of the major newsreel companies charged the Academy's citation with being "irrelevant, perhaps immaterial, and maybe incompetent."

Everyone in Louis's shop was pleased with the award, however, and by way of celebration released the next issue in March 1937 as a "Special Award Edition." The billing was wholly for exploitation purposes inasmuch as the film, though interesting, contained neither a review of past *MOT* features nor new material of award caliber. The principal subject of the issue was a discussion of child labor in the United States which appeared to favor a proposed amendment to the Constitution outlawing the use of minors in industry. On March 24, *Variety* called its pictorial treatment "a strong convincer, with the arguments against the amendment from the Catholic Church and Massachusetts and Vermont officials tepid in comparison." The issue also included a pictorial description of the introduction of voodoo into New York's Harlem. This episode, based on a special feature appearing in New York's *World-Telegram,* exposed voodoo worship as a racket for unscrupulous confidence men and bogus "witch doctors." The reel concluded with a discussion of England's coronation crisis, pre-

171

cipitated by the abdication of Edward VIII. Shopkeepers and souvenir manufacturers, investing heavily in Edward's coronation, panicked following the abdication. In the end, George V's coronation was scheduled for the original date, Lloyd's of London paid off on modest business losses, and many manufacturers found a ready market in the U.S. for defunct Edwardian souvenirs.

By now, a clear indication of Louis de Rochemont's thematic interests was emerging. They were interests that prevailed with fair consistency during the entire period of his administration, as an examination of subjects in the history of the *March of Time* reveals.

Throughout the entire series, 1935-1951, the percentage of episodes dealing specifically with a single country and its affairs varied between 32.5 and 36, the total number of episodes being far fewer in the later years due to the change in format to a single episode per issue. During the same period, approximately 10 per cent of all episodes dealt with economic matters and 5 per cent with domestic politics.

During the prewar period, 1935-1942, approximately 24 per cent of all episodes dealt with war or the threat of war. From Pearl Harbor until the close of the war, nearly every issue dealt with some aspect of the subject.

The emphasis under Louis de Rochemont's regime (1935-1943) was profoundly personal. His political and historical vision was Carlyleian, interpreting broad political, economic, and military events in terms of the personalities associated with them. During this period 14 per cent of all episodes dealt specifically with particular individuals. After Louis's departure from the series, the number of episodes devoted specifically to individuals dropped dramatically. The other subject emphasized by Louis was that of the navies and waterways of the world and the geopolitical role they played in international affairs. From 1935-1943, 7.5 per cent of all episodes dealt directly with this subject.

In the spring of 1937, the most controversial domestic issue of the day was the attempt by Franklin Roosevelt to "pack" the Supreme Court with extra members in order to ensure a more favorable response to New Deal political innovations. The subject was treated in considerable detail in *March of Time*'s ninth issue released in April. The appearance of the reel was timely, following an important ruling by the Court on the Wagner Labor Act.

The film included several shots, both posed and "stolen," of Supreme Court justices. In those days, the justices were especially reluctant to be photographed, and *MOT* production "dope sheets" indicate that several of the shots were made under great difficulty.

Shots of both President Roosevelt and Montana's Democratic Senator Burton K. Wheeler, respectively defending and opposing Roosevelt's plan, were incorporated into the episode. On the whole the subject was treated impartially by the film's editors, and the film was not thought of as an especially provocative *MOT* release.

In Kansas, however, State censor head Mae Clausen, a recently installed political appointee, ordered the opposing arguments by Senator Wheeler removed from the film. Cut were Senator Wheeler's remarks:

> You can say that the privilege of appointing postmasters will not be accorded to me. You can say that I'll get no more projects for my state. You can say what you please, but I say to you and to Mr. Farley [postmaster general and Roosevelt's campaign manager] . . . that I will vote against this proposition because it is morally wrong; it is morally unsound; it is a dangerous proceeding.

Clausen ordered the cuts on grounds that Mr. Farley's comments were partisan and biased.

Louis de Rochemont, speaking for the corporation, immediately protested the cut:

> To the best of our knowledge, this is the first time that a statement on a national political issue by an accredited authority like a United States Senator has been censored from the screen by a State board. We are used to censorship like that in our foreign editions (by foreign powers) but it's new to us here. [*Motion Picture Herald,* April 24]

The *March of Time* complied with the censor's ruling by eliminating the sequence for Kansas.

A storm of protest swept across the nation from political leaders, indignant citizens, and the press. An irate Senator Wheeler blamed Kansas Governor Walter Huxman for the ban, charging that the action "ought to qualify the Governor of that State for the dictatorship of the United States (*New York Times,* April 17). "If they can get away with this, they can stop free speech anywhere. They are trying to kill off any criticism of Administration measures. This is in keeping with the trend of the times. It is the Hitler philosophy" (*Variety,* April 21).

According to the April 24 edition of the *Motion Picture Herald* Alf Landon, former governor of Kansas and Republican presidential candidate in the previous election, demanded that Governor Huxman "correct the foolish act of the Kansas Censor Board. . . . the maintenance of a true Democracy demands that people never forget the truth. . . . We must not sleep while a government board takes away the very foundation of our freedom." The *Kansas City Star* asked its readers: "Can Kansas afford to have its political discussion thus arbitrarily restricted and appear before the nation as a state in which speech is free except on the screen? On its face, the board's decision represents an ill-considered exercise of censorship and should be rescinded."

In Kansas, Mae Clausen, defending her action, emphasized the bipartisan membership of the board, the other two members of which were Republicans, and described the board's decision as a unanimous one. Governor Huxman, parrying with the press, stated that he had not had time to study Mr. Landon's statement that demanded overruling of the board. The governor suggested that Kansas law did not give his office authority in the matter. The protests continued.

On April 21 the Kansas Censor Board, acting on recommendations from Governor Huxman, reversed itself and restored the censored footage. The uproar gradually subsided, though not before Senator Wheeler, speaking a few days later in Kansas, had the last word on the matter: "I wasn't exactly sure whether I'd be welcome if I came out here. . . . I thought someone might try to stop my speech. You elected a Democratic Governor out here last Fall for the first time in some years. Apparently it went to their [the censors'] heads" (*New York Times,* May 2, 1937).

Invigorated and refreshed by the controversy, the *March of Time* staff pushed new films into production, rushing to meet deadlines, and trying to anticipate world news events and crises by backlogging footage and research data for future releases.

It was becoming clear that this brash and noisy film was capable of stimulating and perhaps influencing large segments of the public. Film critics had previously been impressed with the technique and style of the series. They now viewed the production with a new respect for its propaganda potential. British scholars D. A. Spencer and H. D. Waley, writing in *The Cinema Today* (1939), observed:

> Although the ideal behind these films is to present, as objectively as possible, accounts of world happenings, there is no doubt whatever that they are helping to mould our views on such happenings. In America legislation regulating child labour . . . has at last passed both Houses of Congress by a narrow margin which is believed to be due to the 'March of Time.' Their film on cancer has done a good deal to arouse the national conscience of America to the evils of the quackery that battens on fear of this scourge, while in England, before the present campaign for National Fitness was under way, their film *Food and Physical Training* aroused enormous interest and debate in that it brought home to many people's minds the fact that the animals at the zoo are better fed and housed than many of the nation's children.

Issues 11 and 13 of Vol. 3, and Issues 1 and 3 of Vol. 4, all released during the summer and early fall of 1937, featured a succession of tightly knit, carefully prepared résumés of political crises around the world. The group included "Poland and War," "Rehearsal for War" (in Spain), "War in China," and "Crisis in Algeria."

Although the *March of Time* was professedly nonpartisan, a clear and persistent antifascist tone was becoming apparent in its analysis of world politics and rising militarism. Looking back in 1946, Jean Benoit-Levy wrote in *The Art of the Motion Picture* (1946): "*The March of Time* exercised a considerable influence on public opinion in the various democracies, but could not capture it all alone. . . . *Rehearsal for War in Spain,* for instance, produced in 1937, should have provoked free peoples to action if they had not already been obsessed by the fear of communism which Nazi propaganda had skillfully distilled and spread like a poison."

"Rehearsal for War" was unquestionably anti-Franco, which was exactly what liberal staff members had intended. Jimmy Shute said:

> I was so happy I was going to get my [anti-Franco] point of view across . . . which was exactly the opposite of the viewpoint of *Time, Inc.*, and Laird Goldsborough [politically conservative foreign news editor of *Time*]. Harry Luce was convinced that Franco was the great white knight who was going to save Spain from those dirty communists. So we went ahead and oddly enough he didn't interfere and it went through. . . . I was delighted. And Louis, of course, being nonpolitical, didn't realize how far to the left of *Time* he was in the thing, or if he realized it, he didn't give a damn, because it was the way he chose to do it. He had great courage, and he'd fight for things. . . .

Footage for the Spanish episode came, typically, from a variety of sources, including newsreel libraries, *March of Time* cameramen, and freelancers ("stringers"). The production of this film resulted in the only casualty in *March of Time* ranks that Dick de Rochemont could remember. *Life*'s brilliant still photographer, Robert Capa, was in Spain shooting both still and motion pictures, the latter with a hand-held camera that Dick de Rochemont had given him:

> I was very fond of Capa, but he was completely undisciplined. I sent him to the Spanish War with an Eyemo camera on a sort of stringer basis in 1938, and so he gave the camera to his girl friend to operate, and she was a brave girl and she managed to get herself run over by one of her own people's tanks. It was very sad.

Tom Orchard, the associate producer, added:

> The Spanish thing. That was interesting because it had some shots of the famous Bob Capa . . . now an immortal. . . . Dick hired him and taught him how—or had Jimmy Hodgson show him how to use an Eyemo camera and sent him to Spain. Curious thing was that Bob, being a still photographer, didn't know how to use a movie camera. So as a result we had these perfectly marvelous

shots, but they were perfectly marvelous *still* shots! He'd go ZZzz-zztt! And you'd have five feet. But I think some of these were used in [the film].

September's release, "War in China," featured some of the earliest and, in this case, most brutal of the newsreel clips of the Chinese-Japanese conflict in and around Shanghai. Included were exclusive shots of the Japanese bombing of the Cathay Hotel and the Chinese native quarter, and the explosion of the ship *Augusta*, all photographed by freelance cameraman Harrison Forman. Forman's footage had been smuggled past careless Chinese censors and forwarded to the *March of Time* in New York, arriving barely in time for the China release.

Not all of the footage was genuine, of course. Reenactments made in New York City and reported in the dope sheets included a scene of the British ambassador to China being removed from a car by his aides after being wounded by Japanese aerial gunfire; dead Japanese soldiers (photographed in the Commonwealth Garage in New York); Japanese pilots looking out of their aircraft at the carnage below (ptotographed at Teterboro Airport in New Jersey); and a reenactment of a Chinese woman, lying dead amidst debris in Shanghai, with dust flying ("to give the impression of nearby shelling"). Most astonishing reenactment of all was a miniature of the city of Shanghai aflame, built in the *March of Time*'s New York studios and photographed on August 27, 1937, by *MOT* cameraman John Geisel! (This last shot does not appear to have been incorporated into the finished film.)

In October 1937, gaily colored sparks were struck by an *MOT* episode featuring New York's ebullient, colorful, 54-year-old mayor, Fiorello LaGuardia and his administration. It turned out to be one of the most charming and amusing films in the history of the series. Ideally suited for *March of Time* cameras and microphones, the physically diminutive LaGuardia was amusing, informal, energetic, and unpredictable. Variously known as "The Hat" and "The Little Flower," he was a caricaturist's delight with his high squeaky voice, broad smile, and rotund figure. He was much admired for his administrative competence, civic planning, and apparent honesty—all novelties in the political history of New York. Part Italian and part Jewish, he had a fine sense of humor, which he used with good political effect. (When American Nazis in New York requested a parade permit, he granted it. And, just to ensure their safety, he assigned a substantial number of city policemen—the tallest he could find—to march down the street on each side of them. The policemen were all Jewish.) Politically shrewd, he was delighted to appear in the *March of Time*'s re-enactments, with himself as the principal actor, provided that the extent of his participation did not become known. With an election coming up, the production of the film had to be accomplished with great secrecy over a period of several weeks.

Preproduction planning had begun in earnest on August 18, 1937, when Tom Orchard met with LaGuardia to plan the structure and content of the film, the details of which were outlined in a memorandum of that date from Orchard to de Rochemont. As Orchard discovered, LaGuardia had numerous suggestions. Orchard recalled that LaGuardia talked "a mile a minute, all of the time," reviewing his political history and what he considered the high points of his administration—a reduction in political corruption; the appointment of professionals to the police, fire, correction, and sanitation departments; new parks; a police school; a school for underprivileged young men; new swimming pools; new sewage disposal plants; health centers; hospitals and playgrounds; and a costly but ambitious housing project. LaGuardia expressly wanted his fight against the slot-machine racketeers described in the film, as well as his sitting in night court as a city magistrate. Numerous reenactments were planned by Orchard and LaGuardia at this first meeting. The Mayor even had ideas about the music for the film. "Besides 'Give My Regards to Broadway' at the beginning," reported Orchard, "he wants 'The Halls of Montezuma'—one of his favorite pieces—over the campaign scenes. Says he can clear it for us with the Marine Corps." LaGuardia was even willing to be photographed in his home. "He is a little afraid to have us make shots of his children," said Orchard, "but Mrs. LaGuardia is all right."

Direction of the film was assigned to Jack Glenn, called "Lubitsch" by LaGuardia.

One of the most charming and popular episodes featured effervescent, feisty New York Mayor Fiorello LaGuardia. "The Little Flower" collaborated enthusiastically in the making of the episode, hoped it would assist him in the upcoming 1937 New York election. (Courtesy Time, Inc.)

LaGuardia was very short [recalled Glenn]. He resented anyone trying to make him taller. . . . If I wanted to make him mad, I'd put pillows in his seat for the reenactment. . . . So he came in. I said "Good morning, Mayor." He said, "Good morning, Lubitsch." I said, "You're pretty cheerful this morning, Mr. Mayor." [LaGuardia saw the cushions Glenn had placed on his seat to make him appear larger.] "Who put these God-damned cushions in my chair? You, Lubitsch? My friends know I'm a shrimp, my enemies know I'm a shrimp. When are *you* going to learn I'm a shrimp?"

I figured he was in the right mood [said Glenn], so I said to the cameraman, "Shoot!"

Glenn, the master mechanic of the *March of Time,* discovered a way to photograph LaGuardia during an official City Hall meeting, without his political enemies and the press grasping what was happening:

We wanted to get a scene of him talking to the City Council, near election time, and he was afraid it would hurt him politically to have lights and cameras in there. . . . So I went in, and I said, "We have a way to do it, Mr. Mayor. . . ." He said, "What are you going to do, Lubitsch?" I said, ". . . I'll have the lights all set before the Council gets in there. We'll have the camera hidden. And we'll bring it out as soon as you get in there to open the meeting. Now, I'm going to walk around the room and you just say to me, "Get the damn camera out of here. What's going on here?" And you keep talking to me, and I'll keep moving around, and it'll look like you're making a speech. . . ." "Do you think it'll work?" he said. "I'll really cuss you out!" And he did. We couldn't use the sound, of course. . . .

Thomas E. Dewey, then special prosecutor for the state of New York, also appeared in the film, in reenacted scenes with La-Guardia. The two men had collaborated successfully in their anti-racketeering campaign, but they were political rivals and each was jealous of the other's publicity and press exposure. This applied to the *March of Time*'s coverage, too, as Orchard recalled:

Tom Dewey was getting to be politically very important at that time. And I think the Mayor began to feel that Mr. Dewey was getting a little too much publicity. I remember as we kept putting it together, he [LaGuardia] kept calling up and saying, "How's it going? When can I see it?" One time he said, "How much footage have I got and how much footage has Dewey got?" . . . It turned out they both had about the same. The Mayor exploded. He said, "I thought this was about LaGuardia's administration." What he had totally forgotten is that the Mayor can do more, speak more, get more across in a second than . . . Tom Dewey [could] in five minutes.

LaGuardia was especially eager to have his new garbage trucks featured in the film. He had purchased and introduced a new kind of vehicle whose contents were kept enclosed, an innovation that was both cosmetic and sanitary. According to Tom Orchard's original memo, "He wants us to get up early in the morning and get a 'whole mile' of them. 'That'll make a swell shot.' "

The Mayor's love for chasing fires was an important feature of the film. *March of Time* editors integrated authentic fire scenes

180

with re-creations of fires with LaGuardia in attendance watching the excitement. Jack Glenn had "forbidden" LaGuardia to attend the staged fire while *March of Time* cameras were operating. The election was only a few weeks away, and it was feared it would hurt the Mayor politically, Glenn recalled:

> He loved fires, and I asked him if he would help us stage a fire, and he said, "Of course." So, for four days, we had a number of pieces of fire equipment, and a bunch of the fire department personnel creating false fireplaces inside of an old tenement in Brooklyn, with asbestos in the back, and then blowers to blow smoke out the front. . . . So when we got set up I called him, and I said, "Mr. Mayor, you can't come to the fire."
>
> "What do you mean, I can't come to the fire? It's my fire, isn't it?"
>
> I said, "Look, Mr. Mayor, you put up any camera, right away there are a couple of thousand people, right? Now with fire wagons, there are a couple of thousand [more] people. So what does that make? That makes four thousand people.
>
> He said, "But I think I should come out there and see that fire."
>
> "You're not going to do it," I said. "It's not [politically] good for you."
>
> He said, "How are you going to show me?"
>
> I said, "I'm going to do it in a firehouse, with Commissioner McElligott against a firewagon."
>
> "That's a hell of a way to go to a fire—in a firehouse," he said. "What are you going to do about the smoke?"
>
> I said, "I'm going to have smoke pots bring in the smoke in front of you, and cut you into the close-up in the fire."

"Oh, for God's sake," said LaGuardia, who reluctantly did the staged insert shot that Glenn wanted in a firehouse far from the staged apartment house fire.

In the end, said Glenn, the Mayor got to see the fire anyway. LaGuardia sneaked his official automobile into the mob that showed up to watch *March of Time* cameramen at work, and Glenn saw "The Little Flower" poking his head out of the car, watching the *MOT*-produced conflagration with great interest.

Climax of the film was a visit to LaGuardia's home at the end of an exhausting day. The camera caught him beaming with delight when told that dinner
would include *pasta e fagiuoli*. (Courtesy Time, Inc.)

Glenn ended the film with a scene in which the exhausted
Mayor comes home, kisses his wife, flops down in a chair, and
asks what's for dinner. "Pasta e fagiuoli," she says. LaGuardia
reaches up, touches her face, and beams the sweetest smile ever
put on film. It was pure corn, but enormously effective, and as far
as Glenn was concerned, true to the character of the people he was
photographing.

Altogether, Glenn had worked with LaGuardia on the film for
two months. Back at the studios, with the election deadline approaching fast, editors set to work to make sense out of the mass of
accumulated footage. Finally the film was assembled in fine-cut,
and, on September 30 the Mayor came to *March of Time* headquarters to view it. Assistant producer Lothar Wolff remembers
the screening well. At its conclusion, Louis, ill at ease, looked
down from his six-foot-plus height onto the little, rotund politician.

"Well, Mr. Mayor, what do you think?" said Louis.

LaGuardia was furious. "Mr. de Rochemont," he said, in his high squeaky voice, "you *know* what's wrong with that film!"

"Why no, Mr. Mayor," said Louis, alarmed. "I don't know."

"You *know* what you left out," said LaGuardia.

"No, Mr. Mayor, I really don't know."

"WHERE ARE MY GARBAGE TRUCKS?" screamed La-Guardia.

"We'll shoot 'em; we'll shoot 'em!" said de Rochemont.

And so they did.

With new footage of his splendid garbage trucks incorporated into the film, LaGuardia endorsed it. At a preview screening at the Waldorf Astoria, it was predicted that the film would make votes for the Mayor in the coming election.

The finished film, lavish in its praise of "The Little Flower," was released just four weeks prior to the municipal elections. On October 3, Jeremiah Mahoney, the opposing candidate, attacked the film in the *New York Times* as biased and slanted. Mahoney charged:

"I have been informed that the Mayor has had motion pictures taken of himself. The picture, I am advised, is a pleasant one. It shows my opponent, with characteristic modesty, defying the forces of evil to do their worst, wreaking his fury on a defenseless slot machine, dashing around the city at reckless speed to meddle with our gallent firemen and eventually calling it a day. . . . The picture ends, as all pictures should, with everybody happy—but the taxpayers. In the interests of strict accuracy the picture should have been done in Technicolor with red the predominant hue."

The issue opened at the Music Hall on October 7, after a one-week delay. Because of this delay, the film could not open at the next house under contract—the Embassy—until October 21. In turn, because of contractual limitations, the film could not be shown in smaller neighborhood houses until November 5, three days after the election.

The first showing at Radio City Music Hall had been delayed when evidence of politically inspired threats of reprisals against the theater owners was made public. It was alleged that inspectors of the Manhattan Department of Buildings had threatened to close the Music Hall because of technical violations of the building code. It was also reported that owners of small theaters in residential neighborhoods were threatened with stench-bombs if the films were run in their houses. It was charged that these threats were engineered by LaGuardia's opponents to keep the picture out of circulation until after election day. (Political appointee Samuel Fassler, Manhattan Commissioner of Buildings, later made a vigorous denial of the Music Hall charges in the *New York Herald Tribune,* October 15.).

Despite the limited release, a sufficient number of people saw the *March of Time*'s LaGuardia issue to prompt Bosley Crowther of the *New York Times* to speculate, on October 31, on the power of the *March of Time* as a vote-getting medium.

> When the voters of Greater New York go to the polls on Tuesday, it is a pretty safe odds-on bet that a sizable percentage of them will do so with a fresh reminiscence of one of the most surprising pieces of political persuading that has ever been put to the public. The reference is, of course, to the extraordinary film document in which the familiar March of Time has dramatized the past four years of Mayor LaGuardia's career. And, if that gentleman is duly re-elected, as impartial prophets ordain, a good measure of his success will certainly be due to the wholly inspired and unintended contribution of this film.

Fiorello LaGuardia was reelected.

March of Time's November release included a riveting episode on the human heart and the diseases that afflict it. The sequence was noteworthy for including what *MOT* staffers claimed was the first mention of the word "syphilis" ever made in a theatrically released American film (preceding the feature *The Story of Dr. Ehrlich's Magic Bullet* (1940) by more than two years). Still another "first," Tom Orchard recalled, was the recording onto the sound track of an actual heartbeat, which he described as a technically difficult trick to pull off in 1937. Somehow, soundman Yancy Bradshaw managed to attach a doctor's stethoscope to the sound recorder. The patient they chose at one of New York's hospitals had an especially bad heart. "It was one of the most frightening things you've ever heard," said Orchard.

The last issue of 1937, released on December 24, contained three episodes. The first was an approving look at modern Finland, called "the only one of the European war-debtors to come through with regular payments." The second, "The Laugh Industry," outlined the problems, frustrations, and techniques of the radio comedy business. Mourned Fred Allen, as yet unaware of the even greater problems that television was to bring to performers: "In these hectic days of radio I figure the average comedian tells as many jokes in six months as a famous stage comedian like Raymond Hitchcock told in an entire lifetime." Other performers with speaking roles in the film included Jack Benny, Eddie Cantor, Amos 'n' Andy, and Charlie McCarthy.

The third episode, "Ships-Strikes-Seamen," examined the role of U.S. Maritime Commissioner Joseph P. Kennedy in managing maritime affairs and arbitrating labor problems along the nation's waterfronts. Also included was a discussion of alleged acts of mutiny aboard the merchant marine steamship, *Algic*. Subsequently, the Nationtal Maritime Union picketed the Radio City Music Hall. Three members of the *Algic*'s crew filed suit against the *March of Time*, asking damages in the amount of $350,000, and charging that the picture gave a false version of incidents aboard the *Algic*. This action was subsequently dropped on March 26, 1941, on a voluntary basis. No money was paid and no retraction was made. And so, on a note of controversy, the *March of Time* ended its third year of production.

In its domestic release, the series now reached from 22 to 26 million people each month at 9800 theaters. Internationally, it was screened at another 1200 theaters or so, in English, Spanish, French, and Dutch versions. In New York City alone, over 150,000 people saw each monthly issue at the Radio City Music Hall. In a gigantic, multipage advertisement, running simultaneously in several national magazines in January 1938, the *March of Time*'s publishers claimed that the film played in more theaters than any other regular motion picture attraction.

Considering the size of the audience, it may have been just as well that the public had been conditioned to expect a consistently provocative, sensational, and courageous treatment of current events from this series. Even with such a reputation, the producers released an issue in January 1938 that so aroused the public, startled political observers, and confounded the film industry that for some time thereafter the *March of Time* was in danger of permanent censorship, even within the United States, by pressure-group boycott, government action, and film industry agreement.

The offending film ran a short 1457 feet (16 minutes). It was the first *March of Time* to be limited to one subject—in this respect, it set the format for most subsequent issues. Nearly forgotten by motion picture historians, it was perhaps the most controversial American film of the 1930's. It was entitled "Inside Nazi Germany—1938."

8

"Inside Nazi Germany-1938"

THE ISSUE OF MARCH OF TIME YOU ARE ABOUT TO
SEE HAS CAUSED MUCH CONTROVERSY. OUR POLICY IS
TO FEARLESSLY PRESENT ANY WORTHY FILM RE-
LEASED BY A RECOGNIZED AMERICAN PRODUCER. WE
THEREFORE PRESENT UNCENSORED AND IMPAR-
TIALLY THE FOLLOWING SUBJECT.

This was the announcement flashed upon the screen of the Embassy Theater in New York on the night of January 20, 1938, the
premiere showing of the *March of Time*'s highly publicized new
issue, "Inside Nazi Germany—1938."

The film and its release could not have been more ingeniously
designed to arouse audiences and provoke controversy. It featured
the figure, voice, and hysterical histrionics of German dictator
Adolf Hitler, a man whose motion picture representation, with
or without the usual demagogic pyrotechnics, was usually taboo in
American motion picture houses. On the one hand, so *MOT*
staffers reported, Jewish exhibitors were not enthusiastic about
giving Hitler and his philosophy any more exposure than neces-

sary. At the same time, both producers and exhibitors were reluctant to introduce controversial subject matter of any sort into the entertainment context of their business.

The *March of Time*'s new film examined the insidious Nazi program of "racial purification." It was labeled both pro-Nazi and anti-Nazi at a time when a spirit of isolationism governed the national conscience and few politicians, let alone film producers, dared take a stand on the European crisis. Finally, the film was widely touted by its producers as a provocative, ultracontroversial film issue. Such press-agentry, coming as it did from a film organization with an established reputation for sensational motion picture journalism, did much to make this explosive film irresistible to curious motion picture patrons.

The footage which made up the bulk of the film had been photographed in Germany by Julien Bryan. Bryan did not work on salary for the *March of Time,* but regularly sold them stock footage that he had shot in various corners of the world.

During the late 1930's most American cameramen were banned from Nazi Germany. Such newsreel footage as reached America from that country was made available by the German film companies, and was thoroughly censored and doctored. For most journalistic purposes, it was useless. The dream of every American cameraman was to penetrate Nazi Germany and to get out in one piece with important footage. Bryan succeeded where nearly everyone else had failed.

He engineered his entry into Germany the previous year in the course of a conversation with a high-ranking Gestapo officer at an embassy party in Turkey. The officer had complained petulantly about the unfavorable press treatment that Americans gave to German affairs. "Why can't you Americans report our programs a little more objectively?" he asked. Seizing the opportunity, Bryan suggested that American journalists could hardly cover the German story with any kind of thoroughness when they could not even get into the country and move around freely. "Perhaps the General could make arrangements . . . ?"

It turned out he could. Within a short period of time, Bryan was granted permission to enter Germany and to take motion pictures there. He advised the *March of Time* staff of his good for-

American film producers and exhibitors hesitated to show Adolf Hitler's face on theater screens during the 1930's for fear of upsetting audiences. The *March of Time* flouted this taboo regularly. (Courtesy Time, Inc.)

tune and proposed to shoot footage for them. Louis agreed. He gave Bryan raw stock for photography and approximately $2000 as an advance. Bryan departed for Germany, where he remained for seven weeks and shot 20,000 feet of film. Arriving back in the United States with what he claimed was uncensored material, he advised the *March of Time* staff that he had secured the scoop of the century—exclusive, sensational footage of contemporary Germany. With great anticipation, Louis and the boys in his shop sat down and screened the film.

What they saw was disappointing. Julien's work, as always, was technically excellent and provided extensive general scenes of contemporary German life. However, whether the Germans had censored it or not, it failed in almost every way to reveal anything substantial of a political, military, economic, or racial nature that was occurring within that country. Bryan had managed along the way to take a few shots of Jews sitting on the isolated, yellow benches that were set aside for them, and of anti-Jewish grafitti painted onto shop windows around the city. Otherwise, there was nothing that was politically controversial or revealing—nothing of Goebbels's vast propaganda machine, the repressive political regime, the concentration camps, the anti-Jewish pogroms, or the extensive military rearmament and training then under way.

It can be argued, of course, that Bryan had managed to get more new footage out of Germany at that particular moment than anyone else. But the footage was a disappointment nonetheless. The *March of Time* bought the film and sent Bryan on his way. Then Louis set to work, with re-creations and aggressive narration, to

One of Julien Bryan's authentic shots, showing German children studying anti-Semitic posters. (Courtesy Time, Inc.)

rectify the shortcomings of Bryan's material and to provide the distinctly anti-Nazi thrust he felt the subject warranted.

Jack Glenn was assigned to direct the production. He found a colony of anti-Nazi German-Americans in Hoboken, New Jersey, whose buildings, beer halls, homes, and stores were virtually indistinguishable from those in Germany. "Our [re-created] exteriors were very realistic," said Glenn. "Our studio work was done with great care, not merely to symbolize it—it looked real."

The anti-Nazi German-Americans whom Glenn had located were happy to assist him in his production, and appeared appropriately costumed in a variety of scenes intended to illuminate the more ominous aspects of the Third Reich that Bryan's camera had missed. Included in these re-creations were scenes of propaganda activities; scenes of military men pursuing their studies and training; a scene of an elderly German couple listening with trepidation to one of Hitler's radio speeches; scenes of concentration camps; shots of German censors examining mail; a scene of a

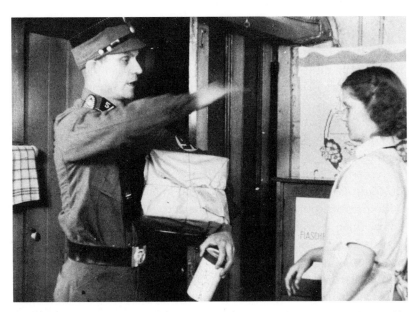

Reenactment of a Nazi storm trooper collecting funds from a housewife. (Courtesy Time, Inc.)

Authentic shot from Julien Bryan's footage showing German officer lecturing on military tactics. (Courtesy Time, Inc.)

storm trooper collecting funds from a housewife; a shot of a German radio announcer; scenes of political prisoners, and many others. George Dangerfield, the *March of Time*'s resourceful property man, played an important role in gathering authentic furniture and props from the homes of German-Americans in Hoboken.

Tom Orchard, at that time the *March of Time*'s production manager, also played a small part in the film's direction. Pressed into service at the last minute, he was told by Louis to get a shot of Catholic nuns in jail—a pictorial comment upon the Nazi's widespread suppression of religious activity. Orchard found some charwomen working in the 369 Lexington Avenue building and put them to work as actresses for $10 each. He sent someone over to Eaves Costume Company, got nuns' habits in the proper sizes, and dressed his charwomen in them. The next problem was to construct a jail. The technicians took a piece of black cardboard, cut a square hole in it, pasted a few strips of black tape from the film cans over the hole to represent bars, and positioned the card-

Hundreds killed in riots
of Communist strikers
in Detroit.

Reenacted shot of a German couple listening to Nazi radio propaganda, which was staged by Jack Glenn with German-American citizens in Manhattan. (Courtesy Jack Glenn)

board "wall" in front of the camera, slightly out of focus, with the bogus nuns in the background. "And then we just sat our lady friends down on a bench in there," said Orchard. "One of them we gave a missal to read and the other had crocheting. . . . We had the shot within three or four hours." This particular re-creation did not escape detection by sharp-eyed film reviewers, but it served the purpose and made the point that Louis wanted at just the right place in the film.

As the principal director on the film, Jack Glenn's greatest coup was in talking the pro-Nazi, German-American Bund leader, Fritz Kuhn, into appearing in staged scenes in Kuhn's offices. Never were Glenn's talents as an advance man, film director, and journalist brought more persuasively to bear than in his efforts to get this American fascist leader onto film. True to his own philosophy, Glenn looked for one subject on which he and Kuhn could agree, as he sought to gain the man's confidence. Said Glenn:

He made himself available because we both hated the recently organized CIO. I was blond and he figured I was Nordic. Took four hours to get into Fritz Kuhn's office. . . . I said, "What do you think about the labor situation in America?" He said, "Terrible, terrible, that God almighty CIO!" I said to myself "Ah, there's my subject." I didn't like the CIO either. I could honestly agree with him on that. . . . I never had to misrepresent anything.

By the time Glenn finished, of course, Kuhn had, without much further prompting, collaborated in a little vignette about his and his followers' activities in the New York area. Intercut with the shots of Kuhn in his office were scenes of Kuhn addressing his followers at an American pro-Nazi rally. (Interestingly, because of Glenn's proximity to Kuhn during this brief period, Glenn's name wound up in the F.B.I.'s files long after the activities of Kuhn and his associates had been terminated following the outbreak of World War II, causing Glenn some embarrassment in later years.)

For all of the footage, both authentic and staged, Louis de Rochemont gradually fashioned an emphatically anti-Nazi narration. He and his researchers were assisted in this task by a German refugee recently escaped from a Nazi concentration camp who served as consultant on the film.

Today, nearly forty years after the film's release, the scenes that the *March of Time* presented do not seem so startling. But in 1938 the film made statements that no other commercially released motion picture had dared, and for that matter precious few newspapers or magazines either.

The following lines are typical of the narration:

Though six years ago, six million Germans voted a communist ticket, every known radical, every known liberal today is either in hiding, in prison, or dead.

Still going on, as pitilessly, as brutally, as it did five years ago is Goebbels's persecution of the Jews. . . . And on the Christian churches, Goebbels's propaganda machine is today bearing down savagely, for these—almost gone—are still offering resistance to the new order. The Nazi state tolerates no rival authority. . . . To the good Nazi, not even God stands above Hitler. . . .

From the time the German child is old enough to understand anything, he ceases to be an individual, and is taught that he was born to die for the Fatherland.

. . . Germany is serving notice that all territories she lost in the World War must eventually be given back to her.

The film ended with lines provided by John Martin which became favorites of many staff members.

Nazi Germany faces her destiny with one of the great war machines in history. And the inevitable destiny of the great war machines of the past has been to destroy the peace of the world, its people, and the governments of their time.

TIME MARCHES ON!

It was only a matter of time, of course, before Julien Bryan found out what they had done with his footage, and he was furious. Bryan agreed with the political sentiment of Louis's work, but his reputation and career as a motion picture journalist depended upon access to foreign countries and upon the keeping of his word. Bryan apparently had arrived at an understanding with German officials that the material he shot would be used in a more or less neutral or possibly favorable fashion. The incorporation of his footage into an anti-Nazi film, on the other hand, would certainly guarantee that his future entry into Germany would be barred. Like Jack Glenn, Bryan believed in honoring his promises to the people he interviewed and worked with—even if they were Nazis. Double-crossing your leads and contacts in the film or newspaper business isn't right, and it isn't smart. Bryan was so upset about the *March of Time*'s anti-Nazi treatment of his footage that he engaged an attorney and considered suing the *March of Time* to secure an injunction against the film's release. In the end, however, he dropped the action, probably because it wasn't feasible. Nearly forty years later Glenn said, "I wanted to sit down some day with Julien over the table and tell him about this, because he never knew where these [re-created] shots came from, and he objected to their being incorporated with his shots. Julien was going to sue us for misrepresenting his pictures. We didn't misrepresent anything. He showed what was going on outside and we showed what was going on inside."

Just before the film's release the staff invited Fritz Kuhn to a private screening of the film at *March of Time* headquarters. Columnist Walter Winchell, a good friend of the *March of Time*'s, also attended. Before everyone arrived, Louis had his technicians bug the projection room with a hidden microphone connected by cable to a recorder. Properly prepared, Louis sat his guests down and ran the picture.

Kuhn was not amused. "If Hitler sees the film, I will be ruint!" he screamed on the recording. "Ruint! Ruint!" Kuhn's hysteria was duly noted by Winchell, who reported it in his column.

An official of the German consulate in New York was also invited to a private preview of the film. According to Louis, he was white-faced with rage when he left the projection room. "De Rochemont, God-damn it," he said, "Germany's no longer a small country and you'll suffer for this!" Louis could not have cared less.

It had been fun making the film. It would be even more fun releasing it. So great was the excitement which accompanied the 16-minute film's opening in New York that fearful municipal authorities assigned detectives from the city's alien squad to mingle with members of the Embassy audience, while a special detail of police was placed outside the theater to regulate the crowds.

Happily, the effect of the film on the opening night audience was less electrifying than authorities had been led to expect. The *New York Times* reported on January 21:

At the first showing the only reaction of the audience was a minor burst of applause from perhaps a dozen spectators in favor of Hitler, immediately matched by about as much hissing. At the second showing there were a few "Heils" for Hitler and an opposing and equivalent quantity of "Pfuis." At the third showing, as the after-dinner crowd assembled, a few fists were waved between shouters of "Heil" and of "Pfui" who happened to be too close together, but order was restored by giving the protagonists more remote seats. The next three showings were similar. There were no arrests.

Following the New York premiere, public interest in the film mounted as descriptions of the controversial issue appeared on the news pages and in the editorial columns of newspapers and magazines.

The film was both praised and damned by motion picture critics and political observers. Regardless of political leanings, all writers criticized the obvious dissimilarity and occasional conflict between the film's visual content and the narrator's comments. Major A. G. Rudd, general manager of the Embassy Theater in New York, stated (*Motion Picture Herald,* January 29): "The film is decidedly controversial and the theatre already has received many protests from those who feel it was unfair to one side or the other." The publishers of *Life* admitted, in the January 31 edition:

> Fact is that a majority of the scenes, showing the German populace, the youth program and the Army, are not unfavorable to Germany and a deaf movie-goer might consider the film more pro-Nazi than anti-Nazi. The MARCH OF TIME, conscious that no camera can portray all the darker aspects of Nazism, has evened the score with a vigorously pro-democratic commentary.

Because of the dissimilarity between the visual material and the narration, politically inclined reviewers found it difficult to determine the exact point of view that the *March of Time* was taking.

"Martin Proctor," allegedly a lifelong resident of Germany, newspaperman, and UFA Studio employee who had recently escaped to the United States, labeled the *March of Time* issue "a flaming pro-Nazi story," as quoted in *Motion Picture Herald,* February 5:

> How can the March of Time offer this newsreel as inside information? . . . Can anyone see from this film how Germany's anti-Hitler citizens are suffering? The whole is a flaming pro-Nazi story, if ever there was one. What do you really see? Youth marching, singing and working. Iron factories and other plants going full blast. Babies cared for, people fed, soldiers and brown shirts well clad and well fed, marching happily, and dictators orating and people cheering. . . . The March of Time editor has done his bit for Nazi Germany. And by order of Herr Goebbels himself, I herewith bestow upon the editor the "Clubfoot Medal," made of

hollow tin, to be worn with a swastika on a ribbon festooned with a blurb.

On February 9 Otis Ferguson, the *New Republic*'s articulate film critic, was delighted with what he felt to be the *anti*-Nazi position of the film's producers, calling it "an editorial with pictures, an editorial for democracy and against suppression, militant nationalism and shoving people around."

> For a while I had a sneaking idea that it might be just as well not to encourage anything so rickety in social theory as Luce enterprises to go in for open crusading, this being the kind of gun as likely to blow its breech out as produce a true salvo. But that is a consideration for the future, which already seems to be in the proper hands. For the present it is heartening to see good young blood making a field-day of the creaky superstitions of the movie trade. The best reassurance in the case of Time's "Inside Nazi Germany, 1938" grows out of the report that around the office in the feverish days before deadline, never had hard work . . . seemed easier. Working under Louis de Rochemont . . . on the shots Julien Bryan brought back from Germany, the majority of this staff seems to have been working on something it believed in. And in making any good thing, belief tells in the end.

During the next few weeks, the clipping files of the *March of Time* continued to swell with both supportive and condemning reviews. Political repercussions quickly followed the film's release. Throughout the nation, German consular and embassy officials, as well as *Bund* leaders, condemned the film and denounced its producers. In Baltimore, German Consul Frederick F. Schneider protested directly to the Maryland Censor Board: in Washington, D.C., it was first announced that the film would not run in R.K.O. houses. This announcement was later withdrawn. In New Orleans, numerous cuts were made in the film before its release to general audiences. And in New York, Radio City Music Hall yielded its first-run right to the Embassy Newsreel Theater, where the film ran for an unprecedented sixteen weeks.

In Chicago, according to the *Motion Picture Herald* of January 29, the Police Board of Censors found the film anti-Nazi and banned it on grounds that "it contained material which was likely to create public ill feelings against a nation 'friendly to the United States.' " Chicago newspapers, supported by civil rights leaders and some church officials, charged the board with suppression of freedom of speech and freedom of the press. The Chicago censors abruptly reversed the order which had banned the release within Chicago city limits. Chicago's Police Commissioner Allman stated: "The film is not censorable—I lifted the ban."

The high point of conflicting reaction was reached a few days later when the Warner Brothers circuit refused to carry the film on grounds that it was *pro*-Nazi propaganda. Henry Luce's reply to Warner's charges was quoted in the *Motion Picture Herald* on January 29:

> Mr. Warner's assertion that the March of Time is "pro-Nazi propaganda" is ridiculous. . . . Mr. Warner also says that movie audiences pay little or no attention to the sound that comes from the screen. This is an amazing observation to come from the man generally credited with introducing the talking picture. . . . Fortunately, Mr. Warner does not control the entire motion picture industry.

In refusing to show the film, Warner Brothers, which had the right to exhibit the *March of Time* in more than 200 theaters across the country, forfeited its exclusive contractual rights to this particular issue. Competing exhibitors scrambled to book the film and ran it profitably throughout the nation.

Within the film industry, the spread of opinion was fully as great as among the critics outside. Motion picture producer David O. Selznick sent this telegram to the producers: "Heartiest congratulations. March of Time's Inside Nazi Germany is one of the greatest and most important reels in the history of pictures. It is exciting to know that at long last someone has the courage to present such facts to the public in this medium and the intelligence and talent to present them so dramatically." Complimentary, too, was the appraisal of British documentarian Basil Wright in the May 13 number of *Spectator,* who found the issue impartial and topical. ". . . it scrupulously avoids the sensational aspects of the case," wrote Wright, "and by an avoidance of physical horrors concentrates our attention on the more unpleasant perversions of human souls and minds which can be so efficiently carried out in the name of a Dictator by a monster propaganda-machine such as that of Dr. Goebbels."

Contrasting with both Selznick's and Wright's enthusiasm was publisher Martin Quigley's hysterical blast in his *Motion Picture Herald*, on February 5, at the looming specter of "idea films" in American theaters:

> The exhibitors of the country ought to tell "The March of Time" that it is welcomed when it behaves itself but only then. They should tell it . . . that they expect it to be mindful of the proprieties of theatrical presentation—that they do not want controversial political material which is calculated to destroy the theatre as the public's escape from the bitter realities, the anguishes and the turmoil of life.

As if in response to Quigley's fulminations, Dorothy Thompson, *New York Herald Tribune* columnist, quoted in the February 5 issue of *Motion Picture Herald,* said:

> The tempest raging around the March of Time's film "Inside Nazi Germany—1938" raises not only the question of screen censorship, but also whether a motion picture can or should deal with an important controversial subject. It is a highly exciting picture, a realistic portrayal of Germany today, and a magnificent piece of journalism. Who on earth can doubt the right or the reason for presenting such a motion picture document?

The protest, anger, and excitement provoked by "Inside Nazi Germany" gradually subsided and, in February it was replaced in most markets by a new and less controversial issue. Nearly a year passed before the closing and perhaps most important comment about this controversial film was made. Speaking in January 1939, by which time it had been widely seen throughout Europe and South America, Adolf Hitler attacked anti-Nazi films planned and produced in the United States, and cautioned the films' makers that if production continued, Germany would answer them with anti-Semitic films, which the dictator felt sure "many countries will appreciate" (*New York Times,* January 31, 1939).

Historians looking back, with memories of events leading up to the Second World War to guide them, can today view "Inside

Nazi Germany" as the first commercially released anti-Nazi American motion picture. Whatever its political importance may have been, "Inside Nazi Germany—1938" is best remembered as a striking example of the vitality and impact of the dramatically conceived informational film. Among contemporary critics, it was British documentary producer John Grierson who most acutely sensed the significance of the *March of Time:*

> There are proper limits, it is true, to freedom of speech which the cinema must regard. Its power is too great for irresponsible comment, when circulations like *March of Time*'s may run to nine thousand theatres across an explosive world. But it seems sensible for the moment that *March of Time* has won the field for the elementary principles of public discussion. The world, our world, appears suddenly and brightly as an oyster for the opening: for film people—how strangely—worth living in, fighting in, and making drama about. And more important still is the thought of a revitalized citizenship and of a democracy at long last in contact with itself.

9

Inside the Sprocket Factory: The House That Louis Built

From the beginning, production at the *March of Time* was carried on under terrifying pressure. Louis, a disorganized perfectionist, could in the absence of union restraints require an 80 to 100-hour work-week from subordinates. Jimmy Shute recalled the sense of things:

> In the early days, we worked as no human beings have ever worked. We would go in, say, at ten in the morning, and then I would stay until perhaps ten the *next* morning, or eleven or twelve—we simply worked until we couldn't work any longer, and became practically unconscious and had to go home to sleep. And I remember that Louis . . . had a little cot—a folding cot outside his door—and he would lie down for ten- or fifteen-minute naps on it, and then keep on—I don't know how he did it. It got to be a kind of contest between him and Roy as to who could work the longest. And Roy was phenomenal—he could do all kinds of things. But after a while, I just gave in. I got so damned tired, I didn't know what I was saying or doing.

There was the occasion, in 1937, now a legend, when Louis worked continuously in the cutting room for eighty-six hours without sleep in order to meet a deadline, having arrived at the

March of Time offices Monday evening and emerged, semicomotose, early the following Friday morning. Larsen kept substantially the same hours.

The directors, cameramen, and sound recordists who worked on location far away from the studio put in just as many hours. "To be a director," said Jack Glenn, "you have to have a certain kind of lunacy, toughness—you've got to have plasticity . . . you never eat properly, you burn yourself out; you consume yourself."

> I'd get home at 3 or 4 o'clock in the morning; here's a message from Roy Larsen and a little clipping from *Time* about trouble in Florida. He'd say, "Jack, here's the research on the Florida Canal [story]. Take your crew immediately and head for Florida. There's a Western Union envelope in the office for you with several thousand dollars for expenses." I'd call the crew. They'd say, "We're very tired." I'd say, "So am I. We're going to Florida. . . . We've got ten days to make the picture. We're going to cover the north of Florida and the south of Florida, and drive in the automobile. What do you think of that?" They'd say, "All right."

The tension and stress under which the *March of Time* staff worked was due in part to the short, inflexible deadlines. Louis and his people were committed to release a new issue of the series every month. Of course, television news producers do something of the same thing once a day, but the technology involved, the quality of film making aspired to, and the journalistic thoroughness achieved are in no way comparable.

The fact that the *March of Time* was able to meet its deadlines using the heavy, tripod-mounted 35mm cameras and the optical sound equipment employed in the 1930's is astonishing by today's television-news standards. The *March of Time*'s cameras, tripods, motors, sound equipment, cables, and batteries together weighed several hundred pounds, compared with the twenty-pound cameras and ten-pound recorders used in 16mm television-film news coverage today. The black-and-white stocks then available were quite insensitive, having a maximum speed of about A.S.A. 100, compared with today's color emulsions rated at A.S.A. 400.

There were qualitative differences as well. Whether network or local, today's television news broadcasters do a remarkable job in getting their hastily photographed, superficially edited images assembled in time for each evening's broadcast. But even the best of its coverage is thin and shallow, compared with the *March of Time*'s carefully crafted productions. Television-news broadcasters employ anchor men/women and field reporters whose on-camera appearances bridge the inevitable gaps in continuity that occur when footage runs out or stops making sense. The *March of Time* enjoyed no such luxury. It used one off-camera narrator, the commentary of which was written and rewritten with meticulous attention to style, accuracy, and impact, assisted from time to time by equally well-written titles. Each *March of Time* issue had to stand on its own, as complete and as professionally made as a theatrical feature film. Editorially, the shots had to cut together properly, and transitions had to be smooth and stylistically consistent—no jump cuts, no swish pans. The photography was rarely elegant, but it was always professional. Each shot was properly lit, compositionally right, accurately exposed, and editorially capable of being cut together with every other shot in the sequence. The sound, both in original dialogue recording, narration and musical accompaniment, and in its final "mix," has to meet Hollywood standards—no static, system noise, ground noise, or extraneous babble. If the sound was not right, Louis would have the whole sequence redone, or dub it in the studio with impersonators. What was good enough for the newsreels—and for the televison news shows that followed them—was never good enough for Louis. And yet, the *March of Time* was indeed a quasi-newsreel, with a monthly deadline to meet, whose subject matter was often closely tied to breaking news events of the day. This combination of high, theatrical-film standards and news-gathering pressures made the business of producing the *March of Time* both a challenge and an agony. If the *March of Time*'s operations are to be compared with anything being broadcast on American television today, it would have to be some kind of cross between an interpretive, feisty documentary series like CBS's "60 Minutes," and a contemporary "docu-drama" such as "Missiles of October" or "Truman at Potsdam," which involves well-researched reenactments of events that transpired in the recent past.

Just to make things a bit more difficult, the parent corporation required the *March of Time* to produce a variety of promotional reels for *Time/Life* magazines, convention films for advertisers, commercial films for sponsors, a 16mm edition of the *March of Time* for schoolroom use, and even political campaign films for Henry Luce's favorite candidates.

For *March of Time* staffers, it was hell on a 30-day cycle. As each month drew to a close and the deadline loomed ahead, the whole crew began putting in their 20-hour days, in a frantic effort to get the film into the can and off to the laboratory for the making and shipping of prints to theaters around the country.

As each issue neared completion, de Rochemont worked continuously in the projection room, passing judgment on the clips, shots, sequences, and tracks brought to him for his appraisal, fulminating all the while on the delays and frustrations that arose.

Even at worst, however, there were grim laughs and good fellowship. Louis may have made life difficult for everyone, but his eccentricities made good material for office legends. During one 36-hour photo-finish in the 1930's, one of Louis's subordinates kept the following transcript of his remarks. Now yellow with age, the transcript, from which the following excerpts are taken, was made available to me:

OVERHEARD IN THE PROJECTION ROOM

Is Van's voice ready?

Is Bev still scoring? What time did they get started?

Is Victor around?

Have I seen all of the cuts, including the barrel cuts on this subject?

How much longer will Lothar be?

Gee, this subject looks lousy! What do you think, Tom?

Is this Shack coffee? You know I don't drink it as much as I used to.

Is the lab working down stairs? Are they getting any better, Jack?

Can Miss Logue start taking key numbers on any subject?

How is Jimmy coming on the script?

Come in for a telegram, and I want some cigarettes—Fatimas.

Now where are those swell steel mill shots that Bonney made?

Does anyone know whether Sozio's shipment has come in?

Who did I ask to get those scenes for me?
Now do we have any shots, in any of our old subjects, of men talk-
in a bar?
Jack, do we need all of these people around here?
I didn't ask for this stuff at all.
Do we have a good print of that Navy subject downstairs, Joe?
Where is that scratch coming from?
This is what I mean by a "falling-off-the-table" shot.
Oh! Do I have to see that scene again? I thought I had told
Charlie to take that out!
Has the fireman been here lately?
Why can't we get these things right the first time?

Oh! That's swell, Lothar—that's swell—perfect—Gee, that's swell—
Oh! What's that title doing there? No! No! I didn't say that—
Stop it! Stop it! Stop the machine! I can't think—Now I thought
it was clear to you—come over here and I will give you a new
line-up.

What is the absolute deadline on this, Wink?
That does it for me.
Well, let's see, what will we have for a line-up for the next release.

The loyalty and enthusiasm of early crews, whether in the editing rooms or out in the field, were astonishing. No matter how difficult Louis's demands, the crew nearly always came through for
him. Lothar Wolff said:

It's really on a whim which in the end may turn out to be journalistically or editorially very effective that he would suddenly
have an idea and ask for something which seemed impossible,
which nobody had ever thought of before, which would have been
very complicated to get. He would phone Jack [Glenn] and say, "I
want three fishing boats in a storm and I need them by day after
tomorrow." And then he'd expect it.

Director Jack Glenn recalled the fishing boat sequence vividly.
Louis had wanted a complicated scene for a sequence in his March
1936 issue "Fisheries." He said, "I want a reenactment of two
schooners out fishing in a storm and twelve dories out from them
trying to do the fishing, caught in the storm, trying to get back to

the ship." "I got my orders on Friday morning," said Glenn. "He wanted the footage on Monday."

Glenn hustled off to Gloucester, Massachusetts, where he found a two-masted fishing boat tied to a pier with full sail, which he leased for the week-end shooting. He hired a group of local fishermen and hangers-on, some of them to appear as actors dressed in oilskins on the boat, the others to pull at a cable attached to the boat to create a rocking effect.

The sequence was filmed on a clear night, but Louis wanted a storm so the local fire department was enlisted to drench the boat and its occupants with water from their hoses. "So it's pitching and the rain is coming down," said Glenn. "They're running around in their oilskins, slipping and sliding, falling down on their asses . . . one guy is bailing . . . damned near sank the boat. I wired Louis: STORM IN CAN, WHAT ELSE YOU WANT?"

As in all enterprises, however, there are limits to one's enthusiasm and endurance. The price paid by *MOT* staff members in both emotional and physical stress was enormous. At least three *March of Time* staff members were certifiable alcoholics; two others had nervous breakdowns; another acquired bleeding ulcers and had to have his stomach removed.

In the end they had little to show for it. Apart from Larsen and de Rochemont, both of whom were officers of the organization, the rank and file had received pitiful salaries. This was especially the case with editorial workers in the cutting rooms, upon whose effectiveness and skill the *March of Time* depended. In 1934, an apprentice's salary was about $16 a week and an experienced cutter's around $50. By 1937, these had risen only slightly to $20 for the former and $55 or $60 for the latter.

Of course, this was the middle of the Depression, and there were many men and women who would have been happy with what the *Time* staff was paid. The salaries themselves would not have been quite so hard to take had it not been for the excessive hours demanded of the staff. According to contemporary memos, the men in the cutting room worked two weekends and every evening overtime for two weeks out of every four—without extra pay! One of these memos—from a cutting room supervisor to Louis de Rochemont—suggests the conditions under which his men worked in the late 1930's:

I know you feel somewhat the same as I do, but if you had seen the physical torture endured by the cutting force the last few days, it would seem as big an imposition to you as it does to me. This last A.N.A. experience [a special-assignment film production for the Convention of the Association of National Advertisers] was only a repetition of the 7 or 8 special reels we have put out in the last six months. . . . it was an amazing achievement to have finished this 1300 ft. subject as quickly and as well as it was done. When it was finished there was no expression of thanks and of course no extra recompense for anyone. And then when I heard there were a few slight criticisms about the finished job, it began to seem that the whole set-up was nothing more than tyranny on one side and slavery on the other. We don't mind and we don't complain about the work on the [regular] *March of Time* release, domestic or foreign. This we feel is our job, even if it does run into a lot of overtime. But is it our job to be expected to do anything extra asked for . . . with no consideration for our personal lives, no thanks in any way, of any kind, even though the work is all done on additional overtime? I think it is nothing but exploitation of the staff.

If the staff members, whether in the cutting room or out in the field, thought they would be rewarded when the *March of Time* began to make some money, they were certainly disillusioned, for the *March of Time* never made any money at all. It was always an expensive series to produce compared with newsreels and other types of motion picture short subjects, especially with Louis's perfectionism and his way of spending money to get what he wanted. According to estimates provided by surviving staff members, the early issues cost between $20,000 and $30,000 each. With the passing of years, and a gradual increase in production costs, this rose to about $40,000 per issue during the war, and then to $50,000 or $60,000 in the late 1940's. Other, competing short subjects, such as travelogues and newsreels, cost much less and were never *intended* to make a profit. Such "intermission fare" was offered as part of the block-booked program that major producers provided for theater owners to support their money-making features. In the *March of Time*'s case, however, the corporation had no other income from feature film production to offset their losses on the short subject—the short subject was their only film product. Because of the *March of Time*'s enormous promotional value to *Time, Life,* and *Fortune* magazines, the corporation was satisfied if it simply broke even. Whether it even managed to do that, however, seems doubtful. More than one former *MOT* staffer has stated that *March of Time* losses were balanced against more profitable properties such as *Time* magazine.

And so, to a considerable extent, Louis's hands were tied in the mid- and late-1930's. The salary scales for his men were set by the corporation, and de Rochemont was obliged to stay within them. For that matter, Louis had his own problems in dealing with the corporation's business managers, who were appalled by his careless administrative procedures and what they considered the reckless way he spent money to get the *March of Time* produced and out on schedule. Louis recalled, for example, that his practice of handing out occasional $5 or $10 bills to police officers on the beat in New York City to gain their cooperation was almost impossible to explain to the business office.

The *March of Time* was underbudgeted by conventional film production standards, and, had it not been for the loyalty and commitment of its rank-and-file staff, it could never have survived on the funds Time, Inc., provided. This lack of funds and Louis's working methods led inevitably to labor-management problems in the late 1930's.

There appear to have been three shocks in the history of the *March of Time*'s corporate body sufficient in their magnitude and duration to alter the nature of operations from that point onward. The first of these occurred in 1937-38 with the unionization by the Newspaper Guild of employees in all divisions of Time, Inc.

By contemporary standards, labor's demands of that day seem modest indeed, but its attempts to stabilize working conditions, reduce unemployment, and provide a measure of job security for American workers involved hard fighting. The systematic, permanent, and widespread organization of labor was a movement whose time had clearly arrived, providing an alternative to a state-controlled socialist economy. And if ever there was an organization ready for unionization, the *March of Time* was it.

The film group's cameramen, sound recordists, and projectionists were already members of the New York locals of the International Alliance of Theatrical Stage Employees, but the more numerous editors, cutters, researchers, and writers were not. It was these unorganized employees whose membership the Newspaper Guild coveted.

Louis fought organization to the bitter end. Many of his *March of Time* issues, such as "Bootleg Coal," "King Cotton's Slaves," and "Strikebreaking," had seemed to champion the plight and right of organized labor, but when it came to Louis's own shop, it was an entirely different matter. There was no doubt that unionization of the film makers would place a strict limit on their working hours or require substantial payments for overtime. With the series just breaking even as it was, it followed that *March of Time* operations would have to be made a great deal more efficient, and that Louis's role as *patrone* of his Lexington Avenue family would draw swiftly to an end.

Louis valued personal and professional loyalty highly. He may have been a difficult boss to work for, but there is ample testimony that he protected loyal subordinates and found ways in which to reward them unexpectedly.

He could be terribly generous [recalled Lothar Wolff]. And he did any number of things which were absolutely amazing in his relationships with me. For instance, in 1939, I had to dash over to Europe because I thought I could get my mother out of Germany, to England. The company paid my trip, on Louis's instigation.

When, in 1938, my brother was dying in Berlin, and I was inconsolable, I was so upset because I was crazy about him and he was supposed to come over here, and [Louis] saw under what a stress I was. When I came home one day, there was a note under my door [which said]: "You are leaving in three days on the maiden voyage of the S.S. *Brazil* to go down with our cameramen to supervise the shooting"—things like that.

I never had to ask for a raise once, during the entire period. Louis would always know when it was appropriate, and when he felt I ought to have one.

The working conditions at the *March of Time* had always had contradictory qualities—punishing hours and demands from Louis combined with the comradeship and a mutual sense of loyalty between the boss and his workers—given which the effect of the Guild's activities was predictably divisive. Many employees supported the Guild. Others lined up behind Louis. A few tried to stay out of the crossfire.

> That was a battle royal . . . [recalled one of the film makers]. And Louis put pressure on me, for example. I remember very clearly, he said, "You can't join, for heaven's sake, you're part of management." I think I made $50 a week, or something like that. Obviously, I had no part in managerial decisions. And I decided not to get into an argument with him, because I didn't want to. . . . I was in no position to.

For those of Louis's employees who played an especially active role in the Guild's activities, life could be grim. One of them, a cutting room supervisor, recalled that Louis asked him to resign "for the mutual good." The supervisor refused. At the time he was making about $75 a week; during his next 3½ years at the *March of Time,* his salary was raised only once, by $5 per week.

Another staff member who was an active Guild supporter and organizer was Mary Losey, who was especially anxious to bring an end to the economic differential that existed throughout Time, Incorporated, between men's and women's salaries.

> I was really very tough on this score, and thanks to that battle it turned out that they couldn't discriminate any longer between a B.A. from Mt. Holyoke and a B.A. from Yale. If they hired you they had to pay you. But it was a real scrap. . . .

Losey left shortly thereafter for a good job at the Rockefeller Foundation, where, as she put it, de Rochemont "couldn't touch me."

In July 1938 the Guild won its fight and became the official representative of workers through the publishing empire of Time, Incorporated. (Still later, the Guild reluctantly relinquished its representation of film workers in the *March of Time* unit to appropriate locals of the International Alliance of Theatrical Stage Employees. Over the years, the *March of Time* also fought a running battle with the Screen Actors Guild, which claimed jurisdiction over *MOT*'s "actors.")

Overnight, as the Guild's supporters had predicted, de Rochemont and Larsen discovered that they *could* produce the *March of Time* on less than an 80-hour work-week. For the first time in years, *March of Time* workers began seeing something of their families and of the world outside.

Routines were readjusted and conditions normalized, but the relationship between de Rochemont and his boys was never quite the same again. Speaking thirty-five years after the event, his comments simplistic but illuminating, de Rochemont was no less bitter than in 1937:

> The Newspaper Guild [people] were nasty. I'm for organizations like that, but I don't think that they should be nasty. . . . We weren't making money. We were *trying* to make money on the thing. You can't make a picture in four-day weeks, and stuff like that. And if we'd gone in and had to pay overtime for all those things, we'd have sunk before we did sink. And I didn't like the people, although I've seen a lot of them since.

In time, everyone adjusted to the new union-management relationship. The *March of Time* was still an exciting place to be, and talented film makers worked just as enthusiastically, although for fewer hours each week, to refine, perfect, and extend their influential film series.

From early 1938 the company was housed in what became its own permanent headquarters in a new building at 369 Lexington Avenue. The facilities were located a block or so from the *Time-Life-Fortune* headquarters. This physical separation was much appreciated by Louis and his staff, for it kept visits by Henry Luce and other corporation executives to a minimum. According to Tom Orchard, William Zeckendorf had built the Lexington Avenue structure with facilities for the *March of Time* to meet de Rochemont's and Larsen's specifications. "It was very nice," said Orchard. "It looks rather plain on the outside, but it was very handsome on the inside. Louis had a beautiful office in front."

Originally, the *March of Time* occupied the second and third floors of the building. The third floor held the executives' and writers' offices, the research library, the conference rooms, and the projection room. The floor below held all of the cutting rooms, shipping and receiving, the film library files, some film storage space, and the processing laboratory. The *March of Time* processed all of its own 35mm negatives and struck its own positive work prints. Release printing was done elsewhere by Deluxe Laboratories. Sound recording, music scoring, and sound "mixes" were also done elsewhere, in RCA's eleventh floor studios at 411 Fifth Avenue.

In those days, all professional 35mm motion pictures, whether features or newsreels, were photographed on nitro-cellulose film, popularly called "nitrate." Chemically akin to gun-cotton, "nitrate" was extremely flammable, oftentimes explosive, capable of spontaneous combustion, poisonous when burning. The amount of nitrate which could be stored within the editing rooms and storage racks was limited because of space, safety considerations, and the law. Visits by the fire marshals were frequent and sometimes unpleasant. *March of Time* cutters operated at high speed and under great stress and were not always as cautious in handling the film as they should have been. On occasion, a $10 or $20 bill was passed to a fire inspector along with a blood oath to clean up the mess at once. Sometimes it worked, sometimes it didn't. By law, smoking was absolutely forbidden in the presence of nitrate; yet some workers smoked. Jack Glenn recalled turning around a corner on the second floor one day to find a city fire inspector giving a fierce tongue lashing to Roy Larsen, then publisher of *Life* magazine and a principal officer of the world's greatest publishing empire. Larsen had been caught, cigarette in his mouth, working in the midst of several thousand feet of nitrate. "I wouldn't give a God-damn if you were editor of the *Saturday Evening Post*," screamed the inspector, and Glenn didn't stay around to hear more.

There were always at least three full-time field production crews on duty within the United States, each ordinarily comprised of a director, a cameraman, an assistant cameraman, a sound recordist, and a grip. These were augmented by a property man and a contact man as needed. Continuously moving throughout the United

States or at work in the *March of Time*'s New York studios, these crews generated the original "background material," the interview sequences, and the reenactments that Louis required for his various issues. The foreign production crews, operating out of the Paris and London offices, did the same thing under Richard de Rochemont's direction. Finally, freelance cameramen, widely scattered throughout the world, were hired as needed to photograph special subject matter to which their geographical location gave them access.

For the issue on the Croix de Feu, for example, Dick de Rochemont used freelance cameramen F. Lelong, Leon Bellet, Alfred Guichard, Lucien Maes, and a man named Ravet, in addition to his regular staff cameraman, Marcel Rebière. Dick explained in a memo to the home office, "I had two ideas in using so many cameramen: the first was to make an impression on the Croix de Feu people, the second, to try out various cameramen who have been applying for work." Dick de Rochemont even operated one of the cameras himself on this occasion, which turned out to be a poor idea. Scenes are out of focus, he explained, "due to the inexperience of the cameraman."

The logistics involved in moving these people from place to place and assignment to assignment were complicated. For example, during production of *MOT*'s 1937 issue on child labor, Louis had five different cameramen (three staff, two freelance) out in the field, together with sound recordists, assistant cameramen, and support technicians, working in widely separated parts of the United States during a 38-day period from February 2 to March 11. According to the production files, work on this issue began on February 2, with cameraman Dick Maedler and recordist Yancy Bradshaw in Washington, D.C., filming government officials involved with a proposed child labor amendment to the Constitution. Between February 24 and March 5, Carl ("Cap") Pryer was in Greenville and Allendale, South Carolina, filming children at work in textile and lumber mills. By February 25, Dick Maedler was back in New York filming in the slums. On March 1 and 2, also in New York, Johnny Geisel was filming young girls at work making veils in the garment district and young boys at work at machines, while Charlie Gilson shot exterior scenes in which chil-

One of Dick de Rochemont's British crews shoots a scene on a London street. (Courtesy Time, Inc.)

dren were seen working at different jobs. On the third of March, Gilson left New York for Boston to film a debate on the child labor amendment in the Massachusetts House of Representatives. A day later, he was in Montpelier, Vermont, to film an interview with Senator George Aiken. On March 3, Jack Haeseler was in southern California photographing children harvesting cabbages and carrots in the fields. Finally, on March 11, Charlie Gilson finished filming inserts at the *March of Time*'s New York studios.

Supplementing the original footage that *March of Time* cameramen shot were thousands of feet of newsreel footage specially ordered by Louis from both American and foreign newsreel companies. Finally, the *March of Time* had its own library of stock-shot material to draw upon which, with the passing of years, grew to a staggering total of 10 million feet of 35mm film. In some cases, all of these different kinds of footage would be stockpiled for months, as Louis waited for the right kind of news break to come along. In other cases, a particular sequence would be rushed to completion within a period of days.

In time, the flood of film which poured into the Lexington Avenue headquarters from around the world mounted to almost alarming proportions. Because of the flammable nature of nitrate, exposed negative could not be sent through the regular mail. Instead, it was shipped by domestic air freight express, automobile, bus, or Railway Express—the fastest available under the circumstances. Footage from Dick de Rochemont's headquarters in Europe arrived by boat during the middle 1930's, this being the only way to transport freight across the Atlantic in the days before regularly scheduled, trans-Atlantic air flight was introduced.

Beginning on July 1, 1936, Dick de Rochemont began shipping his flammable negatives to New York on board the German zeppelin *Hindenburg*, thereby saving a day or two in transit time. Lifting power for this beautiful, lighter-than-air ship was provided by hydrogen, a gas that was even more explosive than the *March of Time*'s nitrate negatives in its hold. In some circles, the *Hindenburg* came to be called "the flying crematorium." When it finally exploded, at Lakehurst, New Jersey, on May 6, 1937, it carried 5701 feet of the *March of Time*'s nitrate negative which had been shot for a story about the British "Defense of the Realm Act." The financial loss for the *March of Time* would, of course, have been substantial.

Funny thing [recalled Dick de Rochemont]. We were shipping by [ocean-going] ship and insuring it. So our broker called me up and said, "I can put your film on the *Hindenburg*." He didn't raise the question of insurance. The *Hindenburg* went up. Naturally, I called up and said, "Did you insure this?" He said, "No." I said, "Why didn't you?" He said, "You didn't tell me to." I said, "Haven't I always insured every shipment?" He said, "Well, I'll take it up." Finally, the Lloyd's people paid on the grounds that since I'd obviously intended to insure, it was the same as insured. We got our money back.

The whole sequence was reshot by de Rochemont, though whether for the better or the worse one will never know. Beginning at least as early as August 1939, Dick began shipping negatives on the Pan-American "Clipper" flying boats.

For each reel of film photographed, a so-called "dope sheet" was prepared by the cameramen and sent to New York independently of the film. Dope sheets indicated the exact order, location, date, and subject of each shot exposed on each roll of film, together with the names of the cameraman and sound recordist, the production number of title, the amount of footage exposed, the kind of film stock used, processing instructions to the laboratory, information about the presence or absence of competing newsreel cameramen, and information about the manner in which the film was being shipped. The names of all individuals shown in each shot were indicated, as were their positions, left-to-right, or vice-versa, within the frame.

Dope sheets were often accompanied by memoranda prepared by cameramen and directors in the field regarding the subject matter being photographed and containing background information that they thought would be helpful to the script writers—economic and political summaries, statistical data, biographical vignettes of the individuals photographed, on-site impressions of social conditions, explanations of complicated issues or problems which would have to be clarified by the Voice of Time, and general gossip about the circumstances under which the film had been photographed. Newspaper clippings, ceremonial programs, press releases, and other relevant documents were also frequently attached. Many of these memoranda which survive in the *March of Time*'s production files, were scribbled late at night on the stationery of hotels scattered all over the United States—hotels which, like the ocean liners on which *March of Time* film was shipped, have long since gone out of business, been torn down, or been virtually forgotten.

Dope sheets were sprinkled regularly with elaborate excuses and explanations from cameramen as to why particular shots that Louis wanted did not turn out properly. These were intended to ameliorate the loss and to pacify the boss when the film was projected for him back at headquarters. Today they make amusing

217

reading, but at the time they were all part of the feedback to the New York offices which could determine over a period of time whether a man kept working or not. Coming from professional film makers, these are also the kind of excuses which should make amateur photographers feel better about their own inadequacies.

British staff cameraman James Hodgson, in London (1939) apologized:

> Note: in one roll a few scenes will be very badly underexposed, because I had to poke the camera through the railings of Buckingham Palace and the shutter spindle of the camera got caught in the railings and so closed the shutter gradually.

From S. R. Sozio, in Egypt (1937):

> On the way back to ABDIN palace. Bad shot. Came pretty close to being run over by His Majesty's horses. . . . Impossible to describe what took place during the mad scramble of all the picture men, police and other strangers. We did the best under the conditions, and I am glad to have gotten an exposure showing the royal couple with a 3.5 lens with no light or very little of it.

Sometimes, the explanations were more dramatic. From Marcel Rebière in Paris (1937):

> Kerenski [leader of the first Russian revolution]—who lives in Paris, since he left Russia in a hurry—coming towards the camera. This shot was made with Kerenski unwilling, and ends with Kerenski knocking down the cameraman with his umbrella.

From Dick de Rochemont at the League of Nations (1935):

> Another attempt to photograph Aloisi. Hustled by fascist bodyguards.

And from Emile Pierre in Addis Ababa (1935):

> I spent an hour at the police station today where I was threatened with a good walloping. It's just a habit to take and we are all used to such things now.

Finally, there were always a few excuses which passed over Louis's or Dick's desks that must have made them wonder whether their people would ever get the act together:

From Jimmy Hodgson in London (1941):

Inside the Sprocket Factory

We have had the R.C.A. sound engineer with us, and he has approved our method of working. . . . However, he has sprung me a little bomb-shell by telling me that the microphones will not function at their greatest efficiency unless we use the transformer supplied with the set. I often wondered what these transformers were doing lying in the spare accessory box, as I am certain that they have never yet been used. Now I know.

Exposed negative, whether domestic or overseas, was nearly always shipped undeveloped to the *March of Time*'s New York laboratory. Exceptions occurred more frequently as political tensions spread throughout Europe in the late 1930's, requiring *MOT* footage to be processed in Europe and censored before shipment. Even when shipped unprocessed, however, footage was often accompanied by instructions from Dick de Rochemont regarding censorship instructions or "understandings" regarding particular scenes:

For a sequence on London shipping (1935):

IMPORTANT: The shots where cargo being unloaded falls off the trucks or out of the slings MUST NOT BE USED. To do so will entail the loss of all future authorizations from the Port of London Authority. It seems unimportant but they are very definite about this and I have therefore promised that this will be taken care of.

For a sequence on the Vichy government (1940):

. . . scene of Marshal Pétain putting his leg on the table, "as Americans do," he said. This last shot is surely the best, but the censors asked us to take it out.

For another sequence on the Vichy government. The note is from Gerald McAllister (1940):

We held the showing of our French film this afternoon for various members of the embassy and they "respectfully request" deletion of the following shots:

1. Scene showing billiard game before [scene of] Ministry of Agriculture.
2. Marshal Pétain tottering to car uncertainly.
3. Shot of banner describing Ministry of Agriculture.

For a sequence on the Red Cross (1939):

The patients must *not* be referred to as "wounded." They can be called "casualties," "sick," or "injured."

The editorial staff in New York who had to make sense out of the mass of material pouring into its rooms, divided each month's work into A, B, C, and D weeks. A-week was devoted to cleaning up the debris remaining from the previous month's D-week. B-week was given to routine and odd jobs that had been held up because of the rush to finish the last release. C-week was the beginning of editorial work on the current month's release. D-week saw every able-bodied cutter at work on the release at hand. Even with Guild limitations on working hours and overtime, the fast pace at which they worked never let up.

As the dope sheets, written in longhand, arrived at the New York office, they were typed by secretaries onto standardized forms. From these were generated the thousands of index cards used in the *March of Time*'s stock-shot library. As many as half a dozen different releases might be in one or another stage of completion at any time, some based largely on original, newly photographed footage, others on newsreel material bought from American and foreign companies. Eventually it was filed in the *March of Time*'s growing film library, the indexing and retrieval system for which had been designed by editor Jack Bradford. *MOT* veterans describe it as a first-rate system that provided for rapid retrieval of tens of thousands of shots, catalogued and cross-indexed into 25,000 categories. "Out-takes" were never thrown away, for one could never tell when a scrap of film could be used at a later date. The millions of feet of film that made up the library were kept in nitrate vaults at Bonded Film Storage Company in Manhattan, with only a minimum amount of footage necessary for editing and completing each monthly release being kept on hand at headquarters.

As each month's issue moved toward fine cut and completion, de Rochemont and his writers laboriously refined the narration to be read by Westbrook Van Voorhis. For years, chief editor Lothar Wolff served as narration supervisor for the English-language version. That he was selected for this assignment always amused Wolff, who, even today, has a noticeable German accent. Van

Voorhis was by that time a quite celebrated figure—the only individual associated with the film's production who was known, at least by ear, to the general public. "The relationship of a dialogue director, which was my function . . ." said Wolff, "and a narrator . . . is always a very tenuous one. And we never had an argument [even after] taking a sentence over twelve times. . . . We didn't do it to picture. . . . We went to the screening room. Someone would read to Van the script [while the picture was screened]. We would come back and adjust the picture to the voice. That means the picture was not frozen before the recording."

In those days, film recordings were made optically, instead of magnetically, and it was necessary to develop the finished sound track chemically before listening to it. Mistakes were time-consuming and costly, often requiring rerecording of the entire reel.

> I remember slipping only once [recalled Wolff], and that time was very upsetting . . . and the word which we mispronounced—Louis hit the ceiling! I can still see him in the projection room!—was spelled "FORECASTLE." How do you pronounce it? "FOSCLE!" Well, we said "FORECASTLE." I don't know whether Van was asleep. Christ! We had to retake [the whole narration for] one sentence.

Different sound tracks, in different languages, were recorded in New York for the foreign countries in which the *March of Time* was released. The British version was narrated at different times by Westbrook Van Voorhis and (beginning in January 1938) by Alistair Cooke. The French version was usually narrated in France by Raymond Destac; occasionally in New York by Fernand Auberjenois.

The American, British, and Canadian versions were virtually identical, although some words were changed in the British to conform to local usage. Also, some sequences were shot exclusively for foreign audiences. This was most likely in the case of the British and French versions. In other cases, particular shots in American-produced sequences might be changed to accommodate foreign sensibilities. In "The Movies March On," for example, a sequence featuring very early motion pictures showed American-made films in the American version and French-made films in the French. Finally, as the result of censorship, particular sequences in the American edition of the *March of Time* were sometimes removed by foreign authorities and so were never seen by overseas audiences.

Whole scripts were sometimes discarded by Louis at the last minute and editors put to work to rebuild the entire structure of the film. Inevitably, reluctantly, and only because the deadline had been reached, Louis would make the last cut, the narration would be recorded, and the film made ready for the final step in its completion—the scoring of the music track.

All of the music for the *March of Time* was original in the sense that it was created expressly for the series. However, for any single issue, only a part of the music would be freshly written, while the other parts would be borrowed from the library of music scores that Jack Shaindlin and staff continually generated for *March of Time* purposes.

The problem [said Shaindlin] was that they could not show me the finished product . . . until about three days before the recording session. . . . Don't forget, we had two reels. We had roughly 17 minutes of music. And obviously we could not do an original score, have an orchestrator copy it into parts because it usually takes about between two and four hours, depending upon the type of music, to orchestrate a one-minute segment. So what would happen is, I would look at a screening of the film, get a detailed cue sheet [which indicated each shot in the film, its sequential order, its description, and its precise length in 35mm feet].

I had an assistant, Robert McBride, who was a very fine musician, a well-known American composer, who's now a professor of music at Arizona. He was with me for 11 years. And what I would do is sit at the piano, and let's say we need two bars of Washington, D.C., then the rifle range [for a film on the F.B.I.]. I'd say, "Bob, supposing it goes something like this" [plays piano]. "Rifle range" [plays piano]. He would kind of write this down and do *something* like that—perhaps not, because he was a composer of stature and he consequently would improve on the detail—but he would do something like that.

From 1942 onward, background music for the series was composed and directed by musical director Jack Shaindlin. (Courtesy Jack Shaindlin)

Once Shaindlin and McBride had finished their sessions at the piano, their rapidly sketched scores were handed to two orchestrators on Shaindlin's staff, who would break down the musical themes and sequences into the various parts for the recording orchestra.

With the passing of years stereotyped, predictable scenes and sequences appeared in *March of Time* issues. In these cases, in order to save time Shaindlin simply went to his library of previously written scores and pulled out the appropriate one for the scene at hand. Shaindlin recalled an example:

There was a sequence which was very predictable. It was a school in session. For instance, Officer's School, and this was a minute and forty seconds of predictable music, so I would pull out an orchestration. . . . And the narration would go like this: "Today, the technical knowledge is passed on to a younger generation. . . ." Then we see a clean young man—you know, without sin—and I would have *this* [plays piano again]. There was no sense in writing it [anew]. It's all obvious—let's pull out No. 379 and we put that in the orchestra book. . . . Then after that, we'd go into a title called "The Pearl Harbor Syndrome" . . . and there'd be narration all over the place. . . . Mind you, it was played each time by the orchestra, but the music was existing.

Shaindlin used a twenty- to twenty-two-piece orchestra, the instrumentation of which was usually as follows: 3 trumpets, 2 trombones, 2 French horns, 4 woodwinds (flute, oboe, clarinet, and bassoon), 1 bass, 6 violins, piano, percussion. Unlike many feature films for which the music is recorded in segments on "A & B rolls," the *March of Time*'s music was recorded straight through, one reel at a time. Because each issue ran two reels, this meant two, nonstop recording sessions.

The selection of musical sequences, the order in which they were played, and the tempo at which they were conducted were related by Shaindlin to the already edited motion picture by means of the footage "counts" shown on the cue sheets provided by the editing department. These same counts (e.g., "110 feet," "235 feet," etc.) were written by him onto his conducting score with a heavy crayon. By varying both the length and tempo of the various musical selections, and comparing the footage counts on his score with a footage counter that operated in front of him during the recording session, Shaindlin could be sure of exact synchronism between his music, the already edited images on the screen, and the previously recorded narration.

Luckily, Louis never attended the recording sessions, or they never would have finished anything. Instead, as with narration recording, he sent Lothar Wolff to oversee the job. Everyone knew what Louis *didn't* want, which was subtle or unconventional music. As a consequence, the music was loud, brassy, and ominous. Shaindlin got along very well with de Rochemont and admired him immensely, but he had no illusions about introducing subtleties into the *March of Time*'s music, nor did anyone else who worked with Louis. De Rochemont may have counterpointed his narration and images, but he wanted his music to state and restate the points that were made on the screen.

Shaindlin recalled an instance when Louis exploded after hearing the final "mix" of a newly completed issue. "What in hell happened to the music?" he asked Shaindlin. "What do you mean, Louis?" asked Jack. "When we cut to Washington, D.C.," said

Perhaps the most famous musical "signature" in the history of the American film were these bars which opened every *March of Time* issue. (Courtesy Jack Shaindlin)

Louis, "we should hear BOOM, deBOOM, deBOOM!" said Louis. "Sure, Louis, you bet," said Jack, and dutifully went back to the recording studio to put in the BOOM, deBOOM, deBOOM's.

Occasionally, as with the release of the *March of Time* issue "One Day of War," the music received special praise from the reviewers. For the most part, however, people either ignored it, forgot it, or forgave it. Shaindlin, very much the professional, viewed the whole experience philosophically, referring to the music that Louis required as "creative banality." "It was quantitative, not qualitative," he concluded. "Of course, you never argue with success. It worked, and Louis knew exactly what would make it work."

One last decision-making step remained before release of the finished film. Without exception, all releases were viewed by *Time*'s legal staff, whose job it was to anticipate actions for libel, slander, and invasion of privacy. There is, of course, no way of knowing what conversations took place over the years between de Rochemont and Larsen, and how many changes may have been required of the former by the latter. It is naïve to believe that a multimillion dollar publishing corporation would allow its progress to be jeopardized in any profound way by the idiosyncrasies of one temperamental film maker. For that matter, journalistic practice throughout the country, led largely by Time-Life publications, was undergoing startling changes during the 1930's, becoming simultaneously more sophisticated, more aggressive, and more outrageous. *Time* and *Life* magazines themselves were regularly sued and censored throughout the United States and in foreign countries. It was a game that Luce, Larsen, and de Rochemont not only enjoyed playing, but also helped to invent and to write the rules for, and the business of irritating both readers and subjects was one of its features. The regular, prerelease examination of *March of Time* issues by the legal staff provided a monitoring function which allowed responsible executives to assess the likelihood of legal actions, to determine the extent of their probable liability, and to prepare for such legal eventualities as seemed likely. As a result, the *March of Time* rarely, if ever, lost a case. Nearly all suits filed were either dropped along the way or settled out of court for symbolic considerations.

Once the lawyers had departed, the final "mix" of music, narration, and sound effects tracks was made for the American edition. For foreign release, the music and effects tracks were retained as is and were remixed with the appropriate foreign-language narration. Cutters then conformed the original negative to the edited work print, and the finished "action" and "track" negatives were sent over to Deluxe Laboratories for the printing of the more than 100 prints required for theatrical release in the United States. (For release in foreign countries, a "married" dupe negative of the finished film, with appropriate narration, was usually shipped to Dick de Rochemont, who arranged for the making of release prints within each of the different countries involved.)

Did *March of Time* staffers ever see their own work in theaters with real audiences? Some did, some didn't.

Researcher Mary Losey:

I got very involved, and I certainly went. I saw it a lot. I was very interested to see how audiences were reacting to it. Curiously enough, I had not been interested at all in film until I started working for the *March of Time*. I thought I wanted to be a journalist.

Writer Jimmy Shute:

Not very often. As a matter of fact, I remember going to see one of the first ones I ever did work on, and I went to Radio City Music Hall to see it, and I could hardly understand it. It all went so fast. . . . I never was much interested in movies, although I was making them.

Writer and associate producer Arthur Tourtellot:

Oh, sure. I did make a point of doing that. . . . I remember long before I ever had any association with the *March of Time* I was always gratified if I went to a theater and, wholly unknown to me, a *March of Time* was going to be shown. I think most people had that attitude.

Assistant producer and chief film editor Lothar Wolff:

Oh, my God! Frequently! That was the only way you could get an impression as to how the public reacted.

Senior associate producer Tom Orchard:

No, I never did, except . . . the first one, I think. We had sort of sneak previews. I have a vague memory of going somewhere up in the Bronx once to look at it and to see how the audience reacted. That's the only time I ever remember.

Director Jack Glenn:

Oh, yes! . . . Greatest joy in life, sitting back in the dark theater and seeing the results of your work.

And so it went, another issue finished. The next day, the whole process began all over again, the same tensions mounting, a new deadline approaching.

10

Eleventh Hour:
A Time for all Things

Needed respite from the excitement created by "Inside Nazi Germany—1938" was provided by the *March of Time*'s second issue of 1938, containing three subjects: "Russians in Exile," an examination of the roles played by white Russian exiles in the United States; "Old Dixie's New Boom," a dramatic announcement of the discovery of new sources of paper and pulpwood in southern slash pine trees; and "One Million Missing," a cinematic trip through New York's Missing Persons Bureau.

In its third release of the year, the *March of Time* returned to its examination of the nearly defunct League of Nations. In a bitter review, the film's editors paraded the failures of the League— Germany rearming; Japan marching into China; Japan, Germany, and Italy quitting the impotent League. The Voice of Time sadly concluded: "With mounting bills the nations move toward war." The film had been put together mostly with newsreel stock-shot footage, although the medium shot of Italian delegates whistling and booing Haile Selassie's speech had been re-created in the staff's New York studios. On March 26 even the usually jocund *New Yorker* found the film sobering: "The chapter on the League of Nations in 'The March of Time,' tracing its story from Wilson to

Eden, deserves all your attention and may well occupy your mind during the long hours of the night."

MOT's April release, entitled "Nazi Conquest—No. 1," was another spirited look at Adolf Hitler and his return to Austria, the place of his birth, following the Anschluss—an event which was, as the *March of Time* pointed out, fully foreshadowed in *Mein Kampf,* Hitler's autobiography. The film's editors prophetically labeled the event a prelude to further steps outlined in the 14-year-old book. Included in the film was an admiring reenactment of the 24-hour scoop and on-the-spot coverage from Vienna of the invasion of Austria by N.B.C.'s radio correspondent Max Jordan.

Although impartial observers endorsed "Nazi Conquest—No. 1" as an unbiased account of Hitler's Austrian coup, the entire episode was rejected by the Warner Brothers theater circuit, as was "Inside Nazi Germany—1938." Joseph Bernhard, general manager of the circuit, announced the ban without further comment.

Issue No. 10 of Volume 4, released in May 1938, was the last of the three-episode issues. Included in it were "Friend of the People," an interesting study of the average day of an American congressman; "Racketeers vs. Housewives," an exposé of the methods of dishonest salesmen and storekeepers; and "England's Bankrupt Peers," a brief examination of the plight of Britain's highly taxed aristocracy.

"Men of Medicine," the June release, was the first *March of Time* issue since "Inside Nazi Germany—1938" to feature a single subject. One of Louis de Rochemont's favorite films, it provided a thought-provoking appraisal of the contemporary medical practitioner and the long-range scientific, social, and professional medical program of which he was a part. Although proudly spotlighting the million-dollars-a-day free medical care donated by U.S. doctors to the needy, the *March of Time* painted a general picture of inadequate medical care for large segments of the public. Warned the Voice of Time: ". . . out of range of any doctor's care are hundreds of thousands of U.S. citizens. And in many out-of-the-way sections, whole counties are too poor to support a single doctor. . . . Among rural Negroes, unattended sickness and uncontrolled disease is pushing up the national death rate."

The film regretted the inability of the medical profession to consolidate its forces and energies into a permanent, workable program of medical aid for the underprivileged. Appearing in the film were Surgeon-General Parran, who urged that appropriations be taken from regular tax funds for medical care of the indigent, and Dr. John Peters of Yale, who advocated a special tax to effect the same revenue. Opposing both plans was Dr. Morris Fishbein, publicist for the American Medical Association, who found in their proposals the specter of government bureaucracy. The film ended on a positive note, with predictions of improved public health programs, new drugs and medical techniques, and the lengthening of the American citizen's life span.

The vagaries of international power politics provided graphic material for the next eight issues, appearing between July 1938 and January 1939. "G-Men of the Sea" examined the role of the United States Coast Guard as protector of American territorial waters. "Threat to Gibraltar" found England and France fighting fascist uprisings among the Moorish natives of the International Zone of Tangier, forty miles away from Gibraltar.

"Prelude to Conquest," the *March of Time*'s September release, provided a striking example of the producers' success in prognosticating news events and backlogging pertinent footage. The film continued the examination of Hitler's rise to power begun by the *March of Time* in its earlier film, "Nazi Conquest No. 1." In this second film, audiences found Hitler in possession of Austria and greedily eyeing Czechoslovakia. The *March of Time* carefully outlined the position of the Sudeten German-speaking population as pawns in the German state's bid for territorial expansion. Cameras showed mobilization of German troops as Czech President Eduard Beñes denied German demands. The film was released on September 2, 1938. Within three weeks after its release, the Czechoslovakian crisis climaxed at Munich. Reviewing this timely film on January 14, 1970, Bosley Crowther of the *New York Times* suggested, "The suspicion is beginning to get around that the boys at the March of Time have an inside wire. . . . [The release] anticipated the event with virtual clairvoyance."

In the same reel, the lighter side of the news was illuminated with the return of the *March of Time*'s crowd pleaser, black religious leader, Father Divine, in an episode directed again by Jack

Glenn. By this time, Divine was running for President of the United States. Increasingly successful in his political/religious activities, he had purchased, or perhaps had been given, the buildings and property at "Crum Elbow" across the river from Franklin Roosevelt's home at Hyde Park.

VOICE OF TIME

And then, on the veranda at Crum Elbow, one of the oldest and proudest estates on the Hudson, dark strangers appeared whose voices, it is said, sometimes floated across the river to Crum Elbow's neighboring estate—the ancestral home of a substantial old Dutch family, the Franklin Roosevelts.

Divine's new estate was called "Crum Elbow" after its original Dutch name "Krum Elbooge." The estate had belonged to a man named Howland Spencer.

VOICE OF TIME

Of all Hudson River squires, none has been so bitter or so violent toward another squire as anti-New Dealer HOWLAND SPENCER has been towards his neighbor Franklin Roosevelt—just across the river. The Spencer-Roosevelt feud dates back to the days when the name of Spencer's estate—Crum Elbow—was appropriated to describe the summer White House.

Spencer explained his gift/sale of the land for *March of Time* cameras:

SPENCER I am turning Crum Elbow over to Father Divine because I believe Father Divine's ideas will triumph over those of Roosevelt. Where President Roosevelt encourages the debtors, Father Divine encourages the thrifty. President Roosevelt is destroying national character—Father Divine is building it up. . . .

I am backing the Divine deal against the New Deal. And we shall see who does the most for this country—a messiah at the White House or a God at Crum Elbow.

Father Divine cooperated with Jack Glenn a second time for a 1938 issue entitled "Father Divine's Deal." The film described the religious leader's acquisition of an estate across the Hudson River from Franklin Roosevelt's property. Divine's new estate had been owned by Howland Spencer, an opponent of Roosevelt's New Deal administration. (Courtesy Jack Glenn)

The film had a surreal ambience throughout. Divine consented to appear in a filmed interview with a *New York Times* reporter named Robert Bird, provided that Glenn, whom he trusted, appeared in the same shot. Glenn did so, entering into the experience with great enthusiasm and asking several of the more important questions.

The original filmed interview, which still exists *in toto* in the *March of Time*'s stock-shot library, ran for several minutes, of which only a few seconds appeared in the fast-moving finished film. Both Glenn and the *New York Times* reporter tried to probe Divine's income-tax position, the matter of financial accountability within his growing organization, allegations of coercion of members of his cult, and purported claims of his divinity, but without success. Like many politicians, Divine had a substantial command of non sequitur.

Eleventh Hour: A Time for All Things

GLENN What is the "Promised Land?"

DIVINE We may take the "Promised Land" to be a place in the consciousness in my—conscious, although a place geographically mine, but set apart from time to time by the work or righteousness to be exemplified in most places as the situation in the consciousness of the people.

GLENN When Father as a person, not working impersonally, needs cash money, what does he do?

DIVINE I do not need any money.

GLENN Well, what they call in a business, petty cash? Do they say Father Divine's heavenly storage of money—how does he work it?

DIVINE It is a matter of the workings of the cooperative system, as it actually is manifest in the material world that they are in the cooperative system, according to the way I see it, is through the individual's harmonizing together for one common purpose.

Glenn enjoyed Divine's personal style. He recalled making a shot in which Divine and his followers were photographed boarding a Hudson River boat to visit their new property up-stream. In the midst of the shot, Divine slipped and tumbled down. Glenn asked him if he'd like to have the scene reshot. "Oh, no, that's fine," said Father. "I want to show 'em that no matter who you are, you can still fall!"

The finished film was adroitly edited. Divine and his "angels" are seen washing the walls of the estate, enthusiastically singing hymns. The film cuts at this point to a stock shot of the Roosevelts inside their Hyde Park home, turning their heads as if listening to the off-screen singing. F.D.R. quipped (as quoted by Walter Winchell, who appeared in the film), "Well, it is good to know we will have some nice neighbors for a change."

"The British Dilemma," also released in September, examined England's position as the one nation specifically excluded from war with Germany in Hitler's *Mein Kampf*. The *March of Time* pictured England's millions praying for guidance as they made ready for the coming war. The film was drastically cut in England by British censors.

Journalistically speaking, the *March of Time* had earned a first-

Divine agreed to be interviewed for the *March of Time* camera and microphone providing Jack Glenn (right) appeared in the scene with him. In center, *New York Times* reporter Robert Bird. Cameraman Johnny Geisel adjusts light at right. Man at left is Divine's secretary. (Courtesy Jack Glenn)

class reputation for calling the shots accurately, just ahead of events, and for hard-headed, accurate judgments of the military capabilities of foreign nations. Still, as with any analyst, it did make mistakes, and when it did, they were big ones. Louis was clearly overimpressed with the "defense mentality" and the fortifications that went with it, all of which had become anachronisms in an age of the devastating *Blitzkrieg*. In July 1937, the Voice of Time had found Hawaii "the most formidably fortified area in the world." The Island of Oahu, on which Pearl Harbor was located, was reported as being "impregnable to attack."

With the release of "Inside the Maginot Line" in October 1938, the *March of Time*'s military judgment hit a real low. A single-subject issue, with exciting, exclusive footage, the film proudly exhibited the French fortifications as France's bid for an invincible defense against German land armies. Extending 125 miles from the Belgian border to the Swiss frontier, and stocked to withstand a year's siege, the Maginot Line was shown supported by an army described in the film as "the most formidable fighting machine in Europe today." The film was lavish in its praise of the French commander-in-chief, described as "able strategist General Marie Gustave Gamelin." This is the same man of whom military writer F. W. Winterbotham wrote thirty-six years later in *The Ultra Secret:* "It seems almost impossible to believe that General Gamelin, the French Commander-in-Chief, had so staked his reputation on his assessment that the Germans could not and would not attack through the Ardennes that he refused to change his mind or his strategy. It is difficult to say more without accusing Gamelin of treason."

If Louis had looked a little more critically at the Francophilic screed that he and his staff had written for Van Voorhis's narration, he would have recognized it for the wishful thinking that it was. Over scenes of a sloppy, disheveled-looking group of French soldiers, we hear the Voice of Time assure:

> In comparison with soldiers in armies where strict attention is paid to every detail of military dress, a company of French recruits may appear slovenly. . . .
>
> After a few months of training, while their bearing may lack traditional military smartness, French recruits are on their way to becoming soldiers. . . .

The film had originally been conceived and produced as a "featurette," running about an hour. Richard de Rochemont scooped the newsreels by gaining access to the impressive fortifications of the Maginot Line, shooting thousands of feet of film of its most intimate and interesting details. It was another "first" for the *March of Time.*

Richard had intended to premier the 60-minute film at a theater on the Champs Élysées, at about the same time it was released in the United States. "We had the cooperation at that point of the army," recalled Dick de Rochemont, "and it [the film] was quite a document." At the last minute, however, the French Foreign Office required that it be withdrawn entirely. "They were afraid that it might irritate the Germans," said Dick, which seemed as preposterous an explanation then as it does now. De Rochemont had to withdraw the film, of course, and after negotiations with the French government, the American version was shortened to a more conventional length of 20 minutes for the October 1938 release. So far as Richard is aware, the longer version no longer exists, although out-takes survive in the *March of Time*'s stock-shot library.

The November release, "Uncle Sam: The Good Neighbor," showed Secretary of State Cordell Hull's efforts to recruit able citizens for careers in the U.S. foreign service. Spotlighted were U.S. efforts to strengthen Latin-American relations and to effect political solidarity in the Western Hemisphere.

The last of this group of "crisis" films was "The Refugee—Today and Tomorrow," which vividly portrayed the plight of homeless, persecuted refugees in Central Europe and Asia. The film was an artful blend of authentic footage and reenactments. The authentic material was powerful, especially that photographed by *March of Time* cameramen in Amsterdam. The following excerpts from their dope sheets, published here for the first time, suggest the grim and bizarre world with which they dealt:

[Dec. 1938]: Shot of sign, Dutch Jewish Hospital. End of reel. All these shots have been made with difficulty; the Jews are so scared and afraid to be photographed, for fear that German agents may recognize them in America and take revenge on their relatives in Germany. This sounds absurd, but many refused to come into the shots.

[December 6, 1938]: At this point a Jew charged the camera, knocked it over and injured the spring. [December 7, 1938]: It is impossible to direct these Dutch Jews, they crowd around the camera when it is on a tripod, refuse to go away, laugh, and play the fool.

The numerous reenactments in the film included shots of Gestapo headquarters (made at *March of Time*'s New York studios), and prisoners and concentration camp grave sites (photographed on Staten Island). Ironically, when *March of Time*'s British cameraman Jimmy Hodgson shipped some very good footage of the interrogation of refugees at London's Woburn House, he enclosed a note which emphasized: "This was *not* a re-enactment, but an authentic case."

The finished film was as up-to-date as possible. Studio re-creations were still being shot for insertion when the final sound mix was completed at midnight on December 18, 1938. The film was well received by critics, and established, beyond question, the antifascist position of the film's producers. Basil Wright, reviewing the film in *Spectator* on January 13, 1939, wrote:

> It attacks Japan and it attacks Hitler and his gang with stinging and unequivocal accusations of barbarisms and the commentator's grim story is punched home point by point by the well-edited scenes, many of which are in themselves accusations, which would take some answering.

Alex Glendinning, writing in the English magazine, *Nineteenth Century* in February, wrote:

> It is encouraging to find, after so much attempted suppression of fact in the cinema, that the latest issue of the March of Time news-reel has been permitted to state the truth about the refugee problem. It is something of a novelty in England to hear a news-reel commentator refer to Japan as an "aggressor" and to the "looting" of Japanese soldiers. The account of Hitler's pogroms, in word and picture, is equally direct. There may have been cuts made in this reel—some of the sequences towards the end seem a little disconnected—but it does give a clear and uncompromising picture of the refugee problem and how it has come about.

From the small group of film workers at the old 54th Street Fox studios in 1935, the *March of Time* staff had now grown to fifty-eight permanent employees, not including numerous contributing cameramen throughout the world and the reportorial manpower of Time, Inc.

Expanding also were the production and editorial facilities of the organization. On April 29, 1938, a portion of the administration offices were moved to the Time and Life Building in Rockefeller Center, where the publishing concern occupied the upper seven floors. A year later, another floor was taken by *March of*

Time at 369 Lexington Avenue for its production facilities, giving them three floors.

The *March of Time,* just celebrating its third anniversary, now reached a monthly theatrical audience of between 20 and 26 million people in between 9000 and 10,000 theaters within the United States alone—an unprecedented audience for a film series. Inevitably, words of caution and criticism mingled with congratulatory birthday greetings.

Frank Nugent, writing for the *New York Times* on March 6, 1938, suspected that *MOT* issues were not reaching audiences intact. Nugent had previously accused exhibitors of cutting scenes from *March of Time* issues in their neighborhood showings:

> The March of Time will have to wait a bit longer to be congratulated and the theatre operators will have to content themselves with a guarded apology; maybe they do not edit down the pictures, but some one does, for we have seen films with scenes missing and lines of dialogue omitted.

Writing years later, Richard de Rochemont confirmed Nugent's suspicions:

> In the United States there was no real [official] censorship problem, but this was amply compensated for by the cowardice of the average exhibitor—the average, I say, not all. These craven businessmen wanted to hear only laughter—and none of that "political" laughter either—and applause. A "boo" would send him quavering to the booth to see what was being protested, and three complaints from patrons would make him talk of pulling out the reel.

Re-creation and staging of unprocurable footage continued as a prominent feature of *March of Time* productions. Perhaps as much as 40 per cent of the controversial "Nazi Conquest No. 1" had been pieced together with staged material, an artifice which did not escape reviewers at *Variety* and other trade papers.

De Rochemont and his people rarely bothered to defend these techniques; they were concerned mostly with justifying their overall treatment. Curiously, it is only in retrospect that this technique appears controversial.

"Looking back," said associate producer Lothar Wolff,

I find it so fascinating to see how our tastes have changed. Take this reenactment, the entire approach to reenactment. It just looks so incongruous to us now and as I think back to the time when the *March of Time* was produced, nobody thought anything about it. . . . The narration carried it, and reenacted footage was used as illustration. . . . It was just an accepted way of communicating—that you used an actor when you couldn't get the real people. Nobody ever questioned it then. . . . Can you imagine doing that today?

Also, [continued Wolff] looking at this equipment. Can you imagine what one could have done with a 16mm camera, which you could take on your shoulder? . . . In those days you had to carry 70 pounds of camera and tripod and lights, which is one of the reasons why reenactment had to be used. You just couldn't be fast enough; that's one of the reasons you had to re-create.

What was so astonishing about the *March of Time*'s reenactments was not its early use of impersonators, but, with the passing of time, its use of famous men and women themselves.

Why did such celebrated figures appear on *March of Time* screens, especially when experience told some of them that they might very well be compromised or even humiliated? They appeared because no matter what the hazards, the *March of Time,* with over 20 million viewers in the United States alone, provided visibility for them and their ideas which was of incalculable value. No matter how minimal a person's contribution to society, or how zany his philosophy or behavior, his appearance on the *March of Time* conferred a measure of legitimacy upon him. "The prestige of the thing was almost inconceivable," recalled writer Jimmy Shute. "The most famous people would turn handsprings for us, and, I remember, I would write speeches for presidents and cabinet members [laughs] and I wasn't telling them exactly what to say, but frequently they did, to my suprise."

Van Voorhis's "Voice of the Tomb," strained with alarm and a prophet's doom, continued to pontificate dramatically over the powerful images that passed across the *March of Time*'s screens as 1938 drew to a close. This characteristic overdramatization of current events was of special interest to John Grierson, whose 1943 comparison of the Voice of Time's presentation with elements of

Greek theater is reminiscent of George Dangerfield's reviews of the first *March of Time* issues.

The voice is authoritative to the point of emphasis. In a world which is sure of nothing, it is supremely sure of itself. Call this oversimplification if you like, yet it gives *March of Time* some of its urgency. Like the buskins on Greek actors it helps to lift puny events to size and significance. There is in *March of Time* always something of an issue. The human mind is beset with a problem; a nation is under threat; deep, devious, and dangerous possibilities open out across some placid sea. A cloud no bigger than a man's hand, but presaging tragedy, appears in some halcyon sky. The dramatic pattern is simple, but it is dramatic. Mr. Van Voorhis, the Voice of Time, is very good at clouds no bigger than a man's hand.

The first release of 1939 was "State of the Nation," a 20-minute appraisal of the U.S. economy, government, and public sentiment. Leaning heavily on the findings of *Fortune* magazine's statistical savant, Elmer Roper, the issue revealed that 59 per cent of the public still supported Franklin Roosevelt's administration. Although optimistically picturing increased production and economic recovery, the film cautiously reminded audiences of the 10 million unemployed across the land.

The February release featured two episodes: "Mexico's New Crisis," a review of President Cárdenas's administration and his programs for modernizing Mexico, and "Young America," an encouraging appraisal of the Boy Scouts of America. This was the last "two-subject" film ever released by the *March of Time*. Henceforth, all issues featured a single subject.

Several other issues released during the spring of 1939 featured domestic issues. "Dixie—U.S.A." provided a cinematic tour of the southern states, nominated by *Time* as the nation's number one economic problem. Cited in the film were the accomplishments of the Civilian Conservation Corps, the Tuskegee Institute, the Berry School of Atlanta, and the National Emergency Council.

"The Movies March On!" produced in association with the Museum of Modern Art, provided an entertaining and affectionate portrait of Hollywood's film industry, in which the medium's remarkable 40-year history was traced from silent shorts to musical comedy features.

"Metropolis—1939" reviewed the problems of the New York police authorities in patroling and supervising a 325-square-mile city of seven and a half million citizens. The accomplishments of Mayor LaGuardia and Police Commissioner Valentine were stressed in this issue.

From March to September 1939 another series of "crisis" films, outlining the spread of war throughout the world, was released. "The Mediterranean—Background for War" found Mussolini seeking control of Tunisia, and with it, control of Europe's inland sea. The *March of Time* showed France's Daladier assembling the French navy and preparing to defend the Mediterranean from fascism.

"Japan—Master of the Orient" reviewed that empire's "record of shameful examples of unprovoked aggression." The Voice of Time stated: "Sober Japanese wonder fearfully how long the patience of the great Western nations will brook this lawless threat to the peace of the world."

"War, Peace, and Propaganda" was a patch job of newsreel clips and staged material, examining the role of British propaganda aimed at Americans. Using techniques reminiscent of "Inside Nazi Germany—1938," the producer of the film incorporated a narration track which did not always follow the visual material, and the issue was severely criticized. On June 17 *Nation* magazine's reviewer concluded:

> However right they may be, words not backed up by pictorial evidence give the impression of propaganda. This is especially bad if the picture wants to expose propaganda. . . . "March of Time" has often done a good job and has won confidence. Its prestige should spur its makers to greater accuracy and not to relax. . . .

"Soldiers with Wings" covered the growth of American aeronautics and the revolutionary changes that air power had brought to the world. United States plans for a vast $200 million program of aircraft construction were revealed. Lamenting American unpreparedness, the Voice of Time pointed ominously to Europe, where citizens lived in constant fear of death from the sky.

VOICE OF TIME

In the years since the First World War there has emerged a new
and powerful weapon—a force so terrible that its threat alone has
conquered weak nations, remade the map of Europe and shifted
the balance of power in the world today. Already, through this
one force—air power—small men have risen to might and stature.
And small nations have become empires by building up armies of
the air, legions of soldiers with wings.

The film was released on September 1, 1939. On the same day,
5000 miles eastward, German bombers swept through European
skies unchallenged as a mighty Nazi army invaded Poland. Within
forty-eight hours, Britain and France were at war with Germany.

By coincidence, Dick de Rochemont was in Warsaw at the time,
trying to acquire footage for a new *March of Time* issue on that
country's military crisis. De Rochemont's progress had been slowed
by the Polish government's discovery that two local cameramen
whom he had hired were Jewish. Anti-Semitism being almost as
strong in Poland as it was in Germany, the Polish government had
withheld the credentials from de Rochemont which would have
permitted him free movement across the country until such time
as he had discharged the Jewish cameramen.

Louis learned of the Germans' march across Poland's border
before Dick knew of it in Warsaw. Louis managed to get a call
through to Dick on *Time*'s leased trans-Atlantic telephone lines,
and Dick and his people made their way safely out of the country
before it fell.

Back in New York, the producers of the *March of Time* began
preparing Americans for war.

11

The Ramparts We Watch

For some time, Louis de Rochemont had been trying to bring Time, Inc., into the production of feature-length motion pictures. The closest he had come to it was "Inside the Maginot Line," described in the previous chapter. Originally produced as a 60-minute "featurette," it had been truncated as a result of political pressure from the French government.

The leadership of Time, Inc., ever sensitive about its image, debated the notion of feature film making for several years. "It obviously couldn't do something with Jimmy Cagney and Greta Garbo," said Tom Orchard. "Certain rules had to be laid down."

At one point in the late 1930's, serious consideration was given to the release of a feature-length documentary based upon footage that expeditionary cameraman Roy Phelps had shot with Armond Denis in the Belgian Congo. The character, problems, and future of colonialism in the world was already being widely debated, and it was thought that the Phelps/Denis footage might provide the point of departure for a provocative discussion of the subject. In the end, the idea was rejected and the Phelps film was subsequently completed and released by others in 1938 under the title, *Dark Rapture*.

By late 1938, de Rochemont and Larsen had begun plans for a film which would draw a parallel between the international tensions, political pressures, and military adventures then operating throughout the world, and similar events which had occurred twenty-five years earlier, and which had led the United States into the First World War.

It was decided to re-create these earlier events, interpreting the political and military issues of World War I through their impact upon the day-to-day lives of the middle-class members of a typical American community in a typical American town. For Louis that meant New England, and the town of New London, Connecticut, was chosen for the story.

The film's script, written by Robert L. Richards and Cedric R. Worth, fictionalized the reluctance of this town's citizens to face political and military realities in 1914; the eagerness of the town's young men to get into the war before it ended; the disruptive effects of the war, once declared, upon the small community and its various racial/national groups; and the inevitable despair of parents, wives, and lovers, who saw their men disappear into the trenches of Europe.

The argument of the script was that world peace, the integrity of small nations, and the American ideal of democratic government were threatened by foreign ideologies and by powerful military forces. The tendency of Americans toward isolationism and the nation's lack of psychological and military preparedness, both in 1914 and 1939, were also emphasized.

Production was authorized by the corporation in 1939. Soon thereafter, dope sheets with this title began to appear in the production records of the *March of Time,* as special newsreel and stock footage was gradually accumulated for it. By the time the film was finally finished, the staff had viewed tens of thousands of feet of both newsreel and official World War I footage for scenes of battle, political and military personalities, and contemporary America. It was intended that, whenever possible, authentic locations were to be used for the film's dramatic scenes—a lawyer's office, a newspaper's editorial offices and linotype rooms, the kitchens, dining rooms, and parlors of real homes, and the streets, sidewalks, houses, and store fronts of New London. The practice of filming stories in authentic locations, rather than on Hollywood sound stages or studio back lots was a novelty in 1940; it was not until well into the 1950's that the practice became commonplace for dramatic productions. Many of the settings in *The Ramparts We Watch* were undeniably real, imparting a heightened credibility to de Rochemont's film. For the sake of convenience an abandoned silk mill in the New London area was rented for $150 a month to provide headquarters and necessary studio space for the group. As with all *March of Time* films, the cinematic treatment throughout was to be technically direct—"No panning, trucking, or trick shots through the strings of a harp," as one staff member put it.

Instead of using professional actors, as in an historical drama, it was decided to cast ordinary citizens in the various roles that were required. As documentary film makers have discovered over the years, the direction of nonprofessional performers in a scripted show has both advantages and hazards. If they pantomime their roles and do not speak their lines their performances are often quite convincing, especially when they move through familiar environments, performing actions that are typical for them in their everyday lives. Directors who prefer to use "real" people in such roles argue that no professional can imitate the original properly, and, in the work of film artists from Flaherty to Rouquier, many splendid documentary films support this point of view. Unfortunately, the realism that one achieves through such casting usually disappears when these untrained actors speak. Lacking the long, disciplined training and the necessary talent that the professional brings to his or her work, the amateur's utterances are often wooden, unconvincing, and embarrassing. And so it was to be, to some extent, with *The Ramparts We Watch*.

More than 1400 townspeople and other nonprofessionals played parts in the production. Of these, seventy-three were said to have speaking parts. The role of an elderly German professor was played by a physician and his son by a Brown University undergraduate. The parts of a clergyman and a Hungarian housewife were played by their real-life counterparts. No more appropriate hero for the film could have been found than the fictitious editor of the small town's newspaper, played by John Adair. Smoothly

245

intercut throughout, in typical *March of Time* style, were authentic shots of well-known World War I figures—Woodrow Wilson, General Pershing, Theodore Roosevelt, Herbert Hoover, and many others. The costuming and "dressing" of sets was as authentic as the producers could make it. For example, the scene of the patriotic parade of townspeople through New London streets (which was shot three times) required removal of all neon signs, post-1915 advertisements, and miscellaneous 1939 bric-a-brac.

Production on the film began in the spring of 1939 and continued until August 1940, the usual chaos of *March of Time* production being compounded by the fact that monthly issues of the regular film series had to be produced and released during the same period. "There was really no script when production started in an empty factory loft in New London," wrote editor Lothar Wolff. "The scenes were usually written the night before. There were several directors on the film—simultaneously—with de Rochemont telling them what to do.

Midway through production, the Second World War, which the film's story foretold, exploded in Europe. The German *Blitzkrieg* rolled across Poland and the Low Countries, nicely illustrating de Rochemont's points but requiring numerous revisions and reshooting during production. Originally budgeted at $200,000, the film is said to have cost twice that figure.

For Louis, it must have been reminiscent of his *March of the Years* series re-creating the past, but this time on a much larger scale. The film's story had been designed in such a manner that only the most obtuse members of the audience could fail to grasp the moral and see the similarities between the totalitarian ambitions of the Kaiser's Germany in 1914 and Hitler's in 1939. Just to make sure that no one missed the point, however, Louis looked around for a sure-fire finish that would bring the film up-to-date in a journalistically flamboyant manner. He finally found his ending in the recently released Nazi propaganda combat film entitled *Feldzug in Polen* (a version of which was released in the United States as *Baptism of Fire*), a bloodcurdling account of the successful invasion and conquest of Poland in September 1939. The film had been intended by Hitler to be seen widely throughout Europe and the western hemisphere, and to intimidate not only French

Publicity still of rehearsal of a scene from *The Ramparts We Watch*. Louis sits behind camera at right. Associate producer Tom Orchard stands at center next to narrator Westbrook Van Voorhis (seated) and Charlie Gilson (standing). John Geisel is at extreme right. (Courtesy Time, Inc.)

and British leaders, then at war with Germany, but also opinion leaders in neutral nations. It was privately screened for officials in many foreign capitals, for whom it provided an impressive portrait of Nazi military might. In the United States, it was shown to members of Congress in Washington, and was licensed by the German film company, UFA, for release in American theaters.

Louis decided to end *Ramparts* with a few minutes of carefully edited and narrated excerpts from this Nazi propaganda film. He had to acquire rights to it from UFA, but the German government, already having had unhappy experiences with the *March of Time,* would not license the film for de Rochemont's use unless he incorporated the original narration, unedited. Louis decided otherwise. In the end, always the professional newsreeler out for his scoop, he got the footage on his own terms, but only after executing some of the most circuitous, devious, and complicated maneuvers ever undertaken by a film producer.

Feldzug in Polen ran eight reels (about 80 minutes) in length. Apparently de Rochemont acquired a print of the film from UFA in June 1940 and secretly made a copy of it. Out of this, he extracted about 10 minutes' worth of footage and edited a preliminary "rough cut," with new narration, music, and sound. The "rough cut" represented an editing of the sequence which would ultimately be inserted into *The Ramparts We Watch*. The original, pro-Nazi narration had, of course, been replaced with a new one.

Whether because of the legal problems involved in the use of this dupe, or the poor quality of Louis's copy, an entirely different print of *Feldzug in Polen* was apparently used to generate the dupe negative for the sequence used in *Ramparts*. This new dupe was lent by John Grierson who was then with the National Film Board of Canada. It was shipped via railway express on August 23, 1940, and received at *March of Time* headquarters the next day by editor Jack Bradford. In a memo dated August 24, Louis instructed Bradford to make from the Grierson print a new dupe negative of the desired scenes and to use it for final printing so that it conformed exactly to the already edited "rough cut." Subsequent to this, as described in a memo dated Jan. 16, 1941, which was prepared by Bradford for business manager John Wood (possibly for legal reasons), all of the original dupe negative footage that had first been made from the UFA print was returned to UFA.

Notwithstanding the evidence in the production files, the exact manner in which Louis acquired the duped footage of *Feldzug in Polen* is not clear. In an interview on June 25, 1975, de Rochemont told me that a print of the film had been brought to his studios by German consular officials and that while he sat in the screening room with them, watching the film, *MOT* technicians secretly duped the film in their laboratory downstairs, a reel at a time. Louis said he then sent the duped print up to Canada by train with Victor Jurgens, having advised the Canadian officials ahead of time of the arrival of this propaganda film into their country. Canadian officials seized the print and sent Jurgens back to the U.S. De Rochemont said that he then arranged with friends at the Canadian Alien Property Custodian's office to buy the print back from Canada for a few dollars, and that he and his wife personally went to Canada to reacquire the print and to bring it back to New York. Quite possibly, it was this "laundered" print that was used for cutting purposes, and the newer, better-quality print that Grierson shipped on August 23, 1940, that was used for final duping purposes. Alternatively, it is possible that the first dupe was used for final integration into the feature negative and that Grierson sent Louis junk footage as a "cover" for the whole operation. The entire business is quite complicated and difficult to piece together today, thirty-five years later. However Louis got the footage, the negative had been well laundered along the way, and he released a story to the press which stated that the footage had come from a copy of the film seized by British authorities in Bermuda.

The Ramparts We Watch, with its explosive, recut and narrated Nazi footage, was finally released on August 30, 1940, opening first at Loew's Palace Theater in Memphis, and booked nationwide by Warner Brothers, Fox-National, R.K.O., and numerous other circuits.

Even before the film's release, reaction to it was swift and noisy. Officials at the German embassy were outraged. It was reported that First Secretary Baron von Gienanth, acting through a Nazi agent named Ernest Hepp, threatened both the *March of Time* and its distributor, R.K.O. Radio Pictures, with legal action and reprisals, including expulsion from Germany of *Time* and *Life* employees. Additionally, UFA notified the two companies that it had arranged to sue for an injunction to restrain use of the *Feldzug in Polen* footage on grounds of infringement. Both *Time* and R.K.O stood pat, so UFA gave up that line of action. Subsequently, however, on August 17, 1940, *all* American films were excluded henceforth from release in Nazi Germany and in all countries then occupied by German troops—France, Belgium, Denmark, Norway, Luxembourg, and Poland. *Chicago Daily News* correspondent Wallace R. Deuel was quoted in the *Los Angeles Times* on that date as reporting that:

249

The Axis exclusion of American films from most of Europe serves several purposes from the German-Italian point of view. First, it affords revenge for Hollywood's production of anti-Nazi and anti-Fascist films. Second, it gives German and Italian films a clear market by excluding their principal competition. Third, it gives Berlin and Rome a bargaining weapon to use in attempts to get trade and other concessions from the United States.

Within the United States, the film was banned by the Pennsylvania State Board of Censors for "fear of the terrifying effect upon the masses." The censors objected explicitly to the reedited and renarrated footage taken from *Feldzug in Polen,* having previously approved a print of the film without that footage. This decision of the Pennsylvania board was the climax of a two-hour meeting with Louis de Rochemont. It must have been a stormy session. Following the announcement of the ban, Louis asserted in the *New York Times* on September 20 that "only the Pennsylvania censors and the Nazis seemed to want to prevent the picture from being exhibited." As for the censor's fears that the film would "terrify" audiences, Louis observed that "he had served seven years in the navy and that he was 'afraid you don't know Americans the way I do. We are not afraid. The thing you are doing is promoting appeasement—surrendering to fear—the most dangerous things facing America today.' " Speaking for the censors, Edna Carroll declared that Mr. de Rochemont had been "highly emotional." "His statements were so foolish, I didn't even answer them," she said.

The *March of Time* and R.K.O. subsequently appealed the ban, but lost the first appeal at the Common Pleas Court in October, when, according to the October 2 issue of the *New York Times,* the three judges ruled that the film did indeed contain Nazi German propaganda "manifestly intended by the Nazi regime in Germany . . . to disseminate Nazi doctrines and to induce other peoples into submitting to German domination, or to the adoption of the Nazi ideology." The court held that the censors had not abused their discretion. Their decision was appealed by the *March of Time* to the Pennsylvania Supreme Court, but this appeal was subsequently dropped by counsel of *Time* and R.K.O., no reason being given for withdrawal of the appeal.

Outside of Pennsylvania, the film played to reasonably large and apparently enthusiastic audiences. Political science professor William Harley, a specialist in motion picture censorship, wrote in his book, *World-Wide Influences of the Cinema* in 1940, that he had "witnessed the showing of this film in San Francisco and Los Angeles, and observed the deep impression it made upon the audiences." Harley judged it "One of the most effective films that has been shown in the United States since the outbreak of war in Europe . . . ," a judgment which was shared by many critics.

The performance of Louis's nonprofessionals may have been a little wooden, but they were a cut better than the "amateur theatricals" the *March of Time* usually offered, and that audiences had become used to. Indeed, the film's performances appear more awkward today than they did at the time of its release, audience tastes having become considerably more sophisticated in the intervening thirty-five years.

New York Times critic Bosley Crowther wrote approvingly on September 20:

> Like the man who was suddenly switched from a diet of cream-puffs to hardtack, we find ourselves this morning with a bite that is tough to chew. . . . A more provocative or challenging motion picture has not been placed before the public in years—or maybe, on second thought, never. For the fact of the matter is that there has never been a motion picture just like this one. . . . By a brilliant conception of Louis de Rochemont, producer of the film, non-actors were used to play the numerous roles of the townsfolk, thus imparting the illusion of photographed actuality. Through this device, the old newsreel and the fictionalized story blend perfectly.

Edgar Anstey, one of the *March of Time*'s enthusiastic foreign supporters, wrote in the British weekly *Spectator* on April 11, 1941:

> . . . the film is so skillfully constructed that it is often hard to tell where news-reel ends and acted scene begins. . . . *The Ramparts We Watch* is a fit climax to Louis de Rougemont's [*sic*] years of experiment in the reconstruction of modern history for the screen, and it will have more influence on the development of cinema than any other film of recent years.

251

Not all the critics were happy with the film, of course. New Deal director/writer Pare Lorentz wasn't sure *what* he thought of it. His review in the October 1940 issue of *McCall's* magazine was glowing, terming it one of "the three most important pictures of the season." "The editors," he wrote, "have done a superb job of matching old newsreels . . . with dramatic interpolations played by a group of amateur professionals." Writing during the same period for *U.S. Camera—1941* (Yearbook), however, he was offended by what he considered its artistic crudities, terming it a "wretched motion picture as far as any technique of direction, photography, words or music are concerned. . . ." And Margaret Frakes, writing in the *Christian Century* on October 16, 1940, scored the film for its "warlike attitude, superficial historiography, and propagandistic omissions." Concluded Frakes: "The result of such omissions, it follows, is that truth takes a holiday."

On the whole, *Time's* first feature film venture was judged a success by its producers. Albert Sindlinger recalls that it was not a financial success. Nonetheless, it had been widely seen and widely reviewed, and had produced the requisite amount of controversy which de Rochemont and Larsen judged appropriate for their productions.

Meanwhile, back at 369 Lexington Avenue, production of the monthly *March of Time* releases continued. Explosive international incidents, increasing domestic tension, and the spreading wars of Europe and Asia provided rich material for the editors from the summer of 1939 to the winter of 1941. Of the thirty-two films released during this period, all but five were concerned with military or political subjects. The tone of the films was predominantly anti-Fascist, their warnings to Americans vividly prophetic in retrospect. Even the five exceptions had political or military implications: "Uncle Sam—The Farmer" reviewed the work of the Department of Agriculture to reclaim land lost through soil erosion and faulty farming techniques. Government programs designed to stabilize the farm economy were also explained.

"The Vatican of Pius XII," released in February 1940, covered various aspects of life in the world's smallest sovereign state. Stressed in the film was Pius XII's leadership of Catholics through-

Jack Glenn on location with crew in mid-America shooting scenes for "Uncle Sam—the Farmer." (1939). Frank Follette is behind the camera, assistant Jim Delavan at left. (Courtesy Jack Glenn)

out the world and his efforts to ensure peace. The release was timely, following the Pontiff's 1939 Christmas broadcast to the world and the subsequent appointment by Franklin Roosevelt of Myron C. Taylor as the President's personal representative at the Holy See. This film production represented the first complete documentation of the city and its distinguished citizens ever made by film producers. Richard de Rochemont had secured permission for cameramen (sometimes dressed in formal attire) to photograph various ceremonies, including an audience with the Pope, a mass at St. Peter's, and an appearance of Pius XII before a group at the Academy of Science. Also photographed for the first time were burial crypts of the Vatican, the Basilica of St. Peter's, the murals of Michelangelo, the vast store of art treasures within the Vatican, the post office, and the library of manuscripts. As a token of gratitude for the Vatican's cooperation, the *March of Time* donated $5000 for distribution amongst the Pope's favorite charities.

Such cordiality between the *March of Time* and the Vatican was in sharp contrast to the strained relationship that prevailed for many years between Time, Incorporated, and the New York Archdiocese of the Catholic Church, whose censor, Monsignor (later Cardinal) J. Francis McIntyre, had strong critical reservations about the subject matter of all *Time* publications.

McIntyre "was always calling us in," recalled Jimmy Shute, "and saying 'Well, you must not do that. You can't do this, and you can't do that,' and we paid no attention to him. And he got furious. He was not only doctrinaire but he was an autocrat. He was always like that. . . . and he'd expect to be obeyed."

The *March of Time*'s April release, "America's Youth," was a salute to the young men and women of the nation. Examining various social and economic groups, the film reviewed the problems, needs, ambitions, and opportunities of contemporary young people. Special credit was given the nation's youth organizations, including the YMCA, the YWCA, the National Youth Commission, and the National Youth Administration. The Voice of Time concluded: "American youth is still the happiest, healthiest, and best cared for in the world."

"Thumbs Up, Texas!," the last of the five nonpolitical issues, took movie audiences on a cinematic tour of the nation's largest state, spotlighting its barren deserts, sweeping mountains, rich cattle ranches and farms, inexhaustible mineral wealth, and booming cities. Also cited were the myriad army training fields, naval stations, and defense factories mushrooming across the state.

A variety of politico-military subjects were covered in the remaining twenty-seven issues. Both the threat and the drama of Europe's spreading wars were vividly reflected in "Battle Fleets of England," "The Republic of Finland," "Spoils of Conquest," "Norway in Revolt," "Crisis in the Atlantic," and "Britain's R.A.F.," all of which were enthusiastically received by both American and British critics. The war in the Pacific was analyzed in a series of releases which included "Crisis in the Pacific," "China Fights Back," "The Philippines," and "Australia at War."

Official political censorship struck again with the release of "Canada at War" in 1940. Pictured in the film were the grim preparations Canada was making to defend its shores from invasion and to take its proper place in the defense of the Empire. Included were sequences depicting the efforts of Canada's defense industry, the recruitment and training of armed forces volunteers, and the departure of Canada's first contingent of troops to Europe, conveyed by units of the British Navy.

Although the film was widely acclaimed by film critics as an accurate and sympathetic appraisal of Canada's war effort, the film was banned on March 4, 1940, in Ontario by Premier Mitchell Hepburn. Premier Hepburn, acting in his capacity as chairman of the Board of Appeals of the Ontario Board of Censors, denounced the film as political propaganda for the Mackenzie King government (which Hepburn opposed), and declared the issue banned until after the general elections, which were to be held in the dominion on March 26, 1940.

On March 5 the *New York Times* reported Louis de Rochemont's variation of his favorite observation on censorship:

> Apparently the March of Time's film "Canada at War" can be shown everywhere throughout the world except in Russia, Nazi Germany and the Province of Ontario.

For good political reasons, the Canadian government did not appeal the ban; however, on March 11, 1940, Harry Nixon, provincial secretary and first assistant to Premier Hepburn, resigned, in part because of the censorship of the *March of Time* issue. Although banned in Ontario, the film was subsequently seen in other provinces of Canada.

It was during this period that the first commercial imitation of the *March of Time* appeared. It was called *Canada Carries On,* and was produced by the National Film Board of Canada. John Grierson had been called to Canada early in 1939 to set up a new film board, to mobilize, supervise, and coordinate its wartime information/propaganda effort, and to serve as its first commissioner. Grierson, always an admirer of the *March of Time,* decided that Canada needed something rather similar, and with de Rochemont's permission sent talented, engineer-turned-film maker,

Stuart Legg, to *March of Time* headquarters in New York some-time in the fall of 1939 to watch Louis's boys in action and to learn what he could about the production of such a series.

Apparently he learned his lessons well. Legg went up to Ottawa and, together with other talented young film makers such as Raymond Spottiswoode, Stanley Hawes, Sidney Newman, Basil Wright, Ross McLean, Tom Daly, and Jim Beveridge, introduced NFB's new "magazine-film" series, *Canada Carries On,* in early 1940. It was a well-made product, partly in the tradition of the editorially dynamic *March of Time,* but leavened with the poetic, personalized, and somewhat more discursive style of the classic British documentary film. The series was well received, both critically and commercially, and represented a real achievement for that young and then quite inexperienced film organization. The Canadians lacked good synchronous sound equipment, strong financial support, the *March of Time*'s news-gathering facilities and expertise, and the extraordinary newsreel stock-shot library resources that were available to their New York mentors.

As the result of the success of this first series, a companion series called the *World in Action* (released overseas as *Empire in Action*) was introduced in 1942. More than an imitation, it was an outright counterfeit of the *March of Time,* of distinctly inferior quality, replete with scenes of continuously marching men, flying banners, smoking steam engines, industrial machinery, and impersonalized masses of fighting working men and women, backed up by continuous music and nonstop, high-speed narration read (as was that of *Canada Carries On*) by Canadian actor Lorne Greene, who later achieved stardom on American television.

Stuart Legg always acknowledged the debt *World in Action* owed to the *March of Time.* All of this would have been well and good, and Louis could have taken some sort of pleasure in seeing the influence of his work spreading northward, had it not been for the fact that both series were released commercially in the United States in direct competition with the *March of Time.* United Artists bought rights to the *Canada Carries On* series, one issue of which ("War Clouds in the Pacific") was said to have grossed $70,000 in North America. As for the *World in Action,* by the end of the war it was seen regularly by an American audience of millions and was grossing between $25,000 and $30,000 per issue. Louis was furious. It was one thing, he argued, to support Canada's war effort by training her young film makers. It was another thing to set up competitors in business, especially when the *March of Time* was barely breaking even, and the Canadian series was subsidized by the government. Such cordiality as had previously existed between de Rochemont and Grierson came to an end, and their relationship was cool thereafter. Even today, some *March of Time* staff members still express anger at the Canadian film makers' behavior.

Whatever the ethics of the matter, the *March of Time* staff could have learned a few things from the Canadians' work. In its time, *Canada Carries On* was very good indeed and critics sometimes rated it more highly than the same month's *March of Time* release. Issues of the series were screened regularly for *March of Time* personnel in New York City. Jimmy Shute recalled them:

> They sent it [*Canada Carries On*] down to us always to look at it, and our people would gather in the projection room—terribly self-satisfied—and they'd sit there jeering "Haw-Haw-Haw." And what we were seeing was much better than what *we* were doing. Their use of sound, for example. Louis had no sense of what sound could do for a film at all. . . . I was fascinated with sound, and then loved the way Stuart Legg used it and John Grierson. That's where the documentary movement, I think, began. And they did wonderful stuff. And I hated it when these . . . self-satisfied people [at the *March of Time*] would scoff at it . . . and I thought it was something that we could very well take lots of lessons from.

Both *Canada Carries On* and the *World in Action* continued in production and release until the end of World War II. There would be other imitations but these were unquestionably the best.

Parodies of the *March of Time* had appeared as early as 1935. Within six months after the introduction of the series, a Hollywood studio, Mascot Pictures, had produced a full-length feature film that exploited the *March of Time*'s name, logo, style, format, and production methods. Rushed into release in June 1935, the film was called *Ladies Crave Excitement,* and was a melodrama of the newsreel business. Norman Foster starred as a newsreel cam-

The first and best imitation of the *March of Time* was *Canada Carries On,* produced by Stuart Legg for the National Film Board of Canada, beginning in 1940. (Courtesy Cinémathèque québécoise)

Canadians spun off a second series entitled *World in Action,* exhibited it widely in Canada, the United States, and countries abroad for several years. (Courtesy Cinémathèque québécoise)

Parodies and other exploitations of the *MOT* style appeared as early as 1935 when Mascot Pictures released "Ladies Crave Excitement," a feature melodrama of the newsreel business which featured a thinly veiled imitation of the *March of Time* called *March of Events.*

Most famous of the *March of Time* parodies appeared in Orson Welles's *Citizen Kane.* Film began with a ten-minute reel entitled *News of the March,* which meticulously imitated *MOT* style. (Courtesy 1977 RKO General Pictures)

projection-room sequence follows in which a Louis de Rochemont figure named Rawlston sends his hapless reporter out to discover the identity of "Rosebud," without which the reel will not be complete. "Rosebud, dead or alive!" says Rawlston amiably. "It'll probably turn out to be a very simple thing." You could almost hear Louis de Rochemont saying the very same thing to Jack Glenn as he sent him out on one of his impossible assignments.

For this parody sequence of *Time on the March,* Welles and his cowriter, Herman Mankiewicz, studied the narrative style of the *March of Time* and matched it closely. Robert Wise, the editor, cut it in the same fashion; Bernard Hermann wrote a musical background score which could have passed for one of Shaindlin's; and William Alland (who also plays the reporter in the film) narrated the parody in the manner of Westbrook Van Voorhis. The supervisor of sound recording on the film, James G. Stewart, recalled that he even went to the trouble to match the "compression" effect that was typical of single-system newsreel sound recording. Some of the footage that purported to be from the newsreel vaults was purposely scratched by running it through a projector hundreds of times. (Actually, this was something of a libel on both the newsreels and the *March of Time,* both of which maintained very high standards of image quality and cleanliness—far higher than obtains today in 16mm television news photography.) Stewart also recalled Welles coaching Bill Alland over a period of weeks, so that Alland could imitate Van Voorhis to Welles's satisfaction.

The people at the *March of Time* were both amused and flattered at Welles's imitation, as they were with another imitation which appeared in Anatole Litvak's 1939 production of *Confessions of a Nazi Spy.* Indeed, according to a contemporary news report in *Variety,* it was Henry Luce's enthusiasm for *Citizen Kane* which ensured the release of the film. The central character of Welles's masterpiece bore a resemblance to William Randolph Hearst, who was not amused with it. Because of the opposition of the powerful Hearst publishing interests, there was apparently some possibility at the time of the film's completion that it might be suppressed and destroyed. According to *Variety,* however, *Time*'s editors thought it quite a plug and Luce let it be known that he was prepared, with Welles's enthusiastic cooperation, to collaborate in mounting an expensive campaign to get the film released if R.K.O. balked. In the end, the film was indeed released, and passed instantly into motion picture history.

Not all *March of Time* imitations were made by outsiders, however. During 1937 and 1938, the *March of Time* itself produced a series of self-parodying "goody reels" or "freak reels" that were shown privately. These featured humorous sound track impersonations of international political figures, laid over authentic newsreel shots of the celebrities, delivering improbable remarks about themselves and their time: Franklin and Eleanor Roosevelt, the Prince of Wales, John L. Lewis, Henry Wallace, Harry Hopkins, Haile Selassie, Mahatma Gandhi, Adolf Hitler, Benito Mussolini, and many others. These films were never seen by the general public, but were made specially, on Roy Larsen's orders, for screening at conventions of business associations in which Time, Incorporated, had an advertising or professional interest. These included the Association of National Advertisers, the Grocer's Association, the American Association of Advertising Agencies, a convention of auto accessory dealers, the R.K.O. exhibitors, a convention of RCA Victor salesmen, the Druggists' Association, and others.

Most of the parodied celebrities were played by the *March of Time*'s repertory company of impersonators. Typical casting included Agnes Moorhead as Eleanor Roosevelt, Ted DeCorsia as Mussolini, Dwight Weist as Hitler, Phil Thompson as Mahatma Gandhi, and Bill Adams as President Roosevelt.

The films carried a recognizable *March of Time* head logo, the cutting and commentary were fashioned in the *March of Time* fashion, and the narration was read by Westbrook Van Voorhis. Beyond that, all similarity with regular *MOT* releases ended.

The humor that illuminated these films was the kind usually found at beer busts, fraternity initiations, and reunions of the Veterans of Foreign Wars—corny and vulgar. Each of the reels was specially tailored to include "in-joke" references to well-known members of the particular association or trade group for which the film was made. Viewed out of context today, the films look inane, but at the time everyone seemed to enjoy them immensely.

The popularity of these convention "goody reels" was a reflection of the manner in which the *March of Time* had ingratiated itself into the public consciousness. The voice of Westbrook Van Voorhis, even more than that of Franklin Roosevelt, was considered the most familiar voice in the United States. Night club comedians and musical performers sometimes integrated parodies of the *MOT* format, and familiar phrases from the Voice of the Tomb, into their acts. To the people back at 369 Lexington Avenue, the parodies were flattering—at the time it seemed a fine compliment. Years later, they saw it differently. "Once this starts," said Jack Shaindlin, "you're going to have a problem with your original. It's going to be smile-inducing instead of thought-inducing." This is a valid point. At the time, however, everyone was too busy to take the parodies seriously.

In the summer of 1940, German armies rolled into France and began moving toward Paris. The moment had arrived for Richard de Rochemont to close down operations in Paris and to evacuate not only his own staff but also the *Time, Life,* and *Fortune* personnel who had operated out of his headquarters.

Dick owned a house at Pontlevoy, about twenty miles from Tours. He sent Jean Pagès down to help Helen de Rochemont, who was already there, to prepare it as a war headquarters and to rent a second house in Tours for the magazine people. Just before the Germans marched into Paris, Dick drove back up to the capital and rounded up the last of his people, including Andrew Heiskell (then a *Life* editor, later chairman of the board of Time, Inc.) and Ralph Delahaye Payne (later publisher of *Fortune* magazine). One of the original Paris group, *Time* correspondent Sherry Mangan, decided to remain in Paris for a while for a first-hand look at the Germans marching in. Otto Dietrich, the German propaganda minister for France, was the first Nazi official to reach Dick's abandoned Paris office. "I see de Rochemont had the good sense to get out in time," he was reported to have said.

De Rochemont and his people didn't stay in Tours long. The city was bombed, the Germans were coming closer, the French government moved out to Bordeaux, and it was decided to move Time, Inc., headquarters again. Dick got the Americans off to Spain and set to work to relocate his European personnel. Everyone headed for Bordeaux, but before they got there, France capitulated, signed an armistice, and began a four-year collaboration with its conquerors. Learning of this, Dick sent Pagès, Oberlin, and the rest of his European staff to Vichy to settle down there and await further instructions. Rebière and Comte had already been mobilized and were in the army. However, Comte turned up in Vichy later and joined the *March of Time* staff there, as did Rebière shortly after the armistice.

All his belongings already left behind and the staff dispersed, Dick, together with his wife and dog, piled into his automobile and headed for the Spanish frontier. They didn't get far.

Some genius trying to be helpful innocently provided me with a supply of gasoline which was watered. I had to get that out of my gas tank and get the carburetor cleaned, which I wasn't capable of doing. I was stuck on the road between St. Jean de Luz and the frontier.

I had emptied the gas tank. Carburetor was filthy. I still had three or four liter cans of gas—enough to get me over the frontier. So I hailed a truck that came along, hoping for a push that would work the gas through. This fellow said, "No, no, that's not the way to do it." He said, "Have you got a wrench?" He took apart the carburetor, cleaned it, put it together again, and we got started—like an angel coming down. And we got over the frontier. That was 1940.

When the de Rochemonts arrived in America, the only possession that Helen carried with her was a silver fork which she used to prepare the dog's food. Back at Pontlevoy at their empty house, the furnishings mysteriously began to disappear, piece by piece. By the time the Germans arrived and the occupation of France had officially begun, the house was partly empty. Later, after the liberation of France and Richard had returned to Pontlevoy, many of the house's furnishings reappeared just as mysteriously—the neighbors had hidden the furniture and linens for safekeeping till the war was over. Unfortunately, the contents of the wine cellar had disappeared for good.

In New York City, Louis appointed Richard managing editor of the *March of Time*. Till then, Richard had run his own shop, with his own people, insulated from Louis's fulminations by the

3600 miles that separated their two offices. What was it like for him now, back in New York?

> Although I had the title of managing editor, my brother was still calling the shots. Which was all right, except I disagreed occasionally.

And how was Louis to work with?

> Well, he could be a pretty frightening character. I used to battle with him when I was there. He was very difficult. He's mellowed a little now [in 1975]. As I say, it was a very personal thing with him. He's got a scratchy disposition. Yet, he'd get an awful lot of work out of people.

In addition to his *March of Time* position, Dick had been accredited to the French Army as a *Life* magazine correspondent from 1939 through 1940. He had done articles for *Life* on Daladier and other French leaders, and was listed briefly on *Life*'s masthead as an associate editor. An intense Francophile, Dick de Rochemont was unhappy with the magazine's general handling of the French situation. *Life* had sent Frank Norris, one of its editors, to Vichy, France, as an invited guest of René DeChambrun, son-in-law of Pierre Laval. In de Rochemont's judgment, the resulting article that Norris wrote for *Life* reflected the Vichy-Pétain point of view. "This Frank Norris thing was malarky," he said. "It didn't seem real to me." On the pretext of taking care of the corporation's French office, Dick slipped back into occupied France and went to Vichy in the spring of 1941. When he returned to the United States a few weeks later, he brought an article that *Life* published in September 1941, entitled "Vichy Versus France." This earned him a lot of attention from the Free French movement, and he was invited to join their American organization, "France Forever." He joined and subsequently became president of the organization. "I felt perfectly free to attack Cordell Hull when he talked about the 'so-called' Free French," said Dick. "I had a lot of fun with this. Made a lot of friends, since I am fairly Francophile. I now found myself labeled . . . a French propagandist." Dick de Rochemont's judgments about France's military capabilities may have been poor, but his enthusiasm for the country's cause was profound, and was to continue throughout the war.

Dick de Rochemont, always an enthusiastic francophile, joined American "France Forever" organization, later became its president. Following World War II, he was made an officer of the French Legion of Honor. He is seen here with General de Gaulle near Siena, Italy, in July 1944. (Courtesy Dick de Rochemont)

Back at the sprocket factory, with Richard on board as stateside managing editor, production of the *March of Time* issues continued. Between the summers of 1940 and 1941, the *March of Time* released a group of issues that outlined the task of arming and manning United States military forces, and consolidating the energies and loyalties of citizens while preparing them for war.

Included in this group were "Gateways to Panama," a timely explanation of the strategic position and military value of the Panama Canal Zone; "The U.S. Navy," an appraisal of U.S. naval power and an examination of current programs for the rebuilding of ships scrapped following the 1922 Washington "20-year naval holiday" agreement; "Men of the F.B.I.," a look at the justice department's most highly publicized agency and its efforts to protect Americans from both domestic crime and foreign intrigue; "Arms and the Men," a review of the selective service system and a look at the U.S. armaments industry; "Labor and Defense," which featured American labor unions and the contribution of their members to the defense effort; and "Americans All," a salute to loyal foreign-born American citizens and a plea for unity and harmony among America's diverse racial and religious groups. Thinly veiled was *Time*'s anxiety about the threat of internal subversion by fascist elements of Italian, German, and Japanese populations then part of the U.S.A.'s 15 million noncitizen immigrants. Whistling in the deepening gloom cast by Nazi Germany's recent military and political successes abroad, the *March of Time* reassured itself and its audiences that American immigrants, whatever their ethnic and national origins, would remain faithful to America's democratic ideals.

"Men of the F.B.I." was an especially interesting film employing extensive "re-creation" sequences with F.B.I. agents as actors. The organization enjoyed a high reputation in those days, and Louis was one of Director J. Edgar Hoover's most enthusiastic admirers. In the film, an apparently authentic, newly inducted special agent named Richard Spellman was shown as he progressed through the training program at Quantico, Virginia. Beginning at an annual salary of $3200 (which was quite good for 1941), the agent was shown undergoing the exhaustive and demanding training in physical fitness, firearms proficiency, and field investigation technique required of F.B.I. agents. Within the F.B.I. building in Washington, D.C., the Bureau's extensive and celebrated crime laboratory was shown, figuring prominently in an apparently fictitious espionage caper called "The Stuart Factory Murder" case, both the plot and dialogue of which sounded like an Agatha Christie novel. It was good melodrama and the film was visually exciting and thematically timely. Mr. Hoover himself appeared toward the end of the film to provide *March of Time* audiences with an unequivocal appraisal of the American political scene:

HOOVER   Never before was there greater need for unity, for a calm appraisal of the forces which work against us—the rabble-rousing communists, the goose-stepping bundsmen [American Nazis]. Their stooges and seemingly innocent fronts, and last but by no means least, the pseudo-liberals, adhere to the doctrines of falsification and distortion.

Hoover subsequently sent Louis a letter thanking him for his support. Louis had it framed and displayed it proudly on the wall of his office.

Two other films, also released during this period, "Newsfronts of War—1940" and "On Foreign Newsfronts" provided résumés of the European and Asiatic conflicts. The former film devoted considerable footage to a searching appraisal of the military might of the Soviet Union. Expressing surprise at the Stalin-Hitler non-aggression pact, the *March of Time* predicted that "Moscow, in 1940, will be one of the world's greatest newsfronts should the Soviet Armies march." The film was more anti-Soviet than any previous issue. It appeared that what irritated the *March of Time* was not Soviet communism, but Soviet support of fascism.

"On Foreign Newsfronts" spotlighted the achievements of the U.S. working press in its service to "the best-informed public in the world." Prominent reporters and commentators from U.S. wire services and newspapers were featured in the film. Also included was spectacular footage of the Battle of Britain filmed by newsreel cameraman Arthur Menken.

Late in 1940, the *March of Time* began publication of a new series of study guides which accompanied releases and were distributed by theater owners to their patrons during the period of each issue's run. The guides proved popular with movie patrons and were later widely distributed to schools and universities.

Angry charges of warmongering followed release of "Uncle Sam—The Non-Belligerent" in 1941. The film incorporated captured German newsreel scenes depicting life aboard German naval ships, heavy German artillery firing cross-Channel, U-boats at work, and England as seen from Nazi bombers. The issue concluded with consideration of a recent Gallup poll which indicated that 60 per cent of American adult citizens favored aid to Britain even at the cost of war. British film critic Edgar Anstey enjoyed the film and, in the March 7, 1941 issue of *Spectator,* found it "perhaps the most important propaganda pictures of the war. . . . March of Time itself is so pro-British," wrote Anstey, "that its editors make no attempt to conceal their support for this majority opinion."

Immediately following the film's release, isolationist leaders who had appeared in the film demanded its withdrawal from film circuits. Verne Marshall, chairman of the "No Foreign War Committee," charged that his comments at a recent press conference had been incorporated into the film without his personal knowledge or consent. In answering this charge, the producers of the film released to the press a photostatic copy of a signed release from Marshall. The "No Foreign War Committee" subsequently dropped the matter without further comment. (Glenn had also employed a technique popular today with some *cinéma vérité* directors. With the sound camera running, he walked into the shot and asked Verne Marshall if he agreed to the use of the footage in the *MOT* release. Marshall agreed. This "out-take" was then filed for legal purposes. "We had the guy anyway he turned," said Glenn.)

Isolationist Senator Burton K. Wheeler, also appearing in the film, demanded that the editors of the *March of Time* delete scenes that represented him as having answered Franklin Roosevelt's "fireside chat" message advocating all-out aid to Britain. The *New York Times,* on January 18, reported that, following a preview of the film, Wheeler termed it "warmongering propaganda" and, in a telegram to Louis de Rochemont, stated that

it was my understanding that my remarks were to be used equally with those of the President's . . . and not just one sentence that you might select. . . . I do not want my name to in any way appear in a warmongering picture which has for its purpose the arousing of the sympathies and the passions of the American people. . . . The picture is deceptive in that it does not equally portray the arguments for and against war. . . . It is so obviously war propaganda that I doubt whether even you will advance the hypocritical plea of impartiality. Delete my picture and statements.

Louis de Rochemont, denying Wheeler's request, replied in a telegram to the Senator:

> Your intemperate and reckless charge of warmongering by the March of Time obscures the fact that the principal portion of this picture deals not with the opinions of American political leaders and statesmen, but with the tragic fate of the millions who have come under the tyranny of the Nazis either as a result of appeasement or as a result of easy conquest. . . . [It is our journalistic duty to] . . . let the public see and hear the men who oppose the policies of those of our leaders who wish to keep the war away from this hemisphere by giving unstinted aid to the British.

Long after the controversy had died, critic Edgar Anstey concluded that "unobjective and partial though it is, this brilliantly photographed film gets near to being a piece of reliable screen history because it attempts no more than the presentation of certain points of view (giving opportunity to both conflicting parties). No history text-book can do more, and film history becomes meaningless when it lays claim to rise superior to such human frailties."

That the *March of Time* embraced a pro-British, anti-fascist, and interventionist point of view seems apparent to us when we see these films today. Happily for de Rochemont and the *March of Time* staff, the verdict of history was on their side. The Second World War turned out to be a "popular" one. The enemy was clearly and easily identifiable in 1939-40, even amongst isolationists, many of whom differed not with respect to the perception of evil, but with the wisdom of involving America in what they considered a losing battle.

It was inevitable even then that the *March of Time* would come under heavy fire from the isolationist wing of the American political system, not only for its interventionist propaganda, but for its frequent, blunt attacks, upon American isolationists. In September 1941, just three months before the Japanese eliminated most of our Pacific fleet at Pearl Harbor, the *March of Time* was cited by a Senate committee, together with seventeen other Hollywood features, as being "warmongering" propaganda designed to bring the United States into the European conflict. (Other titles cited were: "The Great Dictator," "Escape," "Manhunt," "Convoy," "Sergeant York," "The Hamilton Woman," and "Confessions of a Nazi Spy.")

The Senate committee was actually an *ad hoc* "noncommittee," never authorized by a vote of the Senate, but set in motion by isolationist Senators Burton K. Wheeler, Gerald P. Nye, and Bennett Champ Clark. Hearings of the committee were conducted in kangaroo court fashion, with the film industry's defense counsel, Wendell Willkie, prevented from either responding to attacks made upon these films or conducting cross examinations.

On September 22 *Life* magazine summarized the charges that the committee had laid against the films as these:

(1) Though movie houses are losing money on war films, an industry controlled by "foreign-born" producers persisted in making pictures calculated to drag the U.S. into a European Conflict.
(2) Government officials had asked the movies to do this.
(3) Film makers had a stake in a British victory because British rental fees often made the difference between profit and loss on U.S. movies.
(4) The movies are a "tightly controlled monopoly" exercising a rigid censorship that turns 17,000 theaters into "daily and nightly mass meetings for war."

A faint, unpleasant, anti-Semitic haze hung over much of the committee's sessions. "If anti-Semitism exists in America," Senator Nye was quoted as saying, "the Jews have themselves to blame." The committee made a fool of itself when it was learned that its investigators had apparently not seen most of the films that had been singled out by them for censure.

In August of 1941, the company released its second full-length feature, entiled *The Story of the Vatican,* an expanded version of the monthly issue on the same subject that it had released in February 1940. The *March of Time*'s European staff featured prominently in the making of this 53-minute film, with Richard de Rochemont serving as producer, Jean Pagès as director, and Marcel Rebière on camera. Lothar Wolff edited the film, Jimmy Shute wrote the commentary, and Louis De Francesco composed the musical track.

Narrated by then Monsignor Fulton J. Sheen, the film covered much of the same ground as the previous year's issue on the Vatican, with considerable new footage on the Vatican's artistic and bibliographic treasures, radio station, shops, and various ecclesiastical and diplomatic activities throughout the world. Sheen also served as adviser on the film. Staff members recall that he spent a good deal of time with them and was quite helpful from an editorial point of view. The staff felt that Sheen's collaboration would provide a kind of imprimatur for the film and would ensure the church's satisfaction with its treatment of the subject. Apparently, it was hoped that church officials in the United States would also provide some kind of support for its promotion. "It didn't make any money," said Richard de Rochemont. "Didn't lose anything, either, because we didn't spend anything on it. Whether the making of this film on the Vatican had any mitigating influence on the censorship problems that *MOT* had experienced regularly in dealing with the New York Archdiocese, Richard could not recall.

Three politically charged issues brought this troubled year of 1941 to a close. "Peace—by Adolf Hitler," released in August, questioned the peace overtures of Nazi Germany. Hitler's broken promises were graphically reviewed by the film's editors in a montage covering the rapid and conscienceless expansion of the Nazi state during the previous few years. Warned the Voice of Time: "This peace move, originating in Berlin, is being supported by isolationists, Nazi sympathizers, and many who, devoted to the ideal of peace, do not appreciate the danger of dealing with Hitler. . . . Appeasers, credulous, find themselves the victims of their trust. Hitler . . . is simply incapable of truth-telling . . . a psychopathic liar."

In Buenos Aires, the Argentine censorship committee deleted the Voice of Time's comment: "In all history the technique of systematic lying and treachery never has been exploited by the conqueror quite as basely as by Hitler."

"Main Street—U.S.A." showed some of the effects of the European war on the average American town—the disappearance of luxuries from department stores, the hoarding of foodstuffs, the tensions and anxieties that distressed its citizens. The film ended with a fictitious enactment describing the attempt of a hypothetical "New Order" to seize control of a small New England town.

"Battlefields of the Pacific," a special issue, was released during the first week of December. It contained sequences from past issues and presented a review of the Pacific battle areas. Indicated in the film were the strategic values of Malaya, Singapore, the Dutch East Indies, Australia, and New Zealand as possible air bases for counterattack against the Japanese empire. Louis was right on target. The issue was playing in American theaters, from Boston to Honolulu, when Japanese bombs fell on Pearl Harbor.

12

World War II:
The Guard
Changes and Marches On

The Second World War disrupted all of the *March of Time*'s operations, just as it did those of other companies across the nation. It was the second major shock in the company's history, and it altered the character and output of the organization profoundly.

During 1941-42, several staff members were drafted into the army and others volunteered for military duty. Among the latter were key personnel, including Tom Orchard (who played an important role in building the navy's wartime film unit), Lothar Wolff (who was made head of the coast guard's film unit), Jack Bradford, and Arthur Tourtellot.

In August 1941, four months before the Pearl Harbor attack, the *March of Time*, in association with the United States War Department, inaugurated a motion picture service school within its shop, designed to acquaint selected armed forces personnel with the rudiments of newsreel and documentary film production. It was Louis's idea and was conducted at the *March of Time*'s expense. A complete course of studies in the program lasted several months. Most of the trainees were navy, marine, and coast guard personnel; however, the first class of thirty men which graduated in February 1942 was reported to include personnel from the

Royal Canadian Engineers, the Royal Canadian Air Force, and the Royal Norwegian Air Corps as well. The students were exposed to a series of practical film-making experiences, including exercises in cinematography, sound recording, and editing. Much of the class work was informal, the students accompanying the *March of Time*'s professional field crews on location, shooting footage with them, and then working with the editors in New York on the material they had shot. "I don't know what the union would have said today," mused Tom Orchard, "but that was wartime." Although modest in scope, the program was considered a valuable one and was widely praised. Thomas Pryor wrote in the *New York Times* on February 8, 1942: "The cost of the school is borne entirely by March of Time. . . . In return, March of Time will gain only as other newsreel companies will gain—in the improved craftsmanship in film released in the future by the armed forces for public exhibition and use. That, and a fine patriotic glow."

In the months and years that followed, a substantial amount of combat footage which found its way to *March of Time* headquarters turned out to have been shot by the *March of Time*'s students. "Darned good photographers," said Tom Orchard. "Here we'd trained all these boys in the *March of Time* way. . . . Came the war, the First Marine Division went to Guadalcanal, and into history, and these [students of ours] went with it. And they made the great battle shots of Tarawa—all those great close-ups. This was done by our boys . . . training for action, and then in action. . . ."

If things were hectic before the outbreak of war, they were to become more so in the months ahead. *"March of Time*'s schedule for 1942 is tough and tight," said Louis in a January 6, 1942, memo to the staff. "Besides thirteen regular releases, one every four weeks, there will be at least three *MOT* specials, twelve U.S. Navy training films, and an indeterminate number of Service School one-reelers. And we will also have an enlarged Service School, possibly a total of fifty men."

Things *must* have been hectic: in the same memo, Louis took the unprecedented step of writing a more or less coherent description of the titles, responsibilities, and lines of authority of his key people—probably the only such memo he ever wrote. Dick de Rochemont was described as being second in command; John Wood, the business manager, was in charge of all accounting, purchasing, and contractual relations. Al Sindlinger continued as head of publicity and promotion (although Louis required that all promotion copy be sent to him for approval prior to release). Jimmy Shute, with Pete Cardozo, ran the script department. Lothar Wolff (until he joined the coast guard) continued to serve as chief editor. Beverly Jones was in charge of cutting room operations, and served as film editor of the service school. Sam Bryant was head of research and had a lot of other duties, too. "Sam's jobs cannot be defined," explained Louis in the memo, "as he is expected to do most everything; i.e., preparing answers to Producer's mail, escorting film through military censorship, briefing relevant facts and making up first script outlines for service pictures, canvassing newsreel libraries, checking newsreel theaters, and occasionally pinch-hitting as cutter, contact man, and director." Jim Wolcott continued as office manager, personnel supervisor, and production chief, assisted by Jack Savage. Jack Glenn, George Black, and Yancy Bradshaw comprised the directorial staff, assisted by casting director Phil DeLacy. Bradshaw continued to serve as sound chief and technical trouble shooter, in addition to which he headed the service school and was chief contact man for navy aviation training film production.

Typically, after having made this supreme concession of putting job descriptions and a crude organizational table onto paper, Louis concluded the memo with qualifications which appeared to suggest that none of the preceding meant much: "Nothing in this memorandum is to be taken as restricting duties or curtailing the initiative of any member of the staff, and this includes myself. *March of Time* will continue to function as a collaborative enterprise in group journalism."

In early December 1941, before America entered the war, work had begun on a new *March of Time* feature called *We Are the Marines*. Directed by Jack Glenn and Lothar Wolff, it was a competent if not artistically distinguished documentary that traced the training of marines from boot camp to battleground. The film was released in December 1942, by which time Louis and his staff could take pride in the fact that some of the authentic battle footage used in the film had been photographed by their service school graduates. Re-creations were also employed, some of them featuring actual marine corps celebrities, such as Colonel William T. Clement, who had been among the few men to escape from the battles of Bataan and Corregidor. Some scenes of beach landings and close combat were also staged. These were quite convincing and ended up in the marine corps archive. Years later, according to Jack Glenn, some of this staged footage was reacquired by Henry Salomon for use in the celebrated television series, *Victory at Sea*.

> When *Victory at Sea* was shown [said Glenn], it included "authentic" battles from the Solomon Islands—some of them were shot in North Carolina by me. When we were researching it, we knew there wouldn't be enough helmets of the new kind so we mixed them up with the old kind, 'cause we knew we'd have to mix with actual warfare footage from the eight marine cameramen whom we'd trained. So the people who used it [in *Victory at Sea*] found it in the Marine archives, so they figured it was real warfare footage.

Glenn, with a smile, said he used to love to see his re-created shots of Guadalcanal on historical television shows.

A similar incident occurred in the late 1950's when footage of the flooding of the Yellow River in China was acquired from the *March of Time*'s stock-shot library by the producers of the CBS television series, *The Twentieth Century*, and cut into their program on the Sino-Japanese War. Unknown to them, two decades earlier these flood shots, which had appeared in an *MOT* issue on the Far Eastern war, had been lifted by the *March of Time* editors from Pare Lorentz's New Deal documentary film, *The River*. Still other examples of staged *March of Time* footage being incorporated into television documentaries and presented as authentic newsreel coverage are reported by Jay Leyda in *Films Beget Films* (1964).

In addition to the *March of Time*'s special project activity in 1942, the group was still very much involved in its principal business of turning out thirteen issues of the film magazine each year for American theaters. Audiences of that day hungered for information about military events, and about their sons who had been sent overseas to fight a foreign war. Newsreel theaters devoted exclusively to the screening of newsreels and informational short subjects multiplied across the nation and played to capacity houses. In both these and regular theaters, the monthly *March of Time* release more than ever was viewed with great interest by audiences.

Popular though it may have been, though, the *March of Time* began to lose some of its distinctive character after the outbreak of war. It became a less provocative, less imaginative, and more didactic product than audiences had seen in the 1930's.

Overnight, entry into both the European and Pacific wars cut off the company's access to much of its civilian-generated foreign footage. The Allied combat footage that it got from official agencies of the U.S. government was nonexclusive and heavily censored by military authorities. A whole year would pass, for example, before audiences were allowed to see the complete, spectacular coverage of the attack and devastation at Pearl Harbor. As television news broadcasters learned years later, there must be a regular, fresh supply of newsworthy pictures to show audiences. The picture's the thing, both in film and in television, and, beginning in 1942, the *March of Time* had fewer films that were exciting and exclusive to show its audiences.

Also, whether because of choice or necessity, the number and variety of dramatic reenactments was gradually reduced. In their place, more stock-shot footage was employed. The "compilage films" that resulted were quite competent, and not fundamentally different from today's archival productions, such as *World at War,* but it was not the style that audiences were used to. The stock shots were used as "citations" to accompany the Voice of Time's commentary. If the Voice referred to the emperor of Japan, there was a shot of the emperor on his horse, photographed a few years earlier. If the Voice referred to America's industrial production, one saw a quick montage of spinning lathes, sweating workmen, and fiery furnaces, all obviously pulled out of the stock-shot library. The editors "cited" the emperor and the industrial war effort by showing us pictures which represented them at third hand, rather than engineering the scene so that the principals and events spoke and acted for themselves, as in the staged and re-created sequences for which the *March of Time* was famous. There had always been a certain amount of such "citation" during the 1930's, of course, but the proportion increased noticeably after 1941. The more interesting reenacted sequences did not disappear entirely during the war years, but their variety, frequency, and regularity decreased. Gradually, imperceptibly, the series was becoming a slick, illustrated lecture—what Roy Larsen referred to years later as a "mere documentary."

The exigencies of America's war commitment took a lot of the fun and the starch out of the *March of Time,* too. Albert Sindlinger claimed to have foreseen the problems that lay ahead. "It was perfectly clear," he said thirty-five years later, "that we were going to get involved in the war, and there'd be no *March of Time.* . . . You can dramatize someone else's war, but you can't dramatize your own. With censorship, there'd be no *March of Time.*"

Mercifully, the country's communications industry was spared the kind of rigid censorship that had prevailed during World War I. Instead, from 1941 onward, "voluntary" self-censorship prevailed, coordinated by a government office headed by Byron Price. Still, the commitment of Americans to the war was complete. The Second World War was as close to total war as the United States had experienced since the Civil War. There was little room left for the kind of iconoclastic journalism, political muckraking, and sophisticated skepticism for which the *March of Time* was famous. "It just made everything else irrelevant," said Jimmy Shute, "and every damned issue [of the *March of Time*] had to be about some aspect of the war. We'd even do a story about 'Music at War,' and 'The Theater in Wartime,' and things like that. Everything had to be related to war, and that tended to make the whole thing dull."

An examination of the production records confirms Shute's recollection. Between 1941 and 1945, the following percentages of issues were devoted entirely or in part to the war and its various manifestations: 1942: 100 per cent; 1943: 77 per cent; 1944: 77 per cent; 1945 (through August): 25 per cent.

The subject category into which the largest number of wartime issues fell was that of "foreign countries"—issues devoted explicitly to their people, politics, military posture, economics, and social systems. Between January 1942 and August 1945, there were fourteen such issues, one each devoted to Argentina, the Soviet Union, Canada, Spain, Japan, Germany, Italy, Ireland, Portugal, Sweden, and the South American continent as a whole. Two issues were devoted at different times to Great Britain, and a special two-part issue devoted to India was released in May and June of 1942. The Spanish subject, entitled "Inside Fascist Spain," and released in April 1943, was even less friendly than the one the *March of Time* had made in 1937. Spanish authorities had allowed Louis's cameramen into the country on the assumption that the shots they made would have good propaganda value for the Franco government. They were mistaken.

VOICE OF TIME

The crimes of Franco's prisoners are, by today's democratic standards, no crimes at all. Franco and the Falangists ordered the execution of over one million Republican prisoners during the Spanish War. Today, those remaining in Falangist prisons were the least active of those who took part in labor or radical movements, who opposed the rise of Franco's fascists to power. And, in sparing the lives of even these among their former adversaries, Franco's regime feels it has been lenient and, in fact, kind. But only complete submission and repentence on the part of their prisoners can satisfy the new rulers of the new Spain.

"That, of course, was another picture which kept the *March of Time* out of Spain for the rest of its career," said Dick de Rochemont.

The Russian issue, released in January 1943, was made up entirely of footage excerpted from a Soviet documentary feature film. Entitled "One Day of War—Russia, 1943," it purported to show the various military and home front activities that took place within that country's borders in one day. The combat footage was of exceptional quality and the editing was lively. Lothar Wolff recalled that it was the only *March of Time* issue he could recall which went through production without any reediting by Louis.

279

"I took great pride in that," said Wolff. Louis vetoed Wolff's plan to use the original music of the Russian feature behind the images. Instead, Jack Shaindlin composed an excellent score for it.

The second-largest category of subject matter during the war dealt with the day-to-day life of civilians on the home front: both citizens and the press working for victory, in "Mr. and Mrs. America" (November 1942); agricultural activity and the role of food in winning the war, in "America's Food Crisis" (March 1943) and "Post-War Farms" (September 1944); the effect of the war upon America's youth, in "Youth in Crisis" (November 1943); postwar economic prospects, in "Post-War Jobs?" (February 1944); harmony and cooperation between citizens of diverse racial and national origins, in "Americans All" (July 1944—this being the only occasion in the history of the series when the same title was used for two different and chronologically separate issues, the first release having been in February 1941); the shortage of meat in home-front stores, in "Where's the Meat?" (July 1945); the peculiarities and characteristics of "Teen-Age Girls," produced, so the publicity said, with the help of a special teen-age advisory board (June 1945); and the industrial development of America's West Coast and its "colorful inhabitants," in "West Coast Question" (February 1945).

Only two films of the period featured political leaders, and these were adulatory and supportive ("Men in Washington—1942" and "Spotlight on Congress"), contrasting sharply in approach with the aggressive and critical posture that the *March of Time* had assumed while dissecting political figures before the war.

Not surprisingly, Louis saw to it that the navy figured prominently in four issues, whereas only one issue was devoted to the army and two to the air corps. With Louis running the ship, references to the navy were likely to show up in the most unlikely places. "I remember we did a story about agriculture," said Lothar Wolff, "and it starts out with the navy off shore someplace, and to this day I don't know why we did it, but Louis felt it was time to show the navy again."

The F.B.I. was featured for the second time in less than eighteen months, in an issue released in September 1942, entitled "The F.B.I. Front." This issue stressed the role of the Bureau in combating espionage and sabotage during the war.

"Show Business at War" (May 1943) and "Upbeat in Music" (December 1943) featured the role of entertainers in the war effort, with brief vignettes of more than seventy-five well-known personalities in Hollywood, New York, and visiting and entertaining the troops at the front.

Finally, particular battles and campaigns were summarized, including underground resistance in France, the Low Countries, and Scandinavia; the invasion of North Africa in December 1942; preparations of the invasion of Europe (a little prematurely, in June 1943); and Stilwell's jungle march to reopen the Burma Road, in June 1944.

Operationally, the *March of Time* was having severe problems during this period. I have already referred to the loss of key personnel who had gone into the service, as well as the difficulty in securing fresh, exclusive footage from abroad. In addition, the distribution of the *March of Time* was taken from R.K.O. and handed over to Twentieth Century-Fox in the summer of 1942. It turned out to be a grave error, for Ned Depinet, R.K.O.'s distribution head, loved the *March of Time,* and, according to staff members, had always given its release his close attention. The decision to change distributors was an executive one, and no one remembers exactly what the reasoning was at the time, although there was apparently some feeling that R.K.O. wasn't paying enough for the series. Both Louis and his publicity head, Albert Sindlinger, were opposed to the move. They blamed business manager John Wood for talking Roy Larsen into it, and, at the time, begged Larsen not to do it. Whatever the reasoning, the decision was reached, the change was made, and it turned out to be a terrible mistake. "We began to get into trouble," recalled Tom Orchard, "because Fox didn't back us up the way Ned Depinet did. Fox said, 'Oh, we don't want to have the seats torn up in our theaters.' " Thirty-five years after the event, Roy Larsen was quick to agree. "In later years," he told me, "I regretted so much from a personal and company point of view our change to Fox. Spyros Skouras didn't know what to do with the *March of Time.* He handled it like spaghetti—he handled all his films like spaghetti and that was the way he handled the *March of Time.*"

As a consequence of its defection from R.K.O., the *March of*

Time acquired still another imitator in the exhibition market. Ned Depinet, deprived of *Time*'s series, began distributing a rival one that had been developed by Frederick Ullman, Jr., entitled, *This is America*. Its style was frankly patterned after that of the *March of Time*. Even its narrator, Dwight Weist, was a former *March of Time* radio and film actor, who usually played Hitler for de Rochemont. The series was released through R.K.O. exchanges from 1942 till its demise in 1951, consisting of 112 issues, of which Ullman produced the first 63 and Jay Bonafield the last 42.

Optimistic and patriotic in its approach, *This is America* celebrated the U.S.A., its people, and its values. According to one of its early writers and later production supervisor, Philip Reisman, Jr., the series attempted to "relate the small cog to the big wheel instead of showing the big wheel as 'The March of Time' did."

Richard Barsam, one of the few people who remembers *This is America* with anything like affection or respect, concludes in his article in *Cinema Journal* (Spring 1973): "Most of the films in the series blend three viewpoints: a definite nostalgia for the past, a rather unsophisticated awe at the present, and an unbounded optimism and hope for the future." Most film makers and critics, however, remember it as a pale and hackneyed imitation of the *March of Time,* which played its most important role as a training ground for important film and television artists of the future: Stanley Kubrick, Marya Mannes, Burton Benjamin, and Isaac Kleinerman, among others.

As if all of the several operational problems that we have mentioned were not enough, the third and last of what might be called "corporate traumas" occurred in August 1943: Louis de Rochemont left the *March of Time*. He left for Hollywood to begin a brilliant career as a feature film producer. At the time, however, his departure from Time, Inc., and from the film series that he had created was not a happy one.

Once again in his career, he and his superiors had come to a parting of the ways, and his position at the corporation was no longer tenable. Both sides had something to complain about. According to some of Louis's colleagues, he was becoming more difficult to deal with. He had seriously proposed that a substantial proportion of the production operations, together with the entire

March of Time film library, be moved up to his farm in New Hampshire. This was a farfetched idea from any operational point of view. Louis had always been a careless administrator. He ran an expensive operation, spending money lavishly and infuriating the business office with cost overruns. "Louis never believed in nickel and dime terms," said Jack Glenn, sympathetically. "Everything was big. He always thought big." Quite possibly, the corporation was also beginning to tire of his egocentricity. Like John Grierson, Louis regarded the motion picture as a pulpit from which to deliver very personal views of the world. Although history tends to confirm him in the political and moral statements that he enunciated during the late 1930's, his way of doing business was simply too idiosyncratic to survive in a communication corporation as large, as powerful, and as impersonal as Time, Inc.

Louis had his side of the argument, too. He was continually frustrated by what he considered the penny-pinching policies of the corporation. "We had a business manager that thought you could make a picture on 10¢ . . . ," he told me. "[He] was saying, 'What are you writing out these checks for? . . . They didn't realize that you had to pay actors and stuff like that."

According to de Rochemont, he also had a falling out with Henry Luce about this time. "Let me tell you the beginning of the end . . . ," said Louis. "I was invited by Roy Larsen and Harry Luce to meet them at the Biltmore, and Harry Luce said, 'I want you to make a picture that will tell everybody about the freedom of the skies. The heavens must be free. We have freedom of the sea, we must have freedom in the sky.' And I said, 'Well, Mr. Luce, I don't know how the hell I can do a half-hour of film of a plane in the air with somebody giving a lecture on the thing.' " De Rochemont concluded glumly, "So that's when things began to worsen."

There is also testimony to suggest that Louis had grown bored and restless at the *March of Time,* and was ready for a new kind of challenge elsewhere. Arthur Tourtellot said, "I think Louis probably thought the *March of Time* had achieved everything he had in mind as a two-reel documentary, and he wanted to prove a whole lot of things with regard to the making of features, and *Time* didn't see fit to underwrite such things and so there was probably a parting of the ways." De Rochemont's departure from the *March of Time* marked the beginning of an entirely new career for him. From a commercial point of view, Louis revolutionized the theatrical film industry with his production of such successful "semidocumentaries" as *The House on 92nd Street, Walk East on Beacon, Lost Boundaries, Boomerang, Martin Luther, The Whistle at Eaton Falls, Cinerama Holiday,* and *Windjammer.* He also won his second Academy Award for his wartime documentary, *The Fighting Lady.*

A terse memorandum to the staff of Time, Inc., from Roy Larsen, dated August 24, 1943, announced Louis's resignation and the appointment of his brother, Richard de Rochemont, to succeed him. Nearly all of the page-long memorandum was devoted to a review of Richard's experience and qualifications. Larsen's only mention of Louis appeared at the end of the memo, concluding: "To Louis de Rochemont, co-founder of THE MARCH OF TIME and for nine years its Producer, I wish the best of luck in the new field he is entering."

On August 20, Louis sent a confidential memo to his own staff to tell them of his departure. "Until I can talk with each of you personally," he wrote, "I want to express my deep gratitude for the loyalty, skill, energy and unfailing good will which you have consistently shown, often under trying circumstances. . . . To have been your boss has been an honor, to have worked with you a pleasure, and to have known you all as I have known you has been a privilege indeed."

The staff put together a going-away dinner party for Louis. A committee headed by Morrie Roizman, Phil Askling, and George Dangerfield organized the affair, which was held at the Waldorf Astoria on September 10. Eighty people from the *March of Time* staff attended, including Tom Orchard and Lothar Wolff, who were then in the armed forces. About the only people missing were those men who were away on active duty and Roy Larsen. Westbrook Van Voorhis acted as master of ceremonies and several people spoke, reminiscing about the good old days. Louis's wife, Jinny, his boy, Louis, Jr., director Jack Glenn, editors Morrie Roizman and Johnny Dullaghan, and Louis's brother Richard joined him at the head table. Louis made a thank-you speech and someone took a few badly exposed pictures. The climax of the evening was the presentation by the staff of a silver cigarette lighter to Mrs. de Rochemont and an inscribed cigarette box to Louis for his new Hollywood office. Then everyone went home, and that was the end of that.

13

Time Flickers Out

Richard de Rochemont was only four years junior to his brother, but he could have been of a different generation or family, for rarely have two brothers been so unlike.

Louis never went to college and resented it. Dick had gone to Harvard. Louis was a burly, inarticulate extrovert—a diamond in the rough. Dick was urbane, articulate, and sophisticated—well known in social circles, fluent in French, a connoisseur of good wine and good food, and a collector of Impressionist paintings. Louis's life centered on his work. Dick's interests ranged widely—in art, music, politics, and literature. Louis, though respected, was not popular with many of the people who worked for him. Dick was far more diplomatic and democratic, and is remembered, almost without exception, with affection.

From a professional point of view, of course, there were many similarities. Both were widely traveled. Both were intelligent, aggressive, and energetic. Both were honored in their time—Louis was given the Order of Liberation by the King of Norway, Dick was made an officer of the French Legion of Honor, and each of them won an Academy Award for the *March of Time*. Both of them were first-class journalists and film makers, and each of them brought his rich background, personality, and interests to the making of the *March of Time*.

No one had a better view of the two men's idiosyncrasies and differences over the years than Arthur Tourtellot, who began working at *MOT* in 1942 as a writer and who became associate producer and right-hand man to Dick de Rochemont, the position that Tom Orchard had held with Louis.

> . . . the way Louis de Rochemont saw the truth and the way Dick did were different. Both were strong personalities. They're creative men, and they were essentially artists, Louis in a strong, assertive, and not too discriminating way, and Dick in a little bit more sensitive, humanistic, and certainly much more scholarly way. Dick lives in a world of distinction; Louis lives in a world of obvious truths. Dick would start asking questions. Louis wanted to confirm values he already had—and rather obvious ones. . . . Louis had some elements of genius, which I define as a felt instinct that this is the way to do this and it will work. . . . I appreciate genius up to a point, but Dick de Rochemont was one of the most civilized men I know, and Louis, in a sense, is one of the least civilized, but terribly gifted and with this passion. . . . Dick is intellectual in his processes, analytical, and, as compared with Louis, quite sensitive. Dick doesn't live in a world of obvious truth, he lives in a world of subtlety.

For the balance of the war years, there was little noticeable difference in *March of Time* output between Dick's operation and Louis's. On the one hand, as we have seen, the war dominated nearly all of the films. At the same time, Richard inherited an organization, an approach, and a journalistic point of view that was stylistically and commercially fixed. "By the time you get around to this point," said Dick, "this *March of Time* group had pretty much got set in their ways. We weren't making changes in style for the purpose of changing or conforming or anything else. We conformed the material we had to the length limitations we had, and the budget limitations we had, and we really didn't have much time to fool around theorizing."

Nonetheless, with the passing of years substantial changes were introduced by the new boss. Some of these were operational. He created an editorial board headed by Jimmy Shute (whom he also made a producer/director), to originate, develop, and refine the scripts. For the first time, said Shute, a fair amount of the material he wrote actually ended up on the screen. Dick also delegated much more creative authority to his subordinates than Louis had ever allowed. It was a novelty for them, and a pleasant one.

> When Dick asked me whether I would serve as producer [said Shute] which I'd refused to do before, the first thing I did was to use sound [more imaginatively]—and then, the rest of the *March of Time* began following me . . . the first thing I ever did as a producer under Dick, I edited the whole picture in a very long sequence of natural sound and no commentary at all until right at the end [when Van Voorhis says]: "Time Marches on!"

Noticeable changes occurred, too, in the subject matter because Richard had interests that were wide in range. His interest in psychology, psychoanalysis, and medicine, for example, was reflected in "Problem Drinkers" (1946), "Is Everybody Happy?" (1946), "Your Doctors" (1947), "The Case of Mrs. Conrad" (1948), and "The Nation's Mental Health" (1951).

He had many friends in the fashion business, and his interest in this and related subjects was translated into "American Beauty" (1945), "Fashion Means Business" (1947), "Beauty at Work" (1950), and "The Male Look" (1950). The subject of family relations was explored in "Nobody's Children?" (1946), "Life with Baby" (1946), "Marriage and Divorce" (1948), "Life with Junior" (1948), and "Life with Grandpa" (1948). The growth and problems of American education were probed in "The Fight for Better Schools" (1949), "Schools March On" (1950), and "Teacher's Crisis" (1947).

Far more than Louis, Richard was fascinated by the entertainment world, and some of the most interesting postwar issues featured this subject. Television in 1947 was just a blur on the horizon, but radio was very popular indeed. "Is Everybody Listening?" (1947) took a look at the radio broadcasting industry and its performers, with amusing and historically valuable vignettes featuring Fred Allen, Jack Benny, Bob Hope, Fibber McGee and Molly, Edgar Bergen and Charlie McCarthy, and Walter Winchell. This was one of only two issues in the history of the *March of Time* in which the face of Westbrook Van Voorhis, radio's most famous voice, was shown to motion picture audiences. At the end of the film we discover that the announcer standing at a microphone within the radio studio, completing the narration of the film which we have just seen, is the Voice of Time himself. Just before the picture fades out, Van Voorhis turns the microphone so that he can face the audience, and says, "Time Marches On!" Interestingly, staff members recall that an enormous amount of time, energy, and heated argument went into the final decision to put Van Voorhis's image on the screen. Several people argued that this exposure would cheapen and compromise the whole idea of the Voice of Time which had been fashioned so carefully over the years.

"Night Club Boom," released immediately after the war in 1946, featured a tour of New York's most celebrated clubs, interviewing proprietors Sherman Billingsley of the Stork Club, John Perona of El Morocco, Barney Josephson of Café Society, and a variety of night club habitués, performers, and columnists, including Ed Wynn, Elliott Roosevelt, Faye Emerson, Jinx Falkenburg, and Leonard Lyons. "On Stage" (1949) reviewed that year's legitimate stage productions on Broadway and the people who wrote, composed, directed, and performed them. "It's in the Groove" (1949) described the recording industry. "Wish You Were Here" (1949) provided an amusing look at Americans on vacation—on cruise ships, at seashore and mountain resorts, on fishing and camping expeditions, and at dude ranches. "Challenge to Hollywood," released late in 1945, described Britain's bid to compete in American and world markets with her postwar feature films. "Following my brother is always a difficult role for anyone," said Dick, "and I don't take claim to do any innovating, but I'll take credit for broadening the base of the *March of Time*'s point of view— perhaps softening things a little."

One thing that did not change was the continuing preoccupation with international politics. By the late 1940's, the grand alliance of World War II which had joined the U.S. and the Soviet Union for four years had disintegrated and collapsed. One after another of the Soviet's neighbors had been politically absorbed into it, either by military action or subversion, and the parallels between Nazi aggression and those of the U.S.S.R. were becoming

British cameraman Peter Hopkinson joined the organization in 1947, spent most of his time in remote parts of the world. Here, he shoots footage for "Formosa—Island of Promise" (1951), the last *March of Time* issue to be released theatrically. (Courtesy Peter Hopkinson)

apparent to American political leaders and commentators. During the ensuing cold war period the *March of Time* displayed the same kind of crusading spirit that had characterized its prewar, antifascist product. For the first time in its history, it began consistently, systematically, and vigorously to attack communism.

Curiously, during the last six years of the *March of Time* there was an almost complete absence of issues dealing with the domestic political scene—a subject which had been a rich mine for the series in its prewar days. In the more than seventy issues released between 1945 and 1951, there is not the same kind of hard-hitting, iconoclastic, satirical treatment that Louis de Rochemont used to attack Huey Long, Father Coughlin, Gerald L. K. Smith, Dr. Townsend, and other political saviors of the late 1930's. Not a single *March of Time* issue, from 1945 to 1951, questioned, attacked, ridiculed, or otherwise treated the new lunatic fringe that was beginning to infest and flourish so luxuriantly along the right-hand border of America's political flowerbed during the late 1940's and early 50's.

Some of today's film critics and historians who mention the *March of Time* in passing refer to it as a politically conservative product. This is not the case when one looks at the output of its best, most exciting, and most influential years, from 1935 to 1942. Unfortunately, the films that were made during those years were, until recently, virtually inaccessible, and are still quite difficult to obtain. Familiar only with the postwar product (which was available in 16mm versions), unable to view the original prints of the 1930's period, many of today's critics have simply assumed that the *March of Time* attacked only left-wing dictatorships, and that because it was owned by Time, Incorporated, it shared its parent company's conservative point of view with respect to things in general. The time has come for a reappraisal.

Only one of the postwar films emerged as a classic. It was called "Atomic Power," and was released in August 1946, a year after the end of the war. It tells of the making of the atomic bomb, and is a quite remarkable example of film making in the *March of Time* tradition.

In 1945, once the bombing of Hiroshima and Nagasaki had been announced, it became apparent to educated citizens that the door to a new and not altogether happy world had been opened, and that once they had all marched through that door, it would close, permanently, behind them. It was also apparent to Dick de Rochemont that, if the story of the atomic bomb were to be told on film in *March of Time* fashion, it would have to be done quickly, before the scientists, politicians, and military officials involved in its creation died. Dick and his staff set out early in 1946 to tell such a story, using the people involved in the event, and such was the reputation of the *March of Time* that they were able to engage the thespian efforts of nearly every person involved in the bomb's invention and use: J. Robert Oppenheimer, Vannevar Bush, Leslie Groves, James Conant, Arthur Compton, Harold Urey, Enrico Fermi, Ernest O. Lawrence, David Lilienthal, Dean Acheson, Bernard Baruch, Leo Szilard, and Albert Einstein. Every one of them performed as actors before *March of Time* cameras, re-creating for director Jack Glenn the events, decisions, and remembered conversations that had attended the birth of the bomb. "I think they had a sense that they had participated in something historic . . . ," said Dick de Rochemont, "just trying to reproduce the way it happened. Telling us how it was." Even Albert Einstein played his part, re-creating the writing of his famous 1939 letter to President Roosevelt which stressed the wartime applications of atomic energy and the potential of an atomic bomb.

Within the limits of governmental security, every step leading to the creation of the first bomb was staged by the *March of Time:* Lise Meitner demonstrating experimentally that the uranium atom could be split; Enrico Fermi achieving the first controlled chain reaction in uranium fission with an experimental pile set up at the University of Chicago; and Alexander Sachs bringing the Einstein letter to President Roosevelt. The building of entirely new industrial cities at Los Alamos, New Mexico, Oak Ridge, Tennessee, and Hanford, Washington, was described with brief, apparently authentic long shots of the industrial complexes involved. Finally, the test shot, "Trinity," was re-created, with J. Robert Oppenheimer and I. Rabi in the control room at Alamagordo, New Mexico, shortly before detonation, speculating on the consequences of their work.

> OPPENHEIMER   The automatic control's started now. Rab, this time the stakes are really high.
>
> RABI   It's going to work, all right, Robert, and I'm sure we'll never be sorry for it.
>
> OPPENHEIMER   In forty seconds, we'll know.

James Conant and Vannevar Bush are seen a moment later, stretched out on the New Mexico sands, several miles from the tower-mounted bomb. The count down, the conversations, the explosion of the test bomb, the awe-filled faces of the scientists as they viewed the fireball through smoked glasses, all were photographed in the predawn gloom of the day. The sequence ends with a shot of Conant and Bush lying on the sand, reaching across to each other to shake hands. The film continued with a sequence on the bombing of Hiroshima and Nagasaki by planes launched from the Marianas, and footage photographed a few weeks after the bombing by American military cameramen of the devastation at Hiroshima, the latter of which included a grim but fascinating shot of an American soldier pointing out the silhouette cast upon the cement pavement by a Japanese at the moment of detonation.

There was some sarcastic humor in the film, too: a scene in which an official at the U.S. Navy Department in Washington coldly turns away Columbia University scientist George B. Pegram, who had tried to tell them in 1939 that an atomic bomb was a distinct possibility and that it had substantial military and naval implications. "Very interesting, doctor," says an obviously uninterested navy official. "Keep us informed."

Few of the film's scenes were authentic. In typical *March of Time* fashion, not only the performances but the settings had been staged. Conant and Bush, stretched out on the New Mexico sands, had actually been photographed lying on the sand-covered floor of a Boston garage. The entire count-down sequence had been staged on the east coast of the country—only the footage of the explosion and fire-ball was authentic. Nonetheless, the meld of re-created scenes and authentic newsreel footage was so well done that, had it not been for the stilted, wooden dialogue, many of the scenes could pass anywhere, even today, for the real thing.

Dick de Rochemont described the film as one of the most difficult they had ever made. How, for example, does one deal, cinematically and dramatically, with someone like Albert Einstein? How does one capture his monumental genius and compassion on a piece of film? "What were we to do?" asked de Rochemont. "Would we say, 'Einstein, will you think for us?' " In the end, he was photographed silent, in the library and on the porch of his Princeton home, except for one spoken line: "I agree!"

The scientists and politicians in the film were not trained as actor; they were no more skilled in the delivery of lines than the other celebrities who had appeared over the years in *MOT* issues. So long as they did not speak they looked just fine. It was only when they began to read the lines of the script that the artificiality of the film became apparent. For all of this, as in the best of the *March of Time*'s "amateur theatricals," the end result is fascinating, and we shall probably never see this kind of film again. An aesthetic judgment of an artifact can be made at any time in the future, but journalistic appraisals are relevant only to the extent

"Atomic Power" (1946) described the design and creation of the atomic bomb, starred the actual scientists who built it. Here, Leo Szilard reads the draft of a letter from Albert Einstein to Franklin Roosevelt, calling the President's attention to the possibilities of atomic fission. (Courtesy Time, Inc.)

Einstein ponders, then speaks his only line in the film: "I agree!" (Courtesy Time, Inc.)

White House confidant Alexander Sachs brings Einstein's letter to the President, beginning a chain reaction of engineering which led to the atomic bomb. (Courtesy Time, Inc.)

Numerous scientists, such as Ernest O. Lawrence, re-created for *March of Time* cameras their role in building the bomb. (Courtesy Time, Inc.)

Actual government footage of the Alamogordo blast was inter-cut with a re-creation of the count-down at "Trinity." (Courtesy Time, Inc.)

Following the successful test, Drs. James Conant and Vannevar Bush, ostensibly stretched out on the sands of New Mexico, shake hands. Actually, they were filmed lying on the floor of a garage in Boston. (Courtesy Time, Inc.)

that they fit within the context of the period under discussion. The *March of Time*'s re-creations will never survive as dramatic artifacts, nor were they so regarded at the time of their original release, but they were certainly acceptable to audiences of the day as a form of illustration.

From historical, political, and sociological points of view, it is *March of Time* issues such as this, featuring reenactments, which are of greatest interest to audiences and scholars of today. They involve examples of what some theorists call "metacommunication"— the communication of messages beyond the obvious ones of the film—a kind of cinematic hidden agenda. Unfortunately, these are also the most "campy" of the lot, this quality being the price that de Rochemont had to pay for introducing a technique that was fresh and exciting in 1935. They just don't write dialogue like Louis's anymore, and, mercifully, people don't read lines the way they did for him anymore, either. "The *Time* style would be laughed out of court today," said associate producer Arthur Tourtellot.

> It seemed very dramatic then. News had been handled in a very pedestrian way. I think one of the great achievements of Luce was that he hit upon a way of making news exciting and dramatic. So did *March of Time* radio and *March of Time* cinema. Nowadays, that dramatizing would be self-defeating because people are more sophisticated. They see actuality, they see the thing happen. You know, you see Oswald killed on camera. No one's going to believe a re-enactment. The camera's ubiquitous.

Ubiquitous or not, today's cameras still record reenactments, although more sophisticated ones than we find in the *March of Time*. In recent years, the technique of re-creation, using professional actors and impersonators, has again achieved currency in the production of so-called "docu-dramas" for network television. Shows such as "The Missiles of October," "Truman at Potsdam," "Collision Course," "Fear on Trial," and "The Lindbergh Kidnapping Case," and feature films such as *The Battle of Algiers,* are substantially identical in their technique to that of the *March of Time*. They integrate both newsreel and staged scenes, the latter having been written in such a manner as to refashion events as they were believed to have happened (or even *might* have happened), but that occurred in the absence of news-film cameras. When I interviewed Louis de Rochemont in November 1975 he had just seen "The Missiles of October." "All right," he joked. "I can die in peace, My God, that was the *March of Time* all the way through!"

In 1950, Dick de Rochemont produced the last of the regular *March of Time* features. Entitled *The Golden Twenties,* it was an amusing and financially successful compilage documentary, based loosely upon the Frederick Lewis Allen book, *Only Yesterday,* adapted for the screen by Sam Bryant, and edited by Leo Zochling. Comprised entirely of newsreel footage of the 1920's and played for laughs, the film employed several narrators for the different kinds of subject matter that appeared: Elmer Davis handled politics; Red Barber sports; Frederick L. Allen manners and customs; Robert Q. Lewis the entertainment world; and Allen Prescott the lighter moments. According to Dick, Spyros Skouras of Twentieth Century-Fox had given assurance that if Time, Inc., were to produce additional features Fox would release them, but Larsen couldn't agree to the proposal. Also in 1950, the *March of Time* won its second Academy Award "Oscar," for its 1949 issue, "A Chance To Live," a sensitively directed and beautifully photographed study of impoverished and brutalized orphans in postwar Italy. The film won in the short documentary category.

Still another imitation of the *March of Time* had appeared in the fall of 1946, this one in England. Entitled *This Modern Age,* it was produced by Sergei Nolbandov for the J. Arthur Rank organization. Stylistically, it was patterned closely on the *March of Time,* although it was by no means as lively or controversial as its American model. Edgar Anstey described the British series as "a little more pedestrian [than the March of Time]; a little more inclined to describe—call the shots . . . rather than to work for a kind of emotional counterpoint between picture and sound."

What distinguished the series from the *March of Time* was the propaganda function that was provided for it by the Rank organization to encourage and facilitate the economic recovery of Great Britain. "The most pervasive theme running through the *This Modern Age* series," wrote Richard Harkness, "was the promotion

Last feature to be produced by the *March of Time* before the end of its theatrical series was *The Golden Twenties* (1950). It was financially successful but failed to keep the series afloat. The following year, as it must to all men, death came to the *March of Time*. (Courtesy Time, Inc.)

of the intelligent utilization of natural, human and industrial resources [in Great Britain]. . . ." The series lost money consistently and achieved virtually no exhibition within the United
States. By virtue of the Rank organization's sponsorship, however,
it was guaranteed exhibition domestically in 500 Rank theaters
throughout England. Altogether, forty-one issues were released by
the time the series closed in December 1950. By that time the
March of Time was hardly worth imitating.

"I remember once looking over the past 18 issues of the *March
of Time*," said Jimmy Shute, "and I think I found three out of the
whole 18 that were really good. I was alarmed about the quality.
They seemed to be falling apart. . . . That wasn't why I left, but
it was true." Few of the issues sparkled with the same vivacity that
had characterized the prewar product. Most of them were dull and
unimaginative, the narration lacklustre, the images little more
than a continuous series of visual "citations." *MOT*'s amusing re-
creations rarely appeared. Both humor and bite were lacking in
the films, and controversy disappeared altogether. Part of the reason for this blandness apparently followed from Richard's sensitivity to what broadcasters and legislators have since termed "The
Fairness Doctrine"—the notion that every controversial story must
incorporate a proportionate and balanced glance at opposing
points of view. It is a doctrine that invites careful scrutiny, for,
even assuming that one can agree upon what is fair, the effort to
achieve that fairness frequently obscures the point or thrust with
which investigative journalism is concerned. Decades earlier, Winston Churchill had been quoted as saying that as between the fire
and the fire-fighters he planned to side with the fire-fighters. In the
1930's Louis always sided with the fire-fighters. In the 1940's, Dick
seemed to feel obliged to give the fire equal time.

No one has ever accused Richard de Rochemont of lacking journalistic courage, for he displayed an abundance of that during his
entire career. Nevertheless, the days of muckraking film journalism were over. For example, a 1945 *MOT* production entitled
"Where's the Meat?" dealt with the mysterious shortages of meat
products in markets, and raised the suspicion that substantial prof-
its were being engineered through artificially elevated prices. One
member of the staff remembered Dick de Rochemont expressing

concern that the meat-packing industry might be offended by the film. Louis, by contrast, would never have worried about offending anyone. Concluded the staff member, "Once you worry about stepping on someone else's toes, you merely succeed in stepping on your own. . . . When Louis left . . . a feeling of complacency settled in, and then I think there may have been too much advice from the front office. . . . Like the jingle for the soft drink—'It's the real thing.' After that, it wasn't."

For still another of the later *March of Time* issues, resourceful director Jack Glenn, after considerable effort, managed to talk a prominent congressman into repeating for *March of Time* cameras and sound recorders a remark that he had made in a speech in which he referred to a well-known columnist as a "kike." The congressman, who had a notorious reputation as a bigot, was flattered when Glenn asked him to repeat excerpts from several of his "best speeches." To Glenn's astonishment, he repeated the speech in question, with the word "kike" still in it. Glenn was delighted.

It wasn't until the film was in the can and back at the laboratory in New York that the congressman realized what he had committed to celluloid, and what the *March of Time* was likely to do with it. On the telephone to Glenn, he demanded that the footage of him be excised from the reel and that his signed release be returned to him. Glenn refused. The politician threatened suit against Time, Incorporated, and apparently brought considerable political pressure to bear. "After all that work," said Glenn, "they [the corporation's leadership] decided they weren't going to use it because they were afraid of [the] congressman. . . . I said, 'The great days of the *March of Time* are over.' That was the signal for me."

For most of its first decade, the *March of Time* had been an obsession with Louis, an *idée fixe* upon which he focused every moment of his time and every bit of his considerable energy. It was an obsession that Richard did not share.

> What he did not have that Louis had was a passion for film [said Arthur Tourtellot]. Dick knew there was a great big world out there, a world of light, of intellectual interests . . . of aesthetic appreciation. . . . Dick de Rochemont is too civilized to be a producer of films, to the extent of thinking that it was the most im-

300

portant thing in the world. He knew God-damned well it wasn't. Louis did not. Louis believed it was the most important. . . .

If there was a great picture to be looked at, or a performance to be seen, or a great person to meet or a great experience to be gone through, Dick would do it. Louis wouldn't. He'd sit in the God-damned cutting room, clipping one foot off a shot.

Dick de Rochemont seemed to agree: "Louis always had a lot of enthusiasm I may have lacked."

Financially, things went from bad to worse. The *March of Time* had never made any money; the corporation had been happy if it just broke even. Now, in the late 1940's, it could not even do that. The series had always been overbudgeted for the traditionally low-profit, short-subject market. Such a budget, spawned during the lean years of the Depression, could only increase with the passing of years. After World War II, the cost of production rose far beyond income. At the same time, in common with the rest of the film industry, the ranks of its audience were attenuated by the electronic marvels of television. Television, its journalistic capabilities clearly apparent, if not yet fully realized, was an economic competitor so formidable that continued theatrical production of the series became impractical. "We won battles and eventually lost the war," said Dick de Rochemont. "We failed to convince the exhibitor that he should pay for *March of Time* at least as much as for the "B" second feature if he ran double-bill. Television provided the exhibitor with the weapon for his *coup de grace*. He said, 'Why should we pay for what people are seeing at home for free?' This was not strictly true, but it was plausible, and it killed off the newsreels *and* the *March of Time* eventually."

Arthur Murphy, a corporation executive, was assigned the unpleasant job of winding up the *March of Time,* but in the end, it was Larsen himself who had to terminate his own creation. In August 1951, as it must to all men, death came to the *March of Time.* What Huey Long, Adolf Hitler, and a multitude of international censors and litigants had failed to accomplish, television competition had achieved in only a few years. In the fall of 1951, this ubiquitous, impudent film series ceased theatrical production and disappeared from motion picture screens forever.

Amongst film critics, Bosley Crowther, in the July 15, 1951, edition of the *New York Times,* best expressed the dismay and regret that many people felt when the end of the series was announced:

> . . . more than a sentimental sadness over the passing of a cinematic friend will be felt by those toilers in the vineyards who have sweat blood over documentary films. For to them, no matter how they may have snickered at the series' recognized conventional form, the March of Time has stood up as a symbol of real accomplishment in the "pictorial journalism" field. Out of the turbulent Nineteen Thirties, out of those restless years of social change and evolution and growing tension in the world, it emerged with all the eagerness and confidence of the new journalistic approach, pacing off the fruitful innovators and waving the aspirants on.

Fully twenty-five years have passed now since the *March of Time,* with its cinematic bag of tricks, marched off the world's motion picture screens to the oblivion of the film vault. So far, there have been no signs of its reappearance. The production organization itself continued to operate for several years, producing industrial public relations, and television films. Under Arthur Tourtellot, who succeeded Dick de Rochemont as head of the organization when Dick resigned, it produced an archival documentary series for television, based upon the Eisenhower book, *Crusade in Europe,* which was a modest success. This was followed by a spin-off entitled, *Crusade in the Pacific.* In 1960, Morrie Roizman was assigned the job of assembling a 13-week retrospective series of early issues of the *March of Time* for rerelease. This was done and Henry Cabot Lodge was engaged to narrate them. But before the series could be released, Lodge joined the Nixon ticket as vice-presidential candidate. Because of Lodge's political position at that time, the series was shelved. Roizman said that Henry Luce felt that Lodge's appearance made the retrospective look like a plank of the Republican platform.

Still later, in 1965, independent television producer David Wolper gained access to the *March of Time* film library and released a series of eight hour-long documentaries which used the *MOT* title. It was not successful.

Finally, in 1974, North German Television Network commissioned Lothar Wolff to produce a 30-minute film entitled "Report on the March of Time," which summarized the sixteen-year history of the series. With an appropriate German-language sound track, the film was screened on German television and was followed by a complete run of the first year's issues of the *March of Time*—issues that had never been seen in Nazi Germany at the time of the original release. Reception of the series was reported to be enthusiastic.

Considered today, it seems superficial to describe the ultimate failure of the series only in terms of rising costs and aggressive television competition. The point, we suspect, is that the style and format of the *March of Time* had scarcely varied from the day it opened until the day it closed. In 1935 its innovations had had an electrifying effect on other film makers, infusing the documentary movement with new vitality and popularizing the "idea film" for theatrical audiences. A fast freight on the high iron of new journalism, the *March of Time* roared through 1930's America, startling the provincials wherever it went. It was noisy and exciting, and the critics who lined up along the right-of-way to watch it pass didn't always know what to make of it. Today some of them still don't.

If the *March of Time*'s originality had been a growing, changing thing, if it had inspired more emulation than it did imitation, it might have survived the familiarity that breeds net losses in both the film and television businesses. In 1935 Alistair Cooke had cautioned film makers against "witless imitation" of the *March of Time*. So had Grierson. The years that followed brought a rash of copies, most of them poor. Their producers appropriated *March of Time* style and format, but clearly lacked the experience, energy, vision, and resources of the originator.

Whatever the *March of Time*'s faults may have been—and there were many—it was always dynamic, positive, and self-confident. Such qualities, when found in news films, should be counted as virtues. The therapeutic value of the Voice of Time's firm and prescient declarations was not lost on fearful audiences of the day. The movie patron, even when finding *Time*'s solutions inadequate, was at least impressed with the earth-shaking self-confidence with which they had been delivered. The *March of Time*'s very act of examination seemed almost as good as a bona fide solution. The knowledge that *MOT* was "doing" a subject was, in itself, reassuring; it meant that lively debate and public awareness of the issues involved would follow inevitably.

Will the *March of Time* or anything like it again appear on the American motion picture scene? Probably not. In the past, the appeal of the *March of Time* lay largely in its implied assumption that problems could be solved and that answers would be forthcoming—and that the answers would be dramatic ones. Certainly political, economic, and military crises still remain, but the dogged faith of the 1930's appears to have given way to fatalism in the 1970's.

We should not look to the television screen for its reappearance. Television executives, skittishly sensitive to FCC pressures and the protests of vocal minorities, eschew intentionally partisan and provocative programming. Sponsors understandably hesitate to underwrite programs calculated to arouse and possibly alienate substantial portions of their audiences. "I look at today's TV news," said Richard de Rochemont in 1975, "and apart from an occasional Eric Severeid, everything seems to be going right back to the newsreel approach. . . . They [television newspeople] are against the man-eating shark and the boll weevil, as everyone has been since journalism was invented, but apart from that, they treat the most idiotic people . . . with great respect. . . . At least my brother and his people saw through the Huey Long thing and spoke out on it."

Either from preference or conditioning, television viewers appear to reject the unseen, off-stage narrator in favor of the "News Personality"—a flesh-and-blood visitor to their living rooms whom they can recognize and admire or criticize. The powerful and compelling off-stage Voice of Time which narrated the *March of Time* had no distinct personality characteristics. As such, it was a difficult voice to question or attack. In the television years that followed the demise of the *March of Time,* the sententious voice of Edward R. Murrow came closest to approximating the unseen presence of Van Voorhis. For a while, until Murrow's unhappy departure from television news broadcasting in 1961, the omniscient voice remained, but was revealed to have mortal form and substance. Lacking the visual anonymity of Van Voorhis, Murrow and his successors became vulnerable targets for segments of the television audience. (The reference here is to presentation. The journalistic distinction between Murrow and Van Voorhis is, of course, profound. The first was a distinguished commentator who generated his own material; the second was a talented performer who read what was written by others.)

In the years that followed, journalists of Murrow's caliber have been replaced on network levels by bland, wry, and avuncular personalities who seek to maintain that precarious balance required by television's fairness doctrine. Most recently, on the local level, the individual television narrator has been widely replaced by teams of vaudevillians who desperately attempt to infuse accounts of complicated economic trends, intricate political maneuvers, and involved international tensions with light-hearted banter and slapstick humor—television's equivalent of the motion picture newsreel's Lew Lehr and the monkeys.

And so, with a backward glance and a ruffle of drums, *Time* marches off to the film vaults. No competitor was to blame for its demise. No one did it in. It simply grew old and tiresome, telling the same stories in a manner which, once fresh and amusing, finally grew tedious with repetition. No one knew this better than Dick de Rochemont, who concluded in 1974:

> I would not even contemplate the production of *March of Time* today. In 1951 I announced to my employees that the formula or format or idea, whatever it was, had lived out its useful life, and so it had. As one of the chief mourners, for it was the best job I ever had, I wanted it to have a decent burial. Time, Incorporated, made various attempts at resuscitation, but none of them worked. *MOT* still remains an innovation which lasted sixteen years—a respectable life-span for a motion picture series, only rivaled by the newsreels and cartoon shorts (mostly gone now, too)—and won friends and respect. What more can we ask?

Bibliographical Notes

1

In 1974 the *March of Time*'s library of stock-shot footage, as distinct from prints of the finished films, was donated to the U.S. National Archives (together with the production records), where it is now available for research purposes or for film production. A run of prints of the original finished releases from about 1938 to 1951 is also available for study. In 1973 a run of the rarely seen early issues, from 1935 onward, was given by the corporation to the study collection of the New York Museum of Modern Art to commemorate Roy Larsen's fiftieth anniversary with Time, Inc. Selected issues are also available at the archives of Time, Incorporated, in New York. A run of British releases is available at the British Film Institute's archive; however, these differ in many respects from the original American releases. The corporation has retained all rights to its more than 200 finished sound-on-film issues. Beginning in 1939 selected titles were edited for educational use and were made available in 16mm format.

Total footage in the Washington collection is estimated at 10 million 35mm feet, including several million shot or acquired after theatrical release ended in 1951. It will not survive for long, however, because it was photographed on perishable nitrocellulose film stock. Its only hope for survival is a speedy but expensive reprinting onto acetate-based film.

Bibliographical Notes

For background reading on the American newsreel see Raymond Fielding, *The American Newsreel, 1911-1967* (1972).

The founding, evolution, and leadership of Time, Incorporated, are described in Robert Elson, *Time, Inc.* (1968) and *The World of Time, Inc.* (1973); W. A. Swanberg, *Luce and His Empire* (1972); David Cort, *The Sin of Henry R. Luce* (1974); John K. Jessup, ed., *The Ideas of Henry Luce* (1969); John Kobler, *Luce—His Time, Life and Fortune* (1968); Noel F. Busch, *Briton Hadden* (1949); Wolcott Gibbs, "Time . . . Fortune . . . Life . . . Luce," in the *New Yorker*, November 28, 1936; Dwight MacDonald, "Time and Henry Luce," in the *Nation*, May 1, May 8, and May 22, 1937; and Marlen Pew, "Bitten by Ducks," in *Editor and Publisher*, November 3, 1928.

Information about the *March of Time* radio programs was drawn from an interview with Roy Larsen on January 21, 1975; Erik Barnouw, *A Tower in Babel* (1969) and *The Golden Web* (1968); David Campbell, "The Origin and the Early Developments of the Time Incorporated Radio Series, the *March of Time*" (master's thesis, Central Missouri State College, 1969); Frank Tucker, "A Critical Evaluation of the March of Time, 1931-32" (master's thesis, Central Missouri State College, 1969); and Frank Buxton and Bill Owen, *The Big Broadcast, 1920-1950* (1972).

Critical insights were gained from John Grierson, "The Course of Realism," *Footnotes to the Film* (1938) and Andrew Buchanan, *The Art of Film Production* (1936).

Information bearing specifically upon the launching of the *March of Time* film series was secured from a memorandum prepared for me by Time, Inc., executive Arthur Murphy, dated November 3, 1955; *Four Hours a Year* (1936); and *Newsweek*, February 9, 1935. According to the Murphy memorandum, the *March of Time* film organization was incorporated as a subsidiary company of Time, Inc., the first meeting of the corporation being held on November 24, 1934. In September, 1935, the March of Time, Inc., was dissolved and the film organization functioned thereafter as a department of Time, Inc. Roy Larsen served as producer of *MOT* from its beginning until December 10, 1936, at which time he was succeeded by Louis de Rochemont.

I obtained personal reminiscences in interviews with Harry Von Zell (October 1, 1974); Louis de Rochemont (June 25, 1975); Morrie Roizman (March 24, 1975); and Tom Orchard (March 1, 1975). Biographical information about Roy Larsen was obtained from *Current Biography Yearbook* (1950) and various editions of *Who's Who in America*.

A list of the *March of Time*'s experimental reels can be found in the vertical file collection of the Museum of Modern Art and in *MOT* production files 2-11, 25, 40, and 42, United States National Archives (Washington, D.C.). Newspaper and magazine clippings, reviews, photographs, promotion booklets and related documents are available in the vertical file collection of the Museum of Modern Art, the archives of Time, Incorporated, and the Theatrical Collection of the New York Public Library at the Lincoln Performing Arts Center (all in New York City).

Detailed, final, editing continuity scripts of the *March of Time*'s monthly releases and its feature films were originally filed with the U.S. Copyright Office at the time that the individual films involved were submitted for copyright registration. These are available for examination in Washington, D.C.

2

Biographical data about Louis de Rochemont are scarce and contradictory. The information in this chapter is based primarily upon the following interviews: with de Rochement, June 25, 1975; with Jack Glenn, March 8, 1975; with James Shute, January 16, 1975; with Tom Orchard, March 1, 1975; with Arthur Tourtellot, May 15, 1975; with Roy Larsen, January 21, 1975; with Mary Losey Field, February 28, 1975; with Albert Sindlinger, March 17, 1976; with Morrie Roizman, March 24, 1975; with Jack Shaindlin, January 6, 1975; and with Lothar Wolff, April 18, 1975.

Information was also culled from the CBS television show, "Four Hours a Year," 1974, and from the transcript of the program and the out-takes for the production of the North German Television show, "Report on the March of Time," produced in 1974-75.

The following articles and books also proved helpful: Eugene Lyons, "Louis de Rochemont, Maverick of the Movies," *Reader's Digest,* July 1949; Maurice Zolotow, "Want To Be a Movie Star?" *Saturday Evening Post,* March 29, 1952; Harry Lawrenson, "Foreign Editions—Production and Significance of Newsreels," *Journal of the Society of Motion Picture Engineers,* November 1946; *Current Biography Yearbook* (1949), Film Daily Yearbook (1938), and various editions of *Who's Who in America* and *International Motion Picture Almanac.*

Information about the *March of the Years* series was secured from a promotion prospectus in the collection of Jack Glenn, as well as from interviews with Glenn and de Rochemont.

3

The information about the first year of the *March of Time* is based on interviews with Albert Sindlinger on March 17, 1976; James Shute, January 16, 1975; Louis de Rochemont, June 25, 1975; Roy Larsen, January 21, 1975; Mary Losey Field, February 28, 1975; Tom Orchard, March 1, 1975; and Richard de Rochemont, April 18, 1975.

In addition, the following sources were consulted at the United States National Archives in Washington, D.C.: *March of Time* production file numbers 67, 69, 97, and 157. In the latter file I used an undated memorandum; a July 8, 1935 memorandum; a July 14, 1935 memorandum; and a letter to Larsen from Richard de Rochemont dated July 8, 1935. I also made reference to an undated list and synopsis of *March of Time* issues published in the 1950's from my own collection.

Useful background information was provided by *Four Hours a Year* (1936), Robert Elson, *Time, Inc.* (1968), and Neville March Hunnings, *Film Censors and the Law* (1967), and articles appearing in *Variety* April 24, June 12, October 30, and November 13, 1935; *Motion Picture Herald* April 27, May 11, and July 13, 1935; *Newsweek* February 9, 1935; *Life* January 31, 1938; and the *New York Times* October 27, 1935.

The first issue of the *March of Time* was released in England in November 1935 to 190 theaters.

4

Material for this chapter has been drawn from the following secondary sources: John Grierson, "The Course of Realism," in *Footnotes to the Film* (1937); Paul Rotha, *Documentary Film* (1936); and the CBS production of "Four Hours a Year," in the series, *Camera Three* (1974).

I also consulted 192 continuity scripts of the *March of Time* filed with the original prints at the Library of Congress at the time that their copyrights were registered. These scripts provide running footage counts for every shot, a description of each shot, the accompanying narration, and the length of each issue in both 35mm footage and running time.

In addition to the University of Vermont lecture by Lothar Wolff on April 23, 1976, and a July 24, 1974, memorandum by Richard de Rochemont, the following interviews proved helpful: with Louis de

Rochemont, June 25, 1975; Jack Glenn, March 8, 1975; Peter Hopkinson, September 6, 1975; Tom Orchard, March 1, 1975; Arthur Tourtellot, May 15, 1975; Lothar Wolff, April 18, 1975; Morrie Roizman, March 24, 1975; and an interview conducted by Roy Brown with Richard de Rochemont on October 22, 1972.

Willard Van Dyke's definition of documentary appears in the spring 1965 issue of *Film Comment*. Harry Cohn's definition was quoted by Fred Zinneman in the May-June 1976 issue of *Action*.

5

Biographical data on Richard de Rochemont in this chapter are based upon the following: an interview with de Rochemont conducted by Roy Brown on October 22, 1972; another interview that I conducted on April 18, 1975; a memorandum by de Rochemont dated July 24, 1974; a December 1, 1949, biographical summary from the archives of Time, Inc., entitled "How MOT Marches On;" an article by Theodore Strauss in the *New York Times*, January 16, 1944; a December 1, 1937, article in *Variety; Current Biography Yearbook* (1945); and various editions of *Who's Who in America*.

The biographical material on other *March of Time* staff members has been gleaned from interviews with Jack Glenn (March 8, 1975, and September 6, 1975) and a letter from Glenn (August 31, 1976); and interviews with Tom Orchard, March 1, 1975; Harry Von Zell, October 1, 1974; James Shute, January 16, 1975; Jack Shaindlin, January 6, 1975; Albert Sindlinger, March 17, 1976; Lothar Wolff, April 18, 1976; Mary Losey Field, February 28, 1975; Arthur Tourtellot, May 15, 1975; Morrie Roizman, March 24, 1975, and October 28, 1975; Peter Hopkinson, September 6, 1975; Jack Bradford, October 6, 1975; and Roy Larsen, January 21, 1975. Occasionally the sentences have been rearranged for greater clarity.

Among the secondary sources used were Elizabeth Sussex, *The Rise and Fall of British Documentary* (1975); "Van Whangs Into It," the *New Yorker*, November 13, 1937; Lothar Wolff, "Reminiscences of an Itinerant Filmmaker," *Journal of the University Film Association*, vol. 24, no. 4, 1972; Peter Hopkinson, *Split Focus* (1969); Richard Griffith, "Post-War American Documentaries," *The Penguin Film Review No. 8* (January 1949); and *Living Films: A Catalogue of Documentary Films and Their Makers* (1940).

North German Television's 1974-75 production of "Report on the

Bibliographical Notes

March of Time" MOT production file No. 420 and a lecture by Lothar Wolff at the University of Vermont on April 23, 1976, also helped to illuminate the period.

It is possible that Harry Von Zell may have narrated a handful of the very earliest *March of Time* issues or perhaps the experimental reels that Louis de Rochemont and Roy Larsen put together. De Rochemont said that he recalled Von Zell working on some early reels. Also, at least one of the earliest magazine articles about the series lists Von Zell as the narrator. Be this as it may, Von Zell does not recall ever narrating a single film issue of the *MOT* film series.

Although Albert Sindlinger ceased work as a full-time employee of the *March of Time* on December 31, 1939, he continued to serve the organization as a consultant through 1942. His association with the company concluded altogether in January 1943.

The support staff at Richard de Rochemont's Paris office included John Mansfield, Marcel Paulis, Raymond Chaumeret, Solange Croux, Yvonne Oberlin, and Maureen Peschansky; at the London office, William Seibert, Humphrey Swingler, George Benson, James Moynahan, Rita André, Nancy Pessac, Arthur Green, Gwendloyn Rose, Norah Alexander, and John Owens.

Assistant cameramen on the domestic crews were Burt Pike, Frank Calabria, Louis Tumola, Bob Daly, George Stoetzel, and Douglas Downs. Additional sound recordists were Tony Girolami and Pat Fox.

6

Material for this chapter has been drawn from a number of interviews: with Jack Glenn, March 8, 1975; Tom Orchard, March 1, 1975; Edgar Anstey, August 13, 1976; Roy Larsen, January 21, 1975; Albert Sindlinger, March 17, 1976; Richard de Rochemont, April 18, 1975; Mary Losey, February 28, 1975; Jack Shaindlin, January 6, 1975; Morrie Roizman, March 24, 1975; and James Shute, January 16, 1975. A letter from Jack Glenn dated August 17, 1976, and a November 3, 1955, memorandum from Arthur Murphy, Jr., also proved helpful.

With the September 1936 issue, the *March of Time* arbitrarily changed its "volume-issue" numbering system: that issue was shown as Vol. 3, No. 1. For background information, see *MOT* production file number 304; *Four Hours a Year* (1936); Elson, *Time, Inc.* (1968); the *New York Times,* May 23, 1936; *Time,* June 1, 1936; William Troy, "Pictorial Journalism," the *Nation,* February 20, 1935; and Phil Daly, *The Film Daily,* May 19, 1948.

Bibliographical Notes

The entire Father Divine episode was banned in England as being "blasphemous." Divine was claimed by his followers to be God, and in those days the Deity could not be mentioned on English screens. (*Variety*, December 1, 1937).

The alternate ending sequence to the issue on the presidency is available for examination at Time, Inc., archives, as well as in the film entitled, "Report on the March of Time," produced by North German Television Network, 1974-75.

Reaction to British censorship of the League of Nations issue appearing in the London *Daily Herald, News Chronicle,* and *The Times* were quoted in *Time,* June 1, 1936.

7

March of Time production file numbers 363, 448, 453, 517, and 536 at the U.S. National Archives were consulted for this chapter.

In addition to the newspapers and periodicals cited in the text, see the *Motion Picture Herald,* March 27, 1937; the *New York Times,* April 17, 1937, August 27, 1937, September 30, 1937, and February 11, 1938; *Time,* September 13, 1937, January 10, 1938, and February 28, 1938; *Life,* January 10, 1938; and *Variety,* January 26, 1938. Also of interest for this period are John Harley, *World-Wide Influences of the Cinema* (1940); Roger Manvell, *Film* (1950); and both program material and out-takes from North German Television Network's 1974-75 "Report on the March of Time."

The following interviews, of which the sentence order of some were reversed for greater clarity, also provided material for this chapter: Louis de Rochemont, June 25, 1975; James Shute, January 16, 1975; Richard de Rochemont, April 18, 1975; Tom Orchard, March 1, 1975; Jack Glenn, March 8, 1975; and Albert Sindlinger, March 17, 1976. Finally, Tom Orchard's memorandum to Louis de Rochemont, August 18, 1937, and Lothar Wolff's April 23, 1976, University of Vermont lecture were valuable sources.

8

The quotation from John Grierson appears in "The Course of Realism," *Footnotes to the Film* (1938), p. 144. The remarks of David O. Selznick and Dorothy Thompson were featured in a *March of Time* advertisement in the *Motion Picture Herald* on February 5, 1938.

The production file number of "Inside Nazi Germany—1938" in the

Bibliographical Notes

U.S. National Archives collection is 563. Personal reminiscences of the making of the film were culled from interviews with Julien Bryan on November 17, 1959; Louis de Rochemont on June 25, 1975; Tom Orchard on March 1, 1975; Jack Glenn on March 8, 1975; James Shute on January 16, 1975; and Lothar Wolff on November 20, 1975.

For additional material on this subject, see Irving Browning, "Julien Bryan, Film Reporter," *American Cinematographer*, (April 1945); *Living Films: A Catalogue of Documentary Films and Their Makers* (1940); Rotha, *Documentary Film* (1952); John Mosher, *New Yorker*, (December 31, 1938); and "Freedom of Film and Press," the *Christian Century*, (February 2, 1938).

Shots of Hitler, although not unknown, were kept to a minimum in American newsreels during the 1930's. In March 1935, shortly after the *March of Time* was launched, staff member Maria Sermolino issued a press notice which charged the newsreels with suppression of coverage of Hitler, in contrast to the *March of Time*, which, that same month, released the first of its episodes that dealt explicitly with the dictator. Some newsreel companies angrily denied the charge, although they acknowledged in an article in the *Motion Picture Herald*, March 23, 1935, that (1) there had been a time when the newsreels "laid off" Hitler because of the anti-Semitic theme of his government; (2) some exhibitors cut shots of Hitler out of their newsreels before running them for audiences; and (3) there had been complaints from exhibitors regarding coverage of Hitler, and at least one complete circuit of theaters had threatened to cancel a particular newsreel unless coverage of Hitler were excised.

9

For a description of the Newspaper Guild's organizational activities during the 1930's, see Daniel Leab, *A Union of Individuals: The Formation of the American Newspaper Guild, 1933-1936* (1970); and S. Kuczun, "History of the American Newspaper Guild" (Ph.D. dissertation, University of Minnesota, 1970).

Examples from dope sheets, letters, and memoranda were selected from the following production file numbers: 66, 104, 157, 188, 193, 423, 483, 496, 663, 665, 725, 728, 739, 805, 811, and 838.

In addition, the following interviews formed the basis for much of the material presented in this chapter: James Shute, January 16, 1975; Jack Glenn, March 8, 1975; Lothar Wolff, April 18, 1975; Albert Sindlinger, March 17, 1976; Richard de Rochemont, April 18, 1975;

Bibliographical Notes

Jack Shaindlin, January 6, 1975; Mary Losey, February 28, 1975; Louis de Rochemont, June 25, 1975; Arthur Tourtellot, May 15, 1975; Tom Orchard, March 1, 1975; a telephone conversation with Lothar Wolff on August 3, 1976; and an interview with Jack Glenn appearing in the film production, "Report on the March of Time," produced by North German Television Network, 1974-75.

Exact production costs of *March of Time* issues apparently are no longer available from either the corporation or surviving *March of Time* personnel. The estimates shown in this chapter were provided by Lothar Wolff, Morrie Roizman, Tom Orchard, Louis de Rochemont, and Richard de Rochemont.

Original memoranda cited in the text, regarding pay scales and working conditions were given to me by a former *MOT* staff member.

Information regarding disputes between the *March of Time* and the Screen Actors Guild will be found in the *New York Times*, January 8, 1947, and March 23, 1947; and *Variety*, December 1, 1937.

Sixteen millimeter prints of the *March of Time* were first made available for educational use through the Association of School Film Libraries around March 1939. Beginning in October 1944, the *March of Time* organization itself began to release 16mm versions of selected *MOT* releases. These were known as "Forum Editions." Still later, beginning in January 1952, McGraw-Hill became the exclusive distributor.

10

The production file numbers consulted for these years were 588, 614, 637, and 667. The chapter is based primarily on information gleaned from interviews with the following: Tom Orchard, March 1, 1975; Jack Glenn, March 8, 1975; Richard de Rochemont, April 18, 1975; Albert Sindlinger, March 17, 1976; James Shute, January 16, 1975; and Louis de Rochemont, June 25, 1975. I have also made reference to a letter from Richard de Rochemont, July 24, 1974, and the lecture by Lothar Wolff at the University of Vermont, April 23, 1976.

Also of interest for the prewar period are Paul Rotha, *Documentary Film* (1963); "Inside France's Maginot Line," *Life*, October 3, 1938; and John Grierson, "The Documentary Idea," in *The Complete Photographer* (1943), Theodore Strauss, "Richard of the House of de Rochemont," *New York Times*, January 16, 1944; and news items appearing in *Variety*, April 20, 1938, and the *New York Times*, May 2, 1938, and September 23, 1939.

Bibliographical Notes

Estimates of the number of *March of Time* employees vary, depending upon the person making the estimate, the period under discussion, and whether one includes both production and promotion people, both full-time and part-time, both permanent and freelance, and both domestic and foreign workers. Richard de Rochemont told me that at the time the series went out of business in 1951 there were 138 employees, of whom 123 were based in New York City. This figure sounds high, however, and probably includes other kinds of workers associated with Time, Inc. *Scholastic* magazine, in its November 19, 1938, issue estimated a full-time staff of 58. Morrie Roizman, interview on March 24, 1975, estimated the worldwide staff at 100. Tom Orchard, interviewed March 1, 1975, estimated the domestic staff of workers at between 40 and 50 people.

11

In addition to sources indicated in the text, material for this chapter has been drawn from numerous newspaper and periodical accounts, principally from the *New York Times,* October 22, 1939; January 14, 1940; March 12, 1940; March 24, 1940; June 30, 1940; October 26, 1940; January 18, 1941; and January 19, 1941; *Variety,* March 5, 1941; March 19, 1941; September 10, 1941; September 17, 1941; September 20, 1941; and October 21, 1941; the *Los Angeles Times,* August 29, 1940; the *New York World-Telegram,* March 9, 1940; *Life* magazine, February 26, 1940; July 22, 1940; August 12, 1940; September 22, 1941; October 6, 1941; and November 3, 1941; *Spectator,* March 29, 1940; *Motion Picture Reviews,* December, 1940; and *Motion Picture Herald,* March 9, 1940 and September 7, 1940.

The *MOT* production file numbers relevant to the period are 466, 547, 565, 603, 604, 613, 646, 650, 652, 692, 694, 786, and 788 through 795 (U.S. National Archives).

In addition to interviews with Tom Orchard (March 1, 1975), Roy Larsen (January 21, 1975), James Shute (January 16, 1975), Louis de Rochemont (June 25, 1975), Albert Sindlinger (March 17, 1976), Jack Shaindlin (January 6, 1975), James G. Stewart (March 10, 1976), and Richard de Rochemont (April 18, 1975), the following articles and books are helpful for the film student of the period: Lothar Wolff, "Reminiscences of an Itinerant Filmmaker," *Journal of the University Film Association,* vol. 2, no 4 (1972); Siegfried Kracauer, *From Caligari to Hitler* (1947); Peter Morris (ed.), *The National Film Board of Canada: The War Years* (1965); Jay Leyda, *Films Beget Films* (1964); Wil-

Bibliographical Notes

liam Goetz, "The Canadian Wartime Documentaries—*Canada Carries On* and the *World in Action* Revisited" (research paper for the Department of Radio-TV-Film, Temple University, 1975); Elizabeth Sussex (ed.), *The Rise and Fall of British Documentary* (1975); and "The World in Action," *Documentary News Letter*, May, 1942. The remark attributed to Otto Dietrich was quoted in a biographical piece about Richard de Rochemont in *Current Biography Yearbook* (1945).

12

The material on which this chapter is based was obtained from interviews with Tom Orchard (March 1, 1975), Lothar Wolff (April 18, 1975), Louis de Rochemont (June 25, 1975), Jack Glenn (March 8, 1975), Roy Larsen (January 21, 1975), Albert Sindlinger (March 17, 1976), James Shute (January 16, 1975), and Arthur Tourtellot (May 15, 1975).

Other useful sources were a promotion booklet published by Time, Inc., in 1942 entitled "We Are the Marines"; Byron Price, "Freedom of Press, Radio, and Screen," *The Annals of the American Academy of Political and Social Science* (November 1947); and North German Television Network's 1974-75 "Report on the March of Time"; "Marines Attack Solomons," *Life*, August 24, 1942; and news items and reviews appearing in *Variety*, December 9, 1942 and December 14, 1942.

Preparations for, and attendance at, Louis de Rochemont's going-away party are described in documents in the Time, Inc., archives.

13

The sentence order in some of the following interviews has been changed for greater clarity: Richard de Rochemont (April 18, 1975) and his memorandum dated July 24, 1974; James Shute (January 16, 1975); Arthur Tourtellot (May 15, 1975); Louise de Rochemont (June 25, 1975); Jack Glenn (March 8, 1975); and Morrie Roizman (March 24, 1975).

Also of interest for this period are Richard Harkness, "This Modern Age" (research paper, Department of Radio-Television-Film, Temple University, 1974); and *MOT* production file numbers 638 and 1147.

Bibliography

BOOKS AND MONOGRAPHS

Anonymous, *The Factual Film*. London: Oxford University Press, 1947.

———, *The First 59*. New York: Time, Inc., 1936 (pamphlet).

———, *Four Hours a Year*. New York: Time, Inc., 1936.

———, *Introducing the March of Time*. New York: Time, Inc., 1935 (pamphlet).

———, *Living Films: A Catalog of Documentary Films and Their Makers*. New York: Association of Documentary Film Producers, 1940.

Baechlin, Peter and Maurice Muller-Strauss. *Newsreels across the World*. Paris: UNESCO, 1952.

Barnouw, Erik, *Documentary: A History of the Non-Fictional Film*. New York: Oxford University Press, 1974.

———, *The Golden Web*. New York: Oxford University Press, 1968.

———, *The Image Empire*. New York: Oxford University Press, 1970.

———, *A Tower in Babel*. New York: Oxford University Press, 1969.

Barry, Iris, *The Film and Contemporary History* (Museum of Modern Art Film Library Program. Series 2, Program 3). New York: Museum of Modern Art [n.d.].

Benoit-Levy, Jean, *The Art of the Motion Picture*. New York: Coward-McCann, 1946.

Bluem, A. William, *Documentary in American Television*. New York: Hastings House, 1965.

Buchanan, Andrew, *The Art of Film Production*. London: Sir I. Pitman & Sons, Ltd., 1936.

Bibliography

———, *Going to the Cinema*. London: Phoenix House, Ltd., 1947.

Busch, Noel, *Briton Hadden*. New York: Farrar, Straus & Co., 1949.

Buxton, Frank and Bill Owen, *The Big Broadcast, 1920-1950*. New York: Viking Press, 1972.

Cohn, Lawrence, *Movietone Presents the 20th Century*. New York: St. Martin's Press, 1976.

Cort, David, *The Sin of Henry R. Luce*. Secaucus, N.J.: L. Stuart, 1974.

Davis, Richard Harding, *Gallegher and Other Stories*. 1891. Reprint. New York: Arno Press, 1969.

Elson, Robert T., *Time, Inc*. New York: Atheneum, 1968.

———, *The World of Time, Inc*. New York: Atheneum, 1973.

Fielding, Raymond, *The American Newsreel, 1911-1967*. Norman: University of Oklahoma Press, 1972.

Grierson, John, *Grierson on Documentary*. New York: Harcourt Brace & Company, 1947.

Harley, John, *World-Wide Influences of the Cinema*. Los Angeles: University of Southern California Press, 1940.

Hopkinson, Peter, *Split Focus*. London: Rupert Hart-Davis, 1969.

Hunnings, Neville March, *Film Censors and the Law*. London: George Allen & Unwin, Ltd., 1967.

Jessup, John K., ed., *The Ideas of Henry Luce*. New York: Atheneum, 1969.

Kobler, John, *Luce—His Time, Life and Fortune*. Garden City: Doubleday, 1968.

Kracauer, Siegfried, *From Caligari to Hitler*. Princeton: Princeton University Press, 1947.

Leab, Daniel, *A Union of Individuals: The Formation of the American Newspaper Guild, 1933-1936*. New York: Columbia University Press, 1970.

Leyda, Jay, *Films Beget Films*. London: George Allen & Unwin, Ltd., 1964.

Manvell, Roger, *Film*. Rev. ed. Harmondsworth-Middlesex: Penguin Books, 1950.

Morris, Peter, ed., *The National Film Board of Canada: The War Years* (Canadian Film Archives. Canadian Filmography Series, No. 3). Ottawa: Canadian Film Institute, 1965.

Rotha, Paul, *Documentary Film*. 1936. Reprint. New York: Hastings House, 1963.

Seldes, George, *The Facts Are —*. New York: In Fact, Inc. [1942].

Seldes, Gilbert, *The Movies Come from America*. New York: Charles Scribner's Sons, 1937.

Smith, Paul, ed., *The Historian and Film*. Cambridge: Cambridge University Press, 1976.

Spencer, D. A. and H. D. Waley, *The Cinema Today*. London: Oxford University Press, 1939.

Starr, Cecile, ed., *Ideas on Film*. New York: Funk & Wagnalls Co., 1951.

Stott, William, *Documentary Expression and Thirties America*. New York: Oxford University Press, 1973.

Bibliography

Sussex, Elizabeth, *The Rise and Fall of British Documentary*. Berkeley: University of California Press, 1975.

Swanberg, W. A., *Luce and His Empire*. New York: Charles Scribner's Sons, 1972.

Waldron, Gloria and Cecile Starr, *The Information Film*. New York: Columbia University Press, 1949.

Winterbotham, F. W., *The Ultra Secret*. New York: Dell, 1974.

ARTICLES IN BOOKS

Anonymous, "History Makers of 1937: Roy E. Larsen," *The 1938 Film Daily Yearbook*. New York: The Film Daily, 1938, p. 154.

———, "Louis de Rochemont," *Current Biography, 1949*. New York: H. H. Wilson Co., 1950, p. 144.

———, "Louis de Rochemont," *1946-47 International Motion Picture Almanac*. New York: Quigley Publications, 1946, p. 71.

———, "A Report on March of Time's War Effort," *1943 International Motion Picture Almanac*. New York: Quigley Publications, 1943, p. 208.

———, "Richard de Rochemont," *Current Biography, 1945*. New York: H. H. Wilson Co., 1946, p. 147.

———, "Richard de Rochemont," *1946-47 International Motion Picture Almanac*. New York: Quigley Publications, 1946, p. 71.

———, "Roy Larsen," *Current Biography, 1950*. New York: H. H. Wilson Co., 1951, p. 324.

Elson, Robert T., "De Rochemont's *The March of Time*." In Lewis Jacobs, ed., *The Documentary Tradition*. New York: Hopkinson & Blake, 1971, p. 104.

———, "Time Marches on the Screen." In Richard Meran Barsam, *Nonfiction Film Theory and Criticism*. New York: Dutton, 1976, p. 95.

Grierson, John, "The Course of Realism." In Charles Davy, ed., *Footnotes to the Film*. London: Lovat Dickson, Ltd. (Reader's Union Edition), 1938, p. 137.

———, "The Documentary Idea," *The Complete Photographer*. Vol. 4. New York: National Educational Alliance, Inc., 1943, p. 1374.

Lorentz, Pare, "Movies—1940," *U.S. Camera—1941*. Vol. 2. New York: Duell, Sloan & Pearce, 1940, p. 202.

SIGNED ARTICLES

Abel, "March of Time," *Variety*, Feb. 5, 1935, p. 14.

———, "March of Time" (review of "State of the Nation"), *Variety*, Jan. 25, 1939, p. 15.

———, "Short Subject: 'March of Time' (No. 3)," *Variety*, April 24, 1935, p. 13.

Bibliography

———, "Talking Shorts" (review of Issue No. 3 in 1936 series), *Variety,* March 18, 1936, p. 17.

Anstey, Edgar, "The Cinema" (review of "Britain's R.A.F."), *Spectator,* Nov. 8, 1940, p. 475.

———, "The Cinema" (review of "America Speaks Her Mind"), *Spectator,* March 7, 1941, p. 251.

———, "The Cinema" (review of *Ramparts We Watch*), *Spectator,* April 11, 1941, p. 395.

———, "The Cinema" (review of "Australia at War"), *Spectator,* May 30, 1941, p. 580.

———, "The Cinema" (review of "Crisis in the Atlantic—1941"), *Spectator,* June 27, 1941, p. 677.

———, "The Cinema" (review of "China Fights Back"), *Spectator,* August 29, 1941, p. 203.

———, "The Cinema" (review of "Men of Norway"), *Spectator,* Nov. 14, 1941, p. 466.

———, "The Cinema" (review of "Sailors With Wings"), *Spectator,* Dec. 12, 1941, p. 555.

———, "The Cinema" (review of "America at War"), *Spectator,* Feb. 27, 1942, p. 203.

———, "The Cinema" (review of "Argentine Question"), *Spectator,* April 3, 1942, p. 327.

———, "The Cinema" (review of "India in Crisis"), *Spectator,* July 10, 1942, p. 35.

———, "The Cinema" (review of "Challenge to Hollywood"), *Spectator,* March 1, 1946, p. 219.

———, "The Magazine Film," *Penguin Film Review No. 9,* May 1949, p. 17.

Auer, Bernhard M., "A Letter from the Publisher (reissue of *MOT* by David Wolper), *Time,* March 12, 1965, p. 17.

Barsam, Richard, " 'This is America': Documentaries for Theaters, 1942-1951," *Cinema Journal* 12 (spring 1973):22.

Belitt, Ben, "The Camera Reconnoiters," *The Nation,* Nov. 20, 1937, p. 557.

Bige, "Shorts" (review of Issue No. 1 of Vol. 2), *Variety,* Jan. 22, 1936, p. 15.

Birchall, Frederick, "Ontario Bars Film 'Canada at War,' " *New York Times,* March 5, 1940, p. 2:5.

———, "Ontario Official Resigns in Protest," *New York Times,* March 12, 1940, p. 5:1.

Birt, John, "There Is a Bias in Television Journalism. It Is Not against Any Particular Party or Point of View—It Is a Bias against *Understanding,*" *TV Guide,* Aug. 9, 1975, p. 3.

Boehnel, William, "March of Time Editors Bewildered and Amused over That Canadian Ban," *New York World-Telegram,* March 9, 1940.

Bohn, Thomas and Lawrence Lichty, "The March of Time: News as Drama," *The Journal of Popular Film* 2 (fall 1973):373.

Bibliography

Bowles, Stephen, "And Time Marched On," *Journal of the University Film Association* (Winter 1977), p. 7.

Brog, "The Golden Twenties," *Variety*, March 22, 1950, p. 6.

Browning, Irving, "Julien Bryan, Film Reporter," *American Cinematographer*, April 1945, p. 118.

Char, "Shorts" (review of Issue No. 2 of Vol. 3), *Variety*, October 7, 1936, p. 15.

————, "Talking Shorts" (review of Vol. 3, Issue 5), *Variety*, Jan. 20, 1937, p. 14.

Chartier, Roy, "The Newsreels," *Variety*, Jan. 1, 1935, p. 12.

————, "The Newsreels," *Variety*, Jan. 1, 1936, p. 43.

Chic, "Short Subjects" (review of Vol. 2, Issue 4), *Variety*, May 6, 1936, p. 19.

Cook, Bruce, "Whatever Happened to Westbrook Van Voorhis–" *American Film*, March 1977, p. 25.

Cooke, Alistair, "History in the Making," *Listener*, Nov. 20, 1935, p. 931.

————, "The March of Time," *Sight and Sound*, autumn 1935, p. 123.

Crowther, Bosley, "Golden Twenties," *New York Times*, April 10, 1950, p. 15:2.

————, "The Ramparts We Watch," *New York Times*, Sept. 20, 1940, p. 27:1.

————, "Time Goes to the Vatican," *New York Times*, January 14, 1940, p. 5:8.

————, " 'Time' Marches Off," *New York Times*, July 15, 1951, p. 1:7.

————, "Time Marches On and On," *New York Times*, Oct. 31, 1937, p. 6:1.

————, "Time Marches to the Ramparts," *New York Times*, Oct. 22, 1939, p. 5:3.

Cunningham, James, "Weekly Dramatic Newsreel Will Be Launched by 'Time' October 1," *Motion Picture Herald*, Aug. 25, 1934, p. 11.

Daley, Robert, "We Deal with Emotional Facts," *New York Times Magazine*, Dec. 15, 1974, p. 18.

Dangerfield, George, "Time Muddles On," *New Republic*, August 19, 1936, p. 43.

De Rochemont, Richard, "As America Sees It," *Sight and Sound*, spring, 1941, p. 6.

————, "Vichy versus France," *Life*, Sept. 1, 1941, p. 66.

Dispenza, Joseph, "Out of the Studios and into the Streets: Louis de Rochemont and 'The March of Time.' " *AFI Report* No. 3, Nov. 1973, p. 17.

Doan, Richard K., "Wolper's 'March of Time' White House Film Coup," *New York Herald Tribune*, July 20, 1965, p. 13.

Edga, "Shorts: March of Time No. 14," *Variety*, May 20, 1936, p. 12.

Ellis, Peter, "Fascism Marches On," *New Masses*, Sept. 3, 1935, p. 29.

————, "The Screen: The March of Time," *New Masses*, July 9, 1935, p. 29.

————, "Sights and Sounds: The First Offering of Frontier Films," *New Masses*, May 11, 1937, p. 29.

Bibliography

Epstein, Edward, "Onward and Upward with the Arts: Television Network News," *New Yorker,* March 3, 1973, p. 41.

Ferguson, Otis, "Time Steals a March," *New Republic,* Feb. 9, 1938, p. 19.

Fielding, Raymond, "Mirror of Discontent: The *March of Time* and Its Politically Controversial Film Issues," *Western Political Quarterly* 12 (March 1959):145.

———, "Time Flickers Out: Notes on the Passing of the *March of Time,*" *Quarterly of Film, Radio, and Television* 11 (summer 1957):354.

Fortinberry, Alicia, "MOT at MOMA," *FYI* (Time, Inc., house organ), Dec. 8, 1975, p. 1.

Frakes, Margaret, "Time Marches Back," *Christian Century,* Oct. 16, 1940, p. 1277.

Galway, Peter, "Inside Nazi Germany, 1938: The March of Time," *New Statesman and Nation,* April 30, 1938, p. 728.

Gehman, Richard, "De Rochemont—A Pictorial Journalist Who Records the American Scene on Film," *Theatre Arts,* Oct. 1951, p. 58.

Gibbs, Wolcott, "Time . . . Fortune . . . Life . . . Luce," *New Yorker,* Nov. 28, 1936, p. 20. Reprinted in up-dated and revised form in *Scholastic,* Nov. 19, 1938, p. 9.

Glendenning, Alex, "Commentary," *Nineteenth Century,* February 1939, p. 210.

Goetz, William, "The Canadian Wartime Documentary: *Canada Carries On* and *The World in Action,*" *Cinema Journal,* 16, spring 1977.

Greene, Graham, "The Cinema: 'The March of Time,' " *Spectator,* Nov. 8, 1935, p. 774.

Griffith, Richard, "Post-War Documentaries," *Penguin Film Review No. 8,* Jan. 1949, p. 92.

Hart, Henry, "De Rochemont's *Windjammer,*" *Films in Review,* May 1958, p. 235.

Hartung, Philip, "The Stage and Screen: Stay for the Shorts" (review of "One Day of War, 1943"), *Commonweal,* March 5, 1943, p. 496.

Herring, Robert, "Review of Releases: The March of Time," *Life and Letters Today,* Dec. 1935, p. 192.

Hoellering, Franz, "Films" (review of "War, Peace, and Propaganda"), *Nation,* June 17, 1939, p. 708.

Hoffman, Irving, "Tales of Hoffman," *Hollywood Reporter,* Jan. 22, 1945, p. 3.

Hopkinson, Peter, "Letters: The March of Time, *Sight and Sound,* Autumn, 1971.

Hull, Cordell, "Censoring Motion Pictures," *New York Times,* July 19, 1936, p. 8:7.

Kobler, John, "The First Tycoon," *Saturday Evening Post,* Jan. 16, 1965, p. 28.

Kravif, Hy, "Behind the Scenes of 'The March of Time,' " *American Spectator,* March 1936, p. 1.

Bibliography

Land, "Shorts: March of Time No. 6," *Variety,* June 24, 1936, p. 29.
———, "Short Subjects: March of Time (No. 7)," *Variety* Oct. 23, 1935, p. 13.
———, "Talking Shorts: March of Time (No. 4),' *Variety,* June 5, 1935, p. 15.
Lawrenson, Harry, "Production and Significance of Newsreels: Foreign Editions," *Journal of the Society of Motion Picture Engineers,* Nov. 1946, p. 361.
Linen, James, "A Letter from the Publisher" (Forum Editions), *Time,* April 19, 1948, p. 17.
Lorentz, Pare, "The Ramparts We Watch," *McCall's,* Oct. 1940, p. 4.
Ludlow, Ray and Eva Goldbeck, "Time Marches Where?" *New Theatre,* March 1935, p. 19.
Lyons, Eugene, "Louis de Rochemont: Maverick of the Movies," *Reader's Digest,* July 1949, p. 23.
Mabie, Janet, "Pictorial Journalism," *Christian Science Monitor Magazine,* Oct. 30, 1935, p. 3.
MacCann, Richard, "Louis de Rochemont Turns Facts into Fiction—with Care," *Christian Science Monitor Magazine,* Dec. 30, 1950, p. 14.
MacDonald, Dwight, " 'Fortune' Magazine," *Nation,* May 8, 1937, p. 527.
———, " 'Time' and Henry Luce," *Nation,* May 1, 1937, p. 500.
———, "Time, Fortune, Life," *Nation,* May 22, 1937, p. 583.
McGoldrick, Rita, "School and Screen," *Motion Picture Herald,* May 14, 1932, p. 38.
McManus, John, "An Affair of Honor" (review of Vol. 2, No. 7), *New York Times,* July 19, 1936, p. 3:1.
MacMurrough, H., "The Screen: The March of Time," *New Masses,* Oct, 8, 1935, p. 29.
Menefee, Selden, "The Movies Join Hearst," *New Republic,* Oct. 9, 1935, p. 241.
Mosher, John, "The Current Cinema," *New Yorker,* March 26, 1938, p. 60.
———, "The Current Cinema," *New Yorker,* Dec. 31, 1938, p. 49.
Nugent, Frank, "Slightly Off Color," *New York Times,* March 6, 1938, p. 5:1.
Odec, "Short Subjects: March of Time" (review of Vol. 3, Issue 7), *Variety,* March 10, 1937, p. 14.
Pew, Marlen, "Bitten by Ducks," *Editor and Publisher,* Nov. 3, 1928, p. 36.
Price, Byron, "Freedom of Press, Radio, and Screen," *Annals of the American Academy of Political and Social Science,* Nov. 1947, p. 137.
Pryor, Thomas, "By Way of Report: March of Time Trains Service Men in Film Techniques—Best Foot Forward," *New York Times,* Feb. 8, 1942, p. 5:7.
———, "Down the Homestretch—after 18 Months, Time Completes 'The Ramparts We Watch,' " *New York Times,* June 30, 1940, p. 3:7.
———, "Film News and Comment," *New York Times,* Aug. 31, 1941, p. 3:6.
Quigley, Martin, "The Exhibitor's Screen—How Shall It Be Used?" *Motion Picture Herald,* Feb. 5, 1938, p. 7.

Bibliography

Reynolds, Capt. Bob, "Filming a News Event for the Screen," *Moving Picture World,* July 21, 1917, p. 421.

Scho, "Talking Shorts: March of Time," (review of Vol. 3, Issue 8), *Variety* March 24, 1937, p. 16.

Sedgwick, Ruth, "The March of Time. The News Recreated on the Air," *Stage,* Feb. 1935, p. 38.

Seldes, Gilbert, "Screen and Radio," *Scribner's Magazine,* July 1937, p. 56.

———, "The Unreal Newsreel," *Today,* April 13, 1935, p. 6.

Sennwald, André, "Rialto Presents 'The First World War,'" *New York Times,* Nov. 8, 1934, p. 27:1.

Shirer, William L., "Inside Wartime Germany: Part I," *Life,* Feb. 3, 1941, p. 67.

Strauss, Theodore, "Richard of the House of de Rochemont," *New York Times,* Jan. 16, 1944, p. 3:5.

Troy, William, "Pictorial Journalism," *Nation,* Feb. 20, 1935, p. 232.

Van Doren, Mark, "What Pictures Mean," *Nation,* Jan. 29, 1938, p. 136.

Walt, "We Are the Marines," *Variety,* Dec. 9, 1942, p. 8.

Wear, Mike, "Shorts: March of Time (Vol. 3, No. 1)," *Variety,* Sept. 9, 1936, p. 16.

———, "Short Subjects: March of Time" (review of Vol. 3, No. 9), *Variety,* April 14, 1937, p. 12.

———, "Talking Shorts: March of Time, Vol. 3, No. 4," *Variety,* Dec. 2, 1936, p. 18.

———, "Talking Shorts" (review of Vol. 3, No. 6), *Variety,* Feb. 3, 1937, p. 14.

Whitebait, William, "The Movies" (review of "India at War"), *New Statesman and Nation,* Aug. 22, 1942, p. 124.

———, "The Movies" (review of "Men in Washington—1942"), *New Statesman and Nation,* Sept. 5, 1942, p. 156.

———, "The Movies" (review of "The Fighting French"), *New Statesman and Nation,* Nov. 21, 1942, p. 338.

———, "Plays and Pictures" (review of "Britain's R.A.F."), *New Statesman and Nation,* Nov. 2, 1940, p. 443.

Willkie, Wendell, "Senate's Threat to Free Speech," *Life,* Nov. 3, 1941, p. 42.

Wolff, Lothar, "Reminiscences of an Itinerant Filmmaker," *Journal of the University Film Association* 24, (1972): 83.

Wright, Basil, "The Cinema" (review of "Inside Nazi Germany—1938"), *Spectator,* May 13, 1938, p. 867.

———, "The Cinema" (review of "Refugee, Today and Tomorrow"), *Spectator,* Jan. 13, 1939, p. 52.

———, "The Cinema" (review of "The Vatican of Pius XII"), *Spectator,* March 29, 1940, p. 448.

———, "The Cinema" (review of "Canada at War"), *Spectator,* April 5, 1940, p. 481.

Wyatt, E. V., "The March of Time," *Catholic World,* Aug. 1936, p. 602.

Bibliography

Zinneman, Fred, "Remembering Robert Flaherty," *Action*, May-June 1976, p. 25.

Zolotow, Maurice, "Want To Be a Movie Star?" *Saturday Evening Post*, March 29, 1952, p. 24.

UNSIGNED ARTICLES

"Alistair Cooke Draws Paramount 'Fargo' Squawk," (Cooke to narrate British edition of *MOT*), *Variety*, Jan. 26, 1938, p. 4.

"Appeal 'Ramparts' Ban," *New York Times*, Sept. 24, 1940, p. 48:2.

"Ban on Wheeler Film Lifted," *New York Times*, April 22, 1937, p. 13:4.

"Biggest Ad for 'March of Time,' " *New York Times*, Dec. 23, 1937, p. 30:2.

"Blames Farley on Film," *New York Times*, May 2, 1937, p. 28:3.

"Buenos Aires Censorship Committee," *New York Times*, Oct. 21, 1941, p. 10:3.

"Cancer Medico Sues RKO-'Time,' " *Variety*, Jan. 26, 1938, p. 7.

"Cecil Assails Cut in War Peril Film," *New York Times*, May 23, 1936, p. 13:3.

"Celluloid Censorship," *Time*, June 1, 1936, p. 40.

"Censorship of Newsreel Made Political Football," *Motion Picture Herald*, April 24, 1937, p. 13.

"Censors Stand Pat on 'Ramparts' Film," *New York Times*, Sept. 20, 1940, p. 23:1.

"Children Present Service Awards," *New York Times*, May 24, 1942, p. 42:1.

"Concerning Certain Cinematic Chat" (production of "Ramparts We Watch"), *New York Times*, March 24, 1940, p. 5:4.

"Court Plan Foe Barred from Film," *New York Times*, April 17, 1937, p. 4:3.

"Cut in Newsreel Stirs Up Kansas," *New York Times*, April 25, 1937, p. 11:1.

"De Rochemont Back in Expansive Mood," *New York Times*, Sept. 8, 1945, p. 6:6.

"De Rochemont To Be Producer for 20th-Fox," *Motion Picture Herald*, Aug. 28, 1943, p. 25.

"Diplomats View 'Time' Reel as Hull Answers Dominicans," *Motion Picture Herald*, July 25, 1936, p. 26.

"Drops 'Ramparts' Ban Appeal," *New York Times*, Oct. 26, 1940, p. 7:2.

"Film of Papal City Opens at Belmont," *New York Times*, Sept. 20, 1941, p. 11:3.

"First Issue of Time's Two-Reel News Opens in Theatres Dec. 20," *Motion Picture Herald*, Nov. 17, 1934, p. 9.

"Freedom of Film and Press," *Christian Century*, Feb. 2, 1938, p. 136.

"French Fascist Pic from 'Time' Footage," *Variety*, Nov. 13, 1935, p. 13.

"Gerald Smith Sues over 'Libel' in Film," *New York Times*, March 19, 1939, p. 5:1.

"Hitler Talk Eases Fears in Britain," *New York Times*, Jan. 31, 1939, p. 5:5.

Bibliography

"Huey Long a Film Censor Now? Kidding Subject Deleted from 'Time' in N.O.," *Variety*, April 24, 1935, p. 1.

"H'wood Being Taken for a One-Way Sleighride, but It's Bumpy for All," *Variety*, Sept. 17, 1941, pp. 4ff.

"Inside France's Maginot Line," *Life*, Oct. 3, 1938, p. 13.

"Inside Nazi Germany-1938" (advertisement), *Motion Picture Herald*, Feb. 5, 1938, p. 58.

"Inside Stuff—Pictures," *Variety*, Oct. 30, 1935, p. 6.

"Inside Stuff—Pictures" (Canadians censor *MOT*), *Variety*, April 24, 1935, p. 30.

"Inside Stuff—Pictures" (Warner Bros. rejects "Nazi Conquest No. 1"), *Variety*, April 20, 1938, p. 10.

"L. de Rochemont at 20th," *Variety*, Aug. 25, 1943, p. 7.

"Life Refugees From France," *Life*, July 22, 1940, p. 74.

"Louisiana Adopts Censorship Law," *Motion Picture Herald*, July 13, 1935, p. 14.

"Luce's Time-Life Steamup by Welles to Force 'Citizen Kane' Release; $800,000 Prod. Now May Be Stalled," *Variety* March 5, 1941, p. 3.

"Mahoney Scoffs at Film on Mayor," *New York Times*, Oct. 3, 1937, p. 4:3.

"Making the March of Time," *National Board of Review Magazine*, November, 1938, p. 8.

"The March of Time," *Motion Picture Reviews*, Jan., 1940, p. 11.

"March of Time," *Vogue*, Aug. 1, 1936, p. 40.

" 'March of Time' Celebrates Its First Anniversary," *Motion Picture Herald*, Jan. 18, 1936, p. 30.

"March of Time Criticizes Other Reels, Cites $1,000,000 Gross," *Motion Picture Herald*, July 18, 1936, p. 67.

"The 'March of Time' Cut in Two States," *New York Times*, Oct. 27, 1935, p. 28:1.

"March of Time in 35 Full Pages," *New York Times*, Jan. 8, 1938, p. 20:4.

"March of Time in 5200 Houses," *Motion Picture Herald*, April 11, 1936, p. 50.

" 'March of Time' Propaganda, Says Omaha Paper," *Motion Picture Herald*, March 2, 1935, p. 32.

" 'March of Time' Released Friday," *Motion Picture Herald*, Feb. 2, 1935, p. 18.

"March of Time's 'Canada at War' Reel Banned in Ont. by Premier Hepburn," *Variety*, March 6, 1940, p. 7.

" 'March of Time' Self-Sponsored" (radio series), *Motion Picture Herald*, July 17, 1937, p. 51.

"March of Time's Foreign Censorship Headaches: How Time and Life Work," *Variety*, Dec. 1, 1937, p. 60.

" 'March of Time's' Movie on 'Vatican of Pius XII' Is Great Newsreel Scoop," *Life*, Feb. 26, 1940, p. 26.

Bibliography

" 'March of Time' Staff Is Increased," *Motion Picture Herald*, July 27, 1935, p. 18.

"The March of Time—Why, How, Where?" *Cue*, Feb. 16, 1935, p. 12.

"The March of Time—Why, How, Where?" *National Board of Review Magazine*, Dec. 1935, p. 4.

"March Stopped," (LaGuardia issue), *Time*, Oct. 25, 1937, p. 25.

"Marines Attack Solomons," *Life*, Aug. 24, 1942, p. 19.

"Marshall in Row over News Movie," *New York Times*, Jan. 19, 1941, p. 28:1.

"Mayor Acts for a Movie," *New York Times*, Aug. 27, 1937, p. 21:8.

"Mayor Is Pleased by Film about Him," *New York Times*, Sept. 30, 1937, p. 9:5.

"Movie Magazine" ("This Modern Age"), *Business Week*, Aug. 10, 1946, p. 102.

"Movie of the Week" ("Inside Nazi Germany"), *Life*, Jan. 31, 1938, p. 24.

"Mud-Slinging the Pix Biz," *Variety*, Sept. 10, 1941, pp. 1ff.

"Nazis Push Attack on March of Time for German War Shots in 'Ramparts,' " *Motion Picture Herald*, Sept. 7, 1940, p. 23.

"New *March of Time* Program Features Books," *Publishers Weekly*, Oct. 28, 1944, p. 1756.

"New 'March of Time' Sales Plan," *Motion Picture Herald*, March 23, 1935, p. 10.

"News Film Concern Adds Another Floor," *New York Times*, Sept. 23, 1939, p. 31:3.

"News Film Ended by March of Time," *New York Times*, July 6, 1951, p. 21:2.

"Newsreel Policy," *Motion Picture Herald*, June 26, 1937, p. 7.

"Newsreel: Re-Enacted Events Make Bow before Movie Goers," *Newsweek*, Feb. 9, 1935, p. 38.

"Newsreel Signs Pact," *New York Times*, Jan. 8, 1947, p. 28:2.

"Newsreels Answer March of Time on Pictures of Hitler," *Motion Picture Herald*, March 23, 1935, p. 30.

"Newsreels Protest March of Time Award," *Motion Picture Herald*, March 27, 1937, p. 18.

"Newsreels Show Canned Footage on Candidates," *Motion Picture Herald*, Oct. 16, 1948, p. 15.

"Norway Fights on in Invisible War," *Life*, Oct. 6, 1941, p. 49.

"Ontario Official Resigns in Protest," *New York Times*, March 12, 1940, p. 5:1.

"Orchard Rejoins Time," *Motion Picture Herald*, Nov. 3, 1945, p. 18.

"Pictorial Journalism," *New York Times*, Feb. 2, 1935, p. 10:1.

"Plan Paris Office of March of Time," *Motion Picture Herald*, Oct. 6, 1945, p. 43.

"The Press: Anniversary," *Time*, Feb. 28, 1938, p. 37.

"Press Supports Warner's Charge March of Time Is Pro-Nazi," *Motion Picture Herald*, Feb. 5, 1938, p. 33.

Bibliography

"Pros and Cons on 'March of Time's' Nazi Subject Boosts B.O. All Over," *Variety,* Jan. 26, 1938, p. 11.

"Publisher's Letter," (Van Voorhis and the radio series), *Time,* Sept. 5, 1955, p. 9.

"Publishing Concern Leases on East Side," *New York Times,* Nov. 12, 1936, p. 43:7.

"Pull Newsreel Scoop on Basil Zaharoff," *Variety,* March 27, 1935, p. 7.

" 'Ramparts' Ban Upheld," *New York Times,* Oct. 2, 1940, p. 19:4.

"The Ramparts We Watch," *Life,* Aug. 12, 1940, p. 69.

"Real Mobs, Reel 'Extras'—to Which March of Time Objects," *Variety,* Dec. 1, 1937, p. 7.

"RKO To Distrib 'March of Time,' " *Variety,* June 12, 1935, p. 5.

"Rolan Joins Staff of 'Time' Newsreel," *Motion Picture Herald,* March 2, 1935, p. 11.

"Salomon with Time," *Motion Picture Herald,* April 13, 1935, p. 8.

"The Screen: 'We Are the Marines,' " *New York Times,* Dec. 14, 1942, p. 19:2.

"See Free Speech Curtailment in Kans. 'Time' Cuts," *Variety,* April 21, 1937, p. 23.

"Senate Isolationists Run Afoul of Willkie in Movie 'Warmonger' Hearings," *Life,* Sept. 22, 1941, p. 21.

"Shanghai Shambles," *Time,* Sept. 13, 1937, p. 33.

"Showing of Film on Nazis Guarded," *New York Times,* Jan. 21, 1938, p. 14:3.

"Sindlinger of Sindlinger," *Newsweek,* May 18, 1959, p. 67.

"Sindlinger Resigns," *New York Times,* Jan. 20, 1943, p. 24:7.

"Sixteenth Political Ban," *Motion Picture Herald,* March 9, 1940, p. 9.

"Smacking Strongly" (editorial), *Motion Picture Herald,* Nov. 2, 1935, p. 7.

"Sound and Fury Over Free Speech," *Literary Digest,* May 1, 1937, p. 3.

"Sue to Bar Algic Film," *New York Times,* Feb. 11, 1938, p. 3:6.

"Superior Documentary" (review of "Lost Boundaries"), *Newsweek,* July 4, 1949, p. 72.

"Test New Type of Newsreel," *New York Times,* Nov. 21, 1934, p. 22:2.

"Threats Trail 'March of Time' Film on Mayor," *New York Herald Tribune,* Oct. 15, 1937, p. 9.

"Time-First Division Contract Cancelled," *Motion Picture Herald,* May 11, 1935, p. 34.

"Time, Inc. Ends Tonight Task of Occupying Seven Floors at Rockefeller Center," *New York Times,* May 2, 1938, p. 33:1.

"Time, Inc. Enjoined on Sinatra Newsreel," *New York Times,* Dec. 12, 1943, p. 28:5.

"Time Marches On," *Cue,* Sept. 28, 1935, p. 8.

" 'Time' Reel Controversial Subject Matter of Concern to Hays Org.," *Variety,* Oct. 9, 1935, p. 4.

"Twenty in Free for All over Nazi Leader at Embassy Theatre," *New York Times,* May 9, 1940, p. 4:8.

Bibliography

"U.S. 'Regrets' Film Envoy Protested," *New York Times,* July 17, 1936, p. 20:4.

"Van Whangs Into It," *New Yorker,* Nov. 13, 1937, p. 17.

"Warners Call Time Film Pro-Nazi and Luce Replies 'Ridiculous,' " *Motion Picture Herald,* Jan. 29, 1938, p. 21.

"We Are the Marines," *New York Times,* Dec. 14, 1942, p. 19:2.

"Weekly Film of the World's Events, A," *Moving Picture World,* July 29, 1911, p. 187.

"Welles' Threat to Raise 'Kane' Put Him in Spot between Odlum-Schaefer," *Variety,* March 19, 1941, p. 7.

"Wheeler Demands Omission of Photo in Film," *New York Times,* Jan. 18, 1941, p. 3:3.

"The Whistle at Eaton Falls," *Time,* Aug. 13, 1951, p. 100.

"The World in Action," *Documentary News Letter,* May, 1942, p. 72.

RESEARCH PAPERS

Campbell, David, "The Origin and the Early Developments of the Time Incorporated Radio Series, the *March of Time.* Master's thesis, Central Missouri State College, 1969.

Case, Claudia, "An Historical Study of the March of Time Program Including an Analysis of Listener Reaction." Master's thesis, Ohio State University, 1943.

Fielding, Raymond, "The March of Time, 1935-1942." Master's thesis, University of California at Los Angeles, 1956.

Goetz, William, "The Canadian Wartime Documentaries: *Canada Carries On* and *The World in Action* Revisited." Research paper, Temple University, Dept. of Radio-Television-Film, 1975.

Harkness, Richard, "This Modern Age." Research paper, Temple University, Dept. of Radio-Television-Film, 1974.

Kuczun, Sam, "History of the American Newspaper Guild." Doctoral dissertation, University of Minnesota, 1970.

Lunsford, Paul, "A Study of Governmental Inquiries into Alleged Staged News Practices of Two Television News Documentaries." Doctoral dissertation, Ohio State University, 1972.

Tucker, Frank C., "A Critical Evaluation of the March of Time [radio series], 1931-1932." Master's thesis, Central Missouri State College, 1969.

Research Resources

In addition to the published materials listed in the Bibliography, the following research resources were used in the preparation of this study:

(1) The 10-million foot stock-shot library of the *March of Time* is held and administered by the U.S. National Archives in Washington, D.C. Scholars may examine any positive reference prints of this footage that exist. Either positive reference prints or duplicating master positives of footage in the collection may be ordered from the archives by scholars, students, or film producers for a fee.

(2) A fairly complete run of finished sound prints of the monthly *March of Time* releases extending from 1938 to 1951 is available for examination at the U.S. National Archives. At the present time, however, these may not be duplicated without permission of Time, Inc.

(3) A run of finished sound prints of the monthly *March of Time* releases extending from 1935 to 1938 is available for examination at the Museum of Modern Art. At the present time, however, these may not be duplicated without permission of Time, Inc.

(4) The complete production files of the *March of Time*, comprising more than 1500 separate folders of material, are available at the U.S. National Archives for examination or duplication by scholars. Each folder contains an average of from 10 to 50 documents: dope sheets, memoranda, letters, research materials, background information, scripts in various stages of completion, final narration scripts, scripts of foreign versions, and sound mixing scripts.

(5) Newspaper and magazine clippings, reviews, photographs, promotion booklets, and related documents are available in the vertical

file collections of the Museum of Modern Art Library, the Theatrical Collection of the New York Public Library at the Lincoln Center for the Performing Arts, and the Archives of Time, Inc.

(6) Detailed, final, editing-continuity scripts of the *March of Time*'s monthly releases and its feature films were filed with the U.S. Copyright Office at the time that the individual films involved were submitted for copyright registration. The films were all subsequently returned to Time, Inc., by the Library of Congress. However, the scripts are available at the Library for examination by scholars. For the purpose of this study, a microfilmed set of these scripts was made for the author by the Library of Congress with the permission of Time, Inc.

(7) Extensive, tape-recorded interviews were conducted with the following individuals on the dates indicated.

    (1) Edgar Anstey. August 13, 1975. Philadelphia.

    (2) Jack Bradford. Oct. 6, 1975. New York City.

    (3) Julien Bryan. (Not tape recorded—notes only.) Nov. 11, 1959. Los Angeles.

    (4) Louis de Rochemont. June 25, 1975. Newington, N.H.

    (5) Richard de Rochemont. Interviewed by Fielding April 18, 1975, and by Roy Brown, Oct. 22, 1972.

    (6) Mary Losey Field. Feb. 28, 1975. New York City.

    (7) Jack Glenn. March 8, 1975, and Sept. 6, 1975. New York City.

    (8) Peter Hopkinson. Sept. 6, 1975. New York City.

    (9) Roy Larsen. (Not tape recorded—notes only.) Jan. 21, 1975. New York City.

    (10) Tom Orchard. March 1, 1975. New York City.

    (11) Morrie Roizman. March 24, 1975, and Oct. 28, 1975. Philadelphia.

    (12) Jack Shaindlin. Jan. 6, 1975. New York City.

    (13) James Shute. Jan. 16, 1975. New York City.

    (14) Albert Sindlinger. March 17, 1976. Wallingford, Pa.

    (15) James G. Stewart. (Not tape recorded—notes only.) March 10, 1976. Los Angeles.

    (16) Arthur Tourtellot. May 15, 1975. New York City.

    (17) Harry Von Zell. Oct. 1, 1974. Los Angeles.

    (18) Lothar Wolff. April 18, 1975 (New York City); April 23, 1976 (Burlington, Vermont).

These interviews were augmented by correspondence with some of the individuals above, parts of which are cited, where appropriate, in the notes.

Filmography

A chronological list of the March of Time*'s monthly issues and feature films released to American theaters from 1935 to 1951.*

In all, 204 regular issues and 1 special issue (comprising a total of 290 episodes) and four feature films are listed here. In addition the *March of Time* produced numerous one-, two-, and three-reel shorts for the United States government, the United States armed forces, political parties, and private corporations, none of which is listed here. Information about these latter films may be secured from the *March of Time*'s production files at the U.S. National Archives and the cumulative index of the United States Copyright Office, as well as from motion picture yearbooks and other film reference sources.

British and other foreign releases of the *March of Time* are not listed here. Researchers are advised that the contents of such releases, as well as their volume and issue numbers, often differ substantially from those of the American releases. First Division distributed issues from February 1, 1935, through May 31, 1935; R.K.O. those from August 16, 1935, through July 1942; and Twentieth Century-Fox those from September 1942 through August 1951.

Volume	Issue	Titles of Episodes	Date of U.S. Release
1	1	"Saionji" "Speakeasy Street" "Belisha Beacons" "Moe Buchsbaum" "Fred Perkins" "Metropolitan Opera"	Feb. 1, 1935
1	2	"Germany" "New York Daily News" "Speed Camera" "Mohawk Disaster" "Leadbelly"	March 8, 1935
1	3	"Trans-Pacific" "Munitions" "Huey Long" "Mexico"	April 19, 1935
1	4	"Navy War Games" "Russia" "Washington News"	May 31, 1935
1	5	"Army" "Father Coughlin" "Croix de Feu"	Aug. 16, 1935
1	6	"Ethiopia" "Bootleg Coal" "CCC"	Sept. 20, 1935
1	7	"Palestine" "Neutrality" "Summer Theatres" "Safety" ("Sudden Death")	Oct. 18, 1935
1	8	"G.O.P." "Wild Ducks" "Strikebreaking"	Nov. 13, 1935
1	9	"Japan-China" "Narcotics" "Townsend Plan"	Dec. 13, 1935
2	1	"Pacific Islands" "TVA" "Deibler"	Jan. 7, 1936
2	2	"Moscow" "Hartman Discovery" "Father Divine"	Feb. 14, 1936
2	3	"Tokyo, Japan" "Devil's Island" "Fisheries"	March 13, 1936
2	4	"Veterans of Future Wars"	April 17, 1936

Volume	Issue	Titles of Episodes	Date of U.S. Release
		"Arson Squads in Action"	
		"Florida Canal"	
		"Field Trials"	
2	5	"League of Nations Union"	May 15, 1936
		"Railroads"	
		"Relief"	
2	6	"Otto of Hapsburg"	June 12, 1936
		"Texas Centennial"	
		"Crime School"	
2	7	"Revolt in France"	July 10, 1936
		"An American Dictator"	
		"Jockey Club"	
2	8	"Albania's King Zog"	Aug. 7, 1936
		"Highway Homes"	
		"King Cotton's Slaves"	
3	1	"The 'Lunatic Fringe'"	Sept. 2, 1936
		"Passamaquoddy"	
		"U.S. Milky Way"	
3	2	"Labor versus Labor"	Sept. 30, 1936
		"England's Tithe War"	
		"The Football Business"	
3	3	"The Presidency"	Nov. 6, 1936
		"New Schools for Old"	
3	4	"A Soldier-King's Son"	Nov. 27, 1936
		"St. Lawrence Seaway"	
		"An Uncle Sam Production"	
3	5	"China's Dictator Kidnapped"	Dec. 24, 1936
		"Business Girls in the Big City"	
3	6	"Conquering Cancer"	Jan. 22, 1937
		"Mormonism—1937"	
		"Midwinter Vacations"	
3	7	"Father of All Turks"	Feb. 19, 1937
		"Birth of Swing"	
		"Enemies of Alcohol"	
3	8	"Child Labor"	March 19, 1937
		"Coronation Crisis"	
		"Harlem's Black Magic"	
3	9	"Britain's Food Defenses"	April 16, 1937
		"The Supreme Court"	
		"Amateur Sleuths"	
3	10	"Irish Republic—1937"	May 14, 1937
		"U.S. Unemployment"	
		"Puzzle Prizes"	
3	11	"Poland and War"	June 11, 1937

Volume	Issue	Titles of Episodes	Date of U.S. Release
		"Dust Bowl"	
		"Dogs for Sale"	
3	12	"The 49th State"	July 9, 1937
		"Babies Wanted"	
		"Rockefeller Millions"	
3	13	"Rehearsal for War"	Aug. 6, 1937
		"The Spoils System"	
		"Youth in Camps"	
4	1	"War in China"	Sept. 10, 1937
		"Pests of 1937"	
4	2	"Junk and War"	Oct. 1, 1937
		"England's D.O.R.A."	
		"Fiorello LaGuardia"	
4	3	"Crisis in Algeria"	Oct. 29, 1937
		"Amoskeag—Success Story"	
		"U.S. Secret Service"	
4	4	"Alaska's Salmon War"	Nov. 26, 1937
		"Britain's Gambling Fever"	
		"The Human Heart"	
4	5	"Finland's 20th Birthday"	Dec. 27, 1937
		"The Laugh Industry"	
		"Ships-Strikes-Seamen"	
4	6	"Inside Nazi Germany—1938"	Jan. 21, 1938
4	7	"Russians in Exile"	Feb. 18, 1938
		"Old Dixie's New Boom"	
		"One Million Missing"	
4	8	"Arms and the League"	March 18, 1938
		"Brain Trust Island"	
4	9	"Nazi Conquest—No. 1"	April 15, 1938
		"Crime and Prisons"	
4	10	"England's Bankrupt Peers"	May 13, 1938
		"Racketeers vs. Housewives"	
		"Friend of the People"	
4	11	"Men of Medicine"	June 10, 1938
4	12	"G-Men of the Sea"	July 8, 1938
4	13	"Threat to Gibraltar"	Aug. 6, 1938
		"Man at the Wheel"	
5	1	"Prelude to Conquest"	Sept. 2, 1938
		"Father Divine's Deal"	
5	2	"The British Dilemma"	Sept. 30, 1938
		"U.S. Fire Fighters"	
5	3	"Inside the Maginot Line"	Oct. 28, 1938
5	4	"Uncle Sam: The Good Neighbor"	Nov. 25, 1938

Volume	Issue	Titles of Episodes	Date of U.S. Release
5	5	"The Refugee—Today and Tomorrow"	Dec. 23, 1938
5	6	"State of the Nation—1939"	Jan. 20, 1939
5	7	"Mexico's New Crisis" "Young America"	Feb. 1939
5	8	"The Mediterranean—Background for War"	March 1939
5	9	"Japan—Master of the Orient"	April 1939
5	10	"Dixie—U.S.A."	May 1939
5	11	"War, Peace, and Propaganda"	June 1939
5	12	"The Movies March On!"	July 1939
5	13	"Metropolis—1939"	Aug. 1939
6	1	"Soldiers with Wings"	Sept. 1939
6	2	"Battle Fleets of England"	Sept. 1939
6	3	"Uncle Sam—the Farmer"	Oct. 1939
6	4	"Newsfronts of War—1940"	Nov. 1939
6	5	"Crisis in the Pacific"	Dec. 1939
6	6	"The Republic of Finland"	Jan. 1940
6	7	"The Vatican of Pius XII"	Feb. 1940
6	8	"Canada at War"	March 1940
6	9	"America's Youth"	April 1940
6	10	"The Philippines: 1898-1946"	May 1940
6	11	"The U.S. Navy—1940"	June 1940
6	12	"Spoils of Conquest"	Aug. 1940
6	13	"Gateways to Panama"	Aug. 1940
7	1	"On Foreign Newsfronts"	Sept. 1940
7	2	"Britain's R.A.F."	Oct. 1940
7	3	"Mexico—Good Neighbor's Dilemma"	Oct. 1940
7	4	"Arms and the Men—U.S.A."	Nov. 1940
7	5	"Labor and Defense"	Dec. 1940
7	6	"Uncle Sam—The Non-Belligerent"	Jan. 1941
7	7	"Americans All"	Feb. 1941
7	8	"Australia at War"	March 1941
7	9	"Men of the F.B.I.—1941"	April 1941
7	10	"Crisis in the Atlantic"	May 1941
7	11	"China Fights Back"	June 1941
7	12	"New England's Eight Million Yankees"	July 1941
7	13	"Peace—by Adolf Hitler"	Aug. 1941
8	1	"Thumbs Up, Texas!"	Aug. 1941
8	2	"Norway in Revolt"	Sept. 1941

Volume	Issue	Titles of Episodes	Date of U.S. Release
8	3	"Sailors with Wings"	Oct. 1941
8	4	"Main Street—U.S.A."	Nov. 1941
(Special Issue)		"Battlefields of the Pacific"	Dec. 1941
8	5	"Our America at War"	Dec. 1941
8	6	"When Air Raids Strike"	Jan. 1942
8	7	"Far East Command"	Feb. 1942
8	8	"The Argentine Question"	March 1942
8	9	"America's New Army"	April 1942
8	10	"India in Crisis"	May 1942
8	11	"India at War"	June 1942
8	12	"Men in Washington—1942"	July 1942
8	13	"Men of the Fleet"	July 1942
9	1	"The F.B.I. Front"	Sept. 1942
9	2	"The Fighting French"	Oct. 1942
9	3	"Mr. and Mrs. America"	Nov. 1942
9	4	"Prelude to Victory"	Dec. 1942
9	5	"The Navy and the Nation"	Dec. 1942
9	6	"One Day of War—Russia"	Jan. 1943
9	7	"The New Canada"	Feb. 1943
9	8	"America's Food Crisis"	March 1943
9	9	"Inside Fascist Spain"	April 1943
9	10	"Show Business at War"	May 1943
9	11	"Invasion!"	June 1943
9	12	"Bill Jack vs. Adolf Hitler!"	July 1943
9	13	". . . and Then Japan!"	Aug. 1943
10	1	"Airways to Peace"	Sept. 1943
10	2	"Portugal—Europe's Crossroads"	Oct. 1943
10	3	"Youth in Crisis"	Nov. 1943
10	4	"Naval Log of Victory"	Dec. 1943
10	5	"Upbeat in Music"	Dec. 1943
10	6	"Sweden's Middle Road"	Jan. 1944
10	7	"Post-War Jobs?"	Feb. 1944
10	8	"South American Front—1944"	March 1944
10	9	"The Irish Question"	April 1944
10	10	"Underground Report"	May 1944
10	11	"Back Door to Tokyo"	June 1944
10	12	"Americans All"	July 1944
10	13	"British Imperialism"	Aug. 1944
11	1	"Post-War Farms"	Sept. 1944
11	2	"What To Do with Germany"	Oct. 1944
11	3	"Uncle Sam, Mariner?"	Nov. 1944
11	4	"Inside China Today"	Dec. 1944
11	5	"The Unknown Battle"	Dec. 1944

Volume	Issue	Titles of Episodes	Date of U.S. Release
11	6	"Report on Italy"	Jan. 1945
11	7	"The West Coast Question"	Feb. 1945
11	8	"Memo from Britain"	March 1945
11	9	"The Returning Veteran"	April 1945
11	10	"Spotlight on Congress"	May 1945
11	11	"Teen-Age Girls"	June 15, 1945
11	12	"Where's the Meat?"	July 13, 1945
11	13	"The New U.S. Frontier"	Aug. 10, 1945
12	1	"Palestine Problem"	Sept. 17, 1945
12	2	"American Beauty"	Oct. 5, 1945
12	3	"18 Million Orphans"	Nov. 2, 1945
12	4	"Justice Comes to Germany"	Nov. 30, 1945
12	5	"Challenge to Hollywood"	Dec. 28, 1945
12	6	"Life with Baby"	Jan. 25, 1946
12	7	"Report on Greece"	Feb. 22, 1946
12	8	"Night Club Boom"	March 22, 1946
12	9	"Wanted—More Homes"	April 19, 1946
12	10	"Tomorrow's Mexico"	May 17, 1946
12	11	"Problem Drinkers"	June 14, 1946
12	12	"The New France"	July 12, 1946
12	13	"Atomic Power"	August 9, 1946
13	1	"Is Everybody Happy?"	Sept. 7, 1946
13	2	"World Food Problem"	Oct. 4, 1946
13	3	"The Soviet's Neighbor— Czechoslovakia"	Nov. 1, 1946
13	4	"The American Cop"	Nov. 29, 1946
13	5	"Nobody's Children?"	Dec. 27, 1946
13	6	"Germany—Handle with Care!"	Jan. 24, 1947
13	7	"Fashion Means Business"	Feb. 21, 1947
13	8	"The Teacher's Crisis"	March 21, 1947
13	9	"Storm over Britain"	April 18, 1947
13	10	"The Russians Nobody Knows"	May 16, 1947
13	11	"Your Doctors—1947"	June 13, 1947
13	12	"New Trains for Old"	July 11, 1947
13	13	"Turkey's 100 Million"	Aug. 8, 1947
14	1	"Is Everybody Listening?"	Sept. 6, 1947
14	2	"T-Men in Action"	Oct. 3, 1947
14	3	"End of an Empire?"	Oct. 31, 1947
14	4	"Public Relations—This Means You"	Nov. 28, 1947
14	5	"The Presidential Year"	Dec. 26, 1947
14	6	"The Cold War: Act I—France"	Jan. 23, 1948
14	7	"Marriage and Divorce"	Feb. 20, 1948

Volume	Issue	Titles of Episodes	Dates of U.S. Release
14	8	"The Cold War: Act II—Crisis in Italy"	March 19, 1948
14	9	"Life with Junior"	April 16, 1948
14	10	"The Cold War: Act III—Battle for Greece"	May 14, 1948
14	11	"The Fight Game"	June 11, 1948
14	12	"The Case of Mrs. Conrad"	July 9, 1948
14	13	"White-Collar Girls"	Aug. 6, 1948
14	14	"Life with Grandpa"	Sept. 3, 1948
14	15	"Battle for Germany"	Oct. 1, 1948
14	16	"America's New Air Power"	Oct. 29, 1948
14	17	"Answer to Stalin"	Nov. 26, 1948
14	18	"Watchdogs of the Mail"	Dec. 24, 1948
15	1	"On Stage"	Jan. 21, 1949
15	2	"Asia's New Voice"	Feb. 18, 1949
15	3	"Wish You Were Here"	March 18, 1949
15	4	"Report on the Atom"	April 15, 1949
15	5	"Sweden Looks Ahead"	May 13, 1949
15	6	"It's in the Groove"	June 10, 1949
15	7	"Stop—Heavy Traffic!"	July 8, 1949
15	8	"Farming Pays Off"	Aug. 5, 1949
15	9	"Policeman's Holiday"	Sept. 2, 1949
15	10	"The Fight for Better Schools"	Sept. 30, 1949
15	11	"MacArthur's Japan"	Nov. 11, 1949
15	12	"A Chance To Live"	Dec. 23, 1949
16	1	"Mid-Century—Half-Way to Where?"	Feb. 3, 1950
16	2	"The Male Look"	March 17, 1950
16	3	"Where's the Fire?"	April 28, 1950
16	4	"Beauty at Work"	June 9, 1950
16	5	"As Russia Sees It"	Aug. 18, 1950
16	6	"The Gathering Storm"	Sept. 29, 1950
16	7	"Schools March On!"	Nov. 10, 1950
16	8	"Tito—New Ally?"	Dec. 1950
17	1	"Strategy for Victory"	February 1951
17	2	"Flight Plan for Freedom"	March 1951
17	3	"The Nation's Mental Health"	April 1951
17	4	"Moroccan Outpost"	June 1951
17	5	"Crisis in Iran"	July 1951
17	6	"Formosa—Island of Promise"	August 1951

Filmography

THE RAMPARTS WE WATCH

Released August 1940 by R.K.O. Running Time: 99 minutes

Production Staff:

Producer-Director: Louis de Rochemont
Associate Producer: Thomas Orchard
Associate Directors: { James L. Shute, Shepard Traube, George R. Black, Beverly Jones
Film Editor: Lothar Wolff
Story: Robert L. Richards, Cedric R. Worth
Commentator: Westbrook Van Voorhis
Historical Research: { Samuel W. Bryant, Jr. Capt. Reed M. Fawell, U.S.N.
Production Manager: James L. Wolcott
Photography: { Charles E. Gilson John A. Geisel
Sound Engineers: David Y. Bradshaw, Kenneth Hawk
Musical Score: { Louis De Francesco Jacques Dallin Peter Brunelli
Musical Direction: Louis De Francesco

The Cast:

Dan Meredith, editor of 'The Day' .... John Adair
Joe Kovacs, Hungarian immigrant ..... John Sommers
Mrs. Joe Kovacs .... Julia Kent
Anna Kovacs .... Ellen Prescott
Hon. John Lawton, member of
congress .... C. W. Stowell
Mrs. John Lawton .... Ethel Hudson
Edward Averill, businessman .... Frank McCabe
Mrs. Averill .... Myra Archibald
Walter Averill .... Edward Wragge
Professor Gustav Bensinger .... Alfred U. Wyss
Mrs. Bensinger .... Marguerite Brown
Hilda Bensinger .... Georgette McKee
Fred Bensinger .... Robert Rapelye

343

Filmography

Stuart Gilchrist .... Harry C. Stapher
Ralph Gilchrist .... Elliot Reid
Mrs. Dora Smith .... Augusta Durgeon
Eddie Reed .... Albert Gattiker
Capt. John Kellog,, N.G., U.S.A. ...... H. G. Brady
"Tommy" .... Thomas S. Bernie, Jr.
Mrs. Barbara Davis .... Roberta Maaske
College Students .... John Longwell, Richard
                                     Baker, Jane Avery
Hon. Reginald Denis Phelps, a
British lecturer .... John Williams
Chief of police .... W. W. Pinkerton
Hal Fisher, Lieut. Lafayette Escadrille . Richard McCracken
"Fritz," proprietor of the rathskeller ... Mathew Syben
A singer .... Lorenzo Gallant
Hans, German-American .... Charles Schutz
Louis, German-American .... A. D. Philippse
Businessmen .... John Wallin, H. M. Guilloz,
                                     Norman Kimball, Robert
                                     Donahue, Charles O'Conner,
                                     Lloyd Gallup
"Montana" .... David Dean
Lila Bishop, secretary to Congress-
man Lawton .... Lola Lyman
John Slavetz, laborer .... Andrew Brummer
Mrs. Slavetz .... Myrtle Paseler
Karl Von Schleich, German agent ..... George Jackson
George Wescott, city editor of
'The Day' .... H. G. Westcott
A copy boy for 'The Day' .... Arthur Maxson
Reporters for 'The Day' .... Oliver Bell, Norman Feltcorn
Ticket chopper .... David Pardoll
Telegraph operators .... A. A. Nourie, E. C. Lucey
Lydia Foster, Secretary to Mr. Averill .. Lydia Baratz
A merchant .... Sidney Hatchell
A pacifist .... Marion White
Gordon Hall, captain of marines ...... Gordon Hall
Republicans .... F. T. Matthews, Morris Jones

Filmography

Democrats .... Harry Pettis, Garwood Seipel
Election worker .... Lawrence O'Brien
A stump speaker .... Reginald Reynolds
A Western Union manager .... Bernard Goodenow
A postman .... Harry Feltcorn
Rev. Byron Hatfield .... Rev. Byron Ulric Hatfield
A Y.M.C.A. secretary .... Andrew Bizub
"Ben," a brakeman .... Benjamin Semoskay
"Bill," a baggageman .... W. J. Londregan
"Tom," the barber .... Thomas McElarney
An Austrian consular official .... Gabriel Kerekes
A Department of Justice agent .... Albert Iverson
Henry Jensen, the baker .... Henry Jensen
A French general of infantry .... Jean Hebreard
"Louise" .... Louise Illington
"Mattie" .... Constance Patton
Draftee .... Thomas Rudd
Draftee .... George Ames
"Louis" .... Louis de Rochemont, III

Note: Two versions of *The Ramparts We Watch* were copyrighted, the first on Sept. 30, 1940, running 99 min., 13 sec; the second on Nov. 4, running 87 min. So far as we can tell, the version which was first released to the public on Aug. 30, 1940 was the 99-minute version.

THE STORY OF THE VATICAN

Released August 1941 by R.K.O.　　　　　Running Time: 53 minutes

Production Staff:

Producer: Richard de Rochemont
Director: Jean Pages
Narrator: The Rt. Rev. Monsignor Fulton J. Sheen
Camera: Marcel Rebiere
Film Editor: Lothar Wolff
Musical Arrangement: Louis De Francesco
Publicity: Albert E. Sindlinger

Filmography

Special Representatives: { Donald F. Higgins
James H. S. Moynahan
Commentary Written by James Shute

WE ARE THE MARINES

Released December 1942 by   Running Time: 70 minutes
Twentieth Century-Fox

Production Staff:

Producer-Director: Louis de Rochemont

Associate Directors: { Jack Glenn
Lothar Wolff

Technical Advisor: Major E. R. Hagenah, U.S.M.C.

Photography: { Richard W. Maedler, principal cameraman
John Geisel
Sgt. Arthur Steckler, U.S.M.C.

Film Editors: { John Dullaghan
Morris Roizman

Script: { James L. Shute
J. T. Everitt
J. S. Martin
Lieut. John Monks, Jr. U.S.M.C.

Commentator: Westbrook Van Voorhis

Editorial Associates: { Herbert Andrews
George Black
George Dangerfield
Philippe De Lacy
William Gerrity
William Shaw
James L. Wolcott

Sound Engineers: { Kenneth Hawk
Clarence Wall

Musical Direction: Jack Shaindlin

Musical Score: { Jack Shaindlin
Frederik Block

THE GOLDEN TWENTIES

Released April 1950 by R.K.O.   Running Time: 67 minutes.

Producer: Richard de Rochemont
Based on an original story by Frederick Lewis Allen and Samuel W. Bryant
Editor: Leo Zochling
Assistant Editor: Whitfield Davis
Commentators: Elmer Davis, Frederick L. Allen, Robert Q. Lewis, Allen Prescott, and Red Barber
Assistant Producer: Samuel Wood Bryant
Musical Director: Jack Shaindlin
Research: Lois Jacoby, Leona Carney, Nancy Pessac

AWARDS WON BY THE MARCH OF TIME
ORGANIZATION, 1935-1950

During its 16-year history the *March of Time* won at least 35 national and international awards and citations. The citations came from publications such as *Boxoffice, Fame,* and *Showmen's Trade Review;* from governmental agencies such as the U.S. Treasury and the U.S. Coast Guard; and from organizations such as the American Red Cross, the American Veterans Committee, the U.S. Flag Association, the Youthbuilders Citizenship Forum, the National Conference of Juvenile Agencies, the National Conference of Christians and Jews, and the Civil Service Assembly of the United States and Canada.

The most important of the awards which it received are the following:

March 4, 1937: Academy Award (Special). Academy of Motion Picture Arts and Sciences.
(For "significance to motion pictures and for having revolutionized one of the industry's most important branches, the newsreel.")
1937: Clement Cleveland Award, for "Conquering Cancer" (Vol. 3, No. 6).
Oct. 12, 1938: David S. Beyer Memorial Award, for "Men at the Wheel" (Vol. 4, No. 13).
1944: Medal of Honor for Patriotism—Government of Mexico.
June 1947: Belgium Film Festival Award—a testimonial in recognition of the film "Storm Over Britain."
1950: Academy Award. Best Documentary Short Subject of 1949 ("A Chance to Live"). Academy of Motion Picture Arts and Sciences.

Index

Index

Index

Index

Index

Index

Index

Index

356

Index

Index